bad
boys

Law, Meaning, and Violence

The scope of Law, Meaning, and Violence is defined by the wide-ranging scholarly debates signaled by each of the words in the title. Those debates have taken place among and between lawyers, anthropologists, political theorists, sociologists, and historians, as well as literary and cultural critics. This series is intended to recognize the importance of such ongoing conversations about law, meaning, and violence as well as to encourage and further them.

Series Editors: Martha Minow, Harvard Law School
                            Austin Sarat, Amherst College

bad boys

PUBLIC SCHOOLS IN THE

MAKING OF BLACK MASCULINITY

Ann Arnett Ferguson

Ann Arbor

THE UNIVERSITY OF MICHIGAN PRESS

First paperback edition 2001
Copyright © by the University of Michigan 2000
All rights reserved
Published in the United States of America by
The University of Michigan Press
Manufactured in the United States of America
♾ Printed on acid-free paper

2010   2009   2008   2007   10   9   8   7

A CIP catalog record for this book is available from the British Library.

Library of Congress Cataloging-in-Publication Data

Ferguson, Ann Arnett, 1940
     Bad boys : public schools in the making of black masculinity / Ann
Arnett Ferguson.
        p.   cm. — (Law, meaning, and violence)
     Includes bibliographical references and index.
     ISBN 0-472-11103-5 (cloth : acid-free paper)
     1. Afro-American boys—Education—Social aspects.
2. Masculinity.   I. Title.   II. Series.
     LC2771 .F47   2000
     371.82996'073—dc21   99-006950

ISBN 0-472-08849-1 (pbk. : alk. paper)

ISBN 978-0-472-11103-9 (cloth : acid-free paper)
ISBN 978-0-472-08849-2 (pbk. : alk. paper)

To Cole and Carly Rose

contents

acknowledgments

Though the actual work of writing this text has been a solitary activity, it has never been a lonely one. I wish to acknowledge and thank the colleagues, friends, mentors, and teachers who "kept my company" along the way and gave me critical advice, and much needed encouragement. At the University of California, Berkeley, Michael Burawoy got me started on the ethnographic road in the first place; Troy Duster kept me pointed in the right direction; Arlie Hochschild always insisted that I go deeper; Pedro Noguera offered crucial comments; and Carol Stack was my guide through the writing process.

I could not have survived the anxiety and the isolation of the whole dissertation writing process without my writing group: Debra Gerson, Nadine Gartrell, and Maxine Leeds. I depended on their carefully worded comments on early drafts, the deadlines we set for each other, and, most of all, their emotional support. The discussion group at the Institute for the Study of Social Change (ISSC) gave me the space to present my work and critique the work of others in an atmosphere of mutual respect. I received strong support from colleagues at ISSC for the notion that academic research should be socially relevant and politically responsible. David Minkus deserves special mention for his brilliant conversational riffs that were a welcome respite from hours spent alone in front of the computer. I have been nourished by discussions with the "Gender Girls"—Leslie Salzinger, Debra Little, Terri Pohl.

I am deeply grateful to the staff and the students of the elementary school that I have called Rosa Parks who spared the time to talk to me often at the end of a busy and draining day of work. A very special thanks must go to the boys and the family members whom I interviewed. They put up with my questions and probing into their often difficult and complicated lives with patience, interest, and humor. Juanette made me a part of her family in every way.

At Smith College, there was encouragement and inspiration from the Racial Identity discussion group initiated by Brenda Allen of the Psychology Department who has boundless energy. One member, Bill

Cross of the University of Massachusetts, Amherst, read the entire manuscript, for which I am very grateful.

Vicky Spelman took an early interest in the publishing project, read the dissertation, thought the subject important, and opened doors for me. Martha Minow and Austin Sarat, the coeditors of the series, wrote the perceptive reviews that gave me the impetus to revise the manuscript. Susan Van Dyne egged me on. Chuck Myers and Kevin Rennells of the University of Michigan Press have been unfailingly patient and good listeners. Wynne Ferguson read it with tender loving care and caught all the typos.

A grant from the Social Science Research Council provided me with some funds to help with the initial research. A sabbatical semester from Smith College gave me time to work on revisions for publication.

During the time that I was revising the manuscript, I began knitting classes at Northampton Wools. The circle of women with whom I sat knitting and talking each Monday night kept my life grounded and sane as I was initiated into an ancient art of skill and beauty. Linda Daniels, our knitting guru, a perfectionist herself who would not hesitate to tell one of us to "rip it out and start over," taught me that there was no knot or slipped stitch—no problem—that did not have a very practical solution. My best thinking about my writing took place as I knit one and purled two.

Ed Ferguson has been a true comrade through the whole endeavor. He made sure I didn't spend too many hours at the computer and cooked me delicious meals. He did the first editing of the final draft. His fanatical insistence that I purge pretentious academic jargon and obtuse prose from the text has hopefully made it accessible to the wide audience that I hope to reach. Most important of all, he said, "Don't write another word. You've finished."

Grateful acknowledgment is made to the following publishers for permission to reprint previously published materials.

Hal Leonard Corporation for excerpted lyrics from "Homies," words and music by Bobby Ramirez, Robert Gutierrez, James Carter, William Robinson, Jr., Warren Moore, and Marvin Tarplin. © 1992, 1993 EMI Blackwood Music Inc., Hip Hop to Pop, Hip Hop Loco Music, Jobete Music Co., Inc., Ensign Music Corporation, Jams-R-Us Music, and RMI Songs. All Rights for Hip Hop to Pop and Hip Hop Loco Music Controlled and Administered by EMI Blackwood Music Inc. All Rights for Jobete Music Co., Inc. Controlled and Administered by EMI April Music Inc. All Rights Reserved. International Copyright Secured. Used by Permission. Contains elements of "Tracks Of My Tears" by William Robinson, Jr., Warren Moore, and Marvin Tarplin— Jobete Music Co. Inc.

MCA Music Publishing for excerpted lyrics from "Don't Believe the Hype," words and music by Eric Sadler, Hank Shocklee, and Canton Ridenhour. Copyright © 1987 Universal—Def Jam Music, a division of Universal Studios, Inc. (BMI). International copyright secured. All rights reserved.

Reach Music International, Inc. for excerpted lyrics from "Don't Believe the Hype" by Canton Ridenhour, Hank Shocklee, and Eric Sadler. Copyright © 1988 Reach Back (BMI), a division of Reach Music International, Inc. All rights reserved. Used by permission.

Sugar Hill Music for excerpted lyrics from "The Message," by E. Fletcher, S. Robinson, C. Chase, and M. Glover. Copyright © 1982 Sugar Hill Music (BMI).

Varry White Music for excerpted lyrics from "Principal's Office" by Young MC.

Every effort has been made to trace the ownership of all copyrighted material in this book and to obtain permission for its use.

chapter one

don't believe the hype

The minute they see me, fear me
I'm the epitome—a public enemy
Used, abused, without clues
I refused to blow a fuse
They even had it on the news
Don't believe the hype
Don't believe the hype.

—PUBLIC ENEMY, "DON'T BELIEVE THE HYPE"

Soon after I began fieldwork at Rosa Parks Elementary School, one of the adults, an African American man, pointed to a black boy who walked by us in the hallway.[1] "That one has a jail-cell with his name on it," he told me. We were looking at a ten-year-old, barely four feet tall, whose frail body was shrouded in baggy pants and a hooded sweatshirt. The boy, Lamar, passed with the careful tread of someone who was in no hurry to get where he was going. He was on his way to the Punishing Room of the school. As he glanced quickly toward and then away from us, the image of the figure of Tupac Shakur on the poster advertising the movie *Juice* flashed into my mind. I suppose it was the combination of the hooded sweatshirt, the guarded expression in his eyes, and what my companion had just said that reminded me of the face on the film poster that stared at me from billboards and sidings all over town.

I was shocked that judgment and sentence had been passed on this child so matter-of-factly by a member of the school staff. But by the end of the school year, I had begun to suspect that a prison cell might

---

1. This research was assisted by an award from the Social Science Research Council through funding provided by the Rockefeller Foundation. The names of the city, school, and individuals in this ethnography are fictitious in order to preserve the anonymity of participants.

indeed have a place in Lamar's future. What I observed at Rosa Parks during more than three years of fieldwork in the school, heard from the boy himself, from his teachers, from his mother, made it clear that just as children were tracked into futures as doctors, scientists, engineers, word processors, and fast-food workers, there were also tracks for some children, predominantly African American and male, that led to prison. This book tells the story of the making of these bad boys, not by members of the criminal justice system on street corners, or in shopping malls, or video arcades, but in and by school, through punishment. It is an account of the power of institutions to create, shape, and regulate social identities.

Unfortunately, Lamar's journey is not an isolated event, but traces a disturbing pattern of African American male footsteps out of classrooms, down hallways, and into disciplinary spaces throughout the school day in contemporary America. Though African American boys made up only one-quarter of the student body at Rosa Parks, they accounted for nearly half the number of students sent to the Punishing Room for major and minor misdeeds in 1991–92. Three-quarters of those suspended that year were boys, and, of those, four-fifths were African American.[2] In the course of my study it became clear that school labeling practices and the exercise of rules operated as part of a hidden curriculum to marginalize and isolate black male youth in disciplinary spaces and brand them as criminally inclined.

But trouble is not only a site of regulation and stigmatization. Under certain conditions it can also be a powerful occasion for identification and recognition. This study investigates this aspect of punishment through an exploration of the meaning of school rules and the interpretation of trouble from the youth's perspective. What does it mean to hear adults say that you are bound for jail and to understand

2. Punishment resulted in suspension 20 percent of the time. Records show that in 1991–92, 250 students, or almost half of the children at Rosa Parks School, were sent to the Punishing Room by adults for breaking school rules, for a total of 1,252 journeys. This figure is based on my count of referral forms kept on file in the Punishing Room. However, it by no means represents the total number of students referred by teachers for discipline. I observed a number of instances where children came into the Punishing Room but the problem was settled by the student specialist on the spot and no paperwork was generated. This seemed especially likely to occur when the adult referring the child had written an informal note rather than on the official referral form, when a parent did not have to be called, or when the infraction was judged by the student specialist to be insignificant. So it is likely that a much larger number of children were sent to the Punishing Room over the year but no record was made as a result of the visit.

that the future predicted for you is "doing time" inside prison walls? What does school trouble mean under such deleterious circumstances? How does a ten-year-old black boy fashion a sense of self within this context? Children like Lamar are not just innocent victims of arbitrary acts; like other kids, he probably talks out of turn, argues with teachers, uses profanities, brings contraband to school. However, I will argue, the meaning and consequences of these acts for young black males like himself are different, highly charged with racial and gender significance with scarring effects on adult life chances.

The pattern of punishment that emerges from the Rosa Parks data is not unique. Recent studies in Michigan, Minnesota, California, and Ohio reveal a similar pattern.[3] In the public schools of Oakland, California, for example, suspensions disproportionately involved African American males, while in Michigan schools, where corporal punishment is still permitted, blacks were more than five times more likely to be hit by school adults than were whites. In the Cincinnati schools, black students were twice as likely to end up in the in-house suspension room—popularly known as the "dungeon"—and an overwhelming proportion of them were male.[4] In an ominous parallel to Cincinnati's dungeon, disciplinary space at Rosa Parks is designated the "Jailhouse."

The School and Neighborhood

I was initiated to Rosa Parks Elementary School in 1989 as a member of an evaluation team for a new intervention program for children diagnosed as "at-risk" of failing in school. The program, Partners at Learning Skills (PALS), included in-school counseling, after-school tutoring and recreation, evening and weekend workshops for parents, and in-

3. "Survey: Schools Suspend Blacks More," *Detroit Free Press,* December 14, 1988, 4A; Joan Richardson, "Study Puts Michigan 6th in Student Suspensions," *Detroit Free Press,* August 21, 1990, 1A; Minnesota Department of Children, Families and Learning, *Student Suspension and Expulsion: Report to the Legislature* (St. Paul: Minnesota Department of Children, Families and Learning, 1996); Commission for Positive Change in the Oakland Public Schools, *Keeping Children in Schools: Sounding the Alarm on Suspensions* (Oakland, Calif.: The Commission, 1992), 1; and John D. Hull, "Do Teachers Punish according to Race?" *Time,* April 4, 1994, 30–31.

4. In Oakland, while 28 percent of students in the system were African American males, they accounted for 53 percent of the suspensions. See note 3 for racial imbalance in corporal punishment in Michigan schools ("Survey: Schools Suspend Blacks More"), and the racial discipline gap in Cincinnati (Hull, "Do Teachers Punish?").

service training for teachers. It was just one of hundreds that had been started in schools and communities throughout the United States in response to the erosion of funding and services to urban public schools that had occurred over the previous decade.

The children participating in PALS had been selected by a committee of teachers, school administrators, and a counselor. I was told that the selection committee had had a very difficult time choosing the first group of thirty children since more than three times that number had been proposed by classroom teachers. One of the most difficult questions facing the selection committee, it was said, was whether to choose pupils who might benefit from extra help or to select those who were, in the words of one of the school administrators, "unsalvageable" and on whom precious resources would be wasted. The selection committee could not agree, so they compromised and included both types.

The first time I saw the entire group of children in PALS, they were in the school library taking a pencil-and-paper test designed to measure self-esteem. That was when I first became aware of a disturbing fact: all the children except one were African American, and of those 90 percent were males.[5] I quickly became aware that what was surprising and problematic for me appeared to be taken for granted by the others. No one at the school seemed surprised that the vast majority of children defined as "at-risk" of failing academically, of being future school dropouts, were mostly black and male. My own puzzle over how this raced and gendered pattern had come into being lead me to conduct an in-depth study through participant observation at the Rosa Parks School over a three-and-a-half year period from January 1990 to May 1993.

Rosa Parks School is the largest of five intermediate schools (grades 4 through 6) in the school district of Arcadia, a medium-sized city on the West Coast. The city is best known as the home of a large public university whose prestige and reputation has attracted students and faculty from all over the world. Arcadia has operated a complex plan for school desegregation since 1968 that involves citywide busing to produce a racial/ethnic and socioeconomic mix in its schools. Students attending Rosa Parks come from a population where race, household type, and annual income are skewed into three types of neighborhood

---

5. The one who was not black had a Hispanic surname.

I have called Heartland, Midland, and the Highlands.[6] Each day the buses bring children, the majority of whom are white, from upper-middle-class professional families in the relatively affluent Midland and the wealthy Highlands to Rosa Parks School, where they join the kids from the predominantly low-income African American families living in the Heartland neighborhood surrounding the school.[7]

The racial balance targeted by the Arcadia desegregation program has never been actually attained because of the "white flight" from the public schools that followed the implementation of the desegregation plan in 1968. The percentage of white students in the K–12 grades of the city's schools declined from 60 percent to 30 percent between 1960 and 1993.[8] For a city with a reputation for being one of the most liberal communities in the country, Arcadia has one of the highest percentages of children attending private schools in the region.[9] Many of the white children who attend private or parochial elementary schools eventually return to attend the Arcadia public high school, where classes are de facto segregated as the result of an elaborate tracking system.

---

6. Children are bused in from areas of the city that are vastly different in terms of their social and economic characteristics. I compared 1990 census data from two of the most affluent census tracts from which children are bused (Midland and the Highlands) to data from the tract in which the school is located (Heartland). Heartland has a median family income of $20,192, while Midland has a median family income of $66,234, and that of the Highlands is $97,315. Heartland has the highest percentage of blacks and the lowest percentage of whites, while the reverse is true for the Highlands. Race is therefore an excellent predictor of whether a child comes from a family with limited resources. Children in Heartland are also more likely to be living in female-headed households than those bused in. Sixty-one percent of children under eighteen years in Heartland live in female-headed households, compared with 27 percent for Midland and 8 percent for the Highlands. This is significant because female-headed households in the United States are more likely to be poverty households than married-couple households. This is true of Heartland, where women head three-quarters of the families living below the poverty level. Households headed by females in Heartland had a mean income of $15,150 per year, compared to $38,306 for those of married couples. In the Highlands, however, the mean income of female-headed households is $54,388, and those headed by married couples averaged $153,828 annually.

7. About half of the kids in the school are eligible for the subsidized lunch program, while just over one-third come from families that receive AFDC. Almost all of these are neighborhood kids.

8. Arcadia Schools Enrichment Office, "Comparative Racial Census of the Arcadia School District, Grade K–12," 1991.

9. Diana Walsh, "Money Isn't the Only Factor in School Choice," *San Francisco Examiner,* March 7, 1993, 13.

At the time of my study approximately one-half of the Rosa Parks student body was black and one-third was white. Of the remaining students, 10 percent were Asian American, 4 percent Hispanic, and 8 percent were classified as Other. The racial composition of the teaching staff, however, had changed little since desegregation, continuing to be predominately white and female.[10]

Rosa Parks School itself is far from being one of the run-down, resource-poor facilities documented in several recent accounts of urban schools.[11] The freshly painted two-story building and the asphalt playground occupies a full city block. Beautiful old pine trees stand on either side of the walkway leading up to a wide stone porch set in front of the main entrance to the school. The building faces onto a grassy lawn that is green for a short time in the spring and brown by the end of the summer when the school year begins. After school, children play football on the grass or hang around on the wide stone porch.

Inside the front door I am always struck by the calm atmosphere. The hallways are wide, clean, and lined by bulletin boards displaying children's work. The classrooms are filled with light from big windows. These are not rooms that speak of the bare necessities. Rooms are adorned with books, plants, animals, computers, games. Even so, teachers reminisce about better times in the school when the availability of basic school supplies could be taken for granted, when there was a school nurse, when the playground was open for recreation in the afternoons.

Nor is the neighborhood in which the school stands dilapidated or run-down. There is a mix of small, neat, single-family dwellings with older rambling wood-frame houses converted into multiple family units. Some are shabby, some are newly renovated. A few 1960s vintage apartment buildings, home to many of the poorest families, are interspersed throughout the neighborhood.

In spite of the quiet, ordinary feeling of its surroundings, Rosa Parks School is located in the heart of a major drug-trafficking area in the city. The buying and selling of drugs, the symbolic presence of urban poverty, is signaled through the signposts on a number of street

---

10. There were twenty white, nine African American, and three Asian American teachers, of whom only three classroom teachers were male, one of whom was African American.

11. See, for example, Alex Kotlowitz, *There Are No Children Here* (New York: Doubleday, 1991), and Jonathan Kozol, *Savage Inequalities: Children in America's Schools* (New York: HarperCollins, 1991).

corners that warn that police are watching and that the car license numbers of people buying drugs are being recorded. The area accounted for ten of the city's fourteen murders; one-half of the reported rapes; about a third of the robberies, and almost a half of the aggravated assaults in the city, according to 1991 statistics from the Arcadia Police Department.[12]

Doing Fieldwork

Statistics about school trouble and punishment provide a map that delineates a raced and gendered pattern of who gets punished in school and present the big picture of a disturbing phenomenon, but they can tell us very little about the actual processes that give rise to this configuration. So, my fieldwork was designed to explore these processes. Through a combination of participant observation at the school and a wide range of interviews and conversations with kids and adults, I examined the beliefs, the social relationships, and the everyday practices that give rise to a pattern in which the kids who are sent to jailhouses and dungeons in school systems across the United States are disproportionately black and male.

As a participant observer, I roamed the hallways before, during, and after school, hung out in the student cafeteria and the teachers' lounge at lunchtime, attended assemblies, wandered around the playground during recess. I sat in on classes and in the school library. I also tutored in the PALS after-school program.

During my second year, I began sitting in on Mrs. Daly's sixth-grade class. I had chosen this room because Horace, the boy who I was tutoring after school, was in the class.[13] The first few visits, I spent most of my time sitting at a worktable, quietly watching what was going on. But very soon, with Mrs. Daly's encouragement, I began participating in the regular classroom activities. I often worked with small groups of kids who needed help. I observed Horace and his friends "in action" and also got to know several of the African American girls in the class who were considered "challenges" and who also spent time in the Punishing Room. I accompanied the group on several field trips, including

---

12. Arcadia Police Department statistics as reported in a PALS document.

13. There were twenty-seven children, ten girls and seventeen boys, in Mrs. Daly's class. Fifteen of the children were African American, six were white, three were Hispanic, and three were of Asian descent.

a three-day camping trip, the sixth-grade picnic at the end of the school year, and the orientation at the junior high school to which some of the kids would be transferring the following year.

But the most important site of all was observing in what I came to call the Punishing Room as well as in the other spaces connected with the school's discipline system. I would not have discovered the existence of the Punishing Room on my own. Some of the boys whom I was observing in Mrs. Daly's class led me to it because it was a regular stop on their passage through the day. I had already begun following them into more familiar places: their classroom, the playground, the cafeteria. I had begun to sift through their files in the school office and had learned about their scores on reading and math placement tests, whether their vision had been checked, whether they had moved from another school district. But I had never actually followed them down to "Miss Woolley's office" when they got in trouble until one day Mrs. Daly asked me to accompany two boys who had gotten in trouble right after recess for squirting water at each other. "I want to make sure they make it back to class quickly. Not get lost"—this with a significant look at both boys—"on the way back." So I went with them and discovered the function of one of the spaces of the school that up to that point I had only glanced at as I passed by.

After this first visit I asked permission to observe in the Punishing Room. At first the staff of the Punishing Room, all African Americans, were uneasy about my presence. But they were interested in the fact that my research was looking for answers as to why the majority of children getting into trouble and frequenting their office were African American. It turned out that this was a topic that they had theories about themselves. As a result, they not only gave me access, but urged me to look through the discipline records kept on individual children in the filing cabinets in their office.[14]

I spent many hours sitting in the Punishing Room, and my presence became less obtrusive as time went by. After the first few days, during which I felt that the student specialists were consciously bridling their responses to the children, being "softer" because of my presence, I became a taken-for-granted member of the setting. When this happened, verbal harangues, sympathy, even physical intimidation could

---

14. The student specialists also turned over to me the referral forms from 1992–93 at the end of the school year. I organized the data from the forms according to grade, race, gender, type of infraction, punishment, and noted any comments by teachers.

be expressed without the fear that I was monitoring their activities on behalf of the school district. I became even more "invisible" as I sat copying the data from the discipline files. I would sit there handwriting the contents of referral slips onto a yellow pad while a stream of children came in and out of the room with stories, explanations, complaints. Scathing adult comments and childish declarations of innocence took place as if I were not there at all. Phone calls to parents were made, and families were critically appraised by staff after these conversations. I gained a great deal of insight from these interactions. What I observed confirmed that a trip to the Punishing Room was not necessarily a shameful event but held a variety of meanings for the children. For example, one day a fifth-grade African American boy who was always in trouble saw the file folder with his name on the desk. "I got a lot in there, don't I? Who else got one that big?" he asked. There was awe in his voice at his accomplishment. He had made an important mark on the school.

Troublemakers and Schoolboys

The heart of my research was the time I spent with twenty fifth- and sixth-grade African American boys. These boys had been selected after discussions with school personnel, review of the discipline files, and my own initial observations in and around the school. Ten of the boys, whom I have called *Schoolboys,* had been identified by the school as "doing well," while ten boys, whom I call the *Troublemakers,* were identified as "getting into trouble." I conducted interviews with all and spent time observing, hanging out with, and getting to know a smaller group.

The Troublemakers were no strangers to the Punishing Room. All the members of this group of boys had been suspended at home at least once over the course of the year for school infractions such as fighting, obscenity, bringing toy guns to school. None had ever been charged with illegal acts such as bringing drugs or real guns to school. None were inveterate truants; the vast majority rarely voluntarily missed a day of school and were usually on time. All had been labeled "at-risk" of failing, "unsalvageable," or "bound for jail" by school personnel.

The Schoolboys, on the other hand, had only occasionally been handed a referral slip, and none of them had ever been suspended. At the outset of my study I saw this group as just the opposite of the

Troublemakers, as a control group; I wondered how they were different. What could we learn about the attitude, home-life, experiences of a group of boys who were clearly committed to the school's project that would help explain Troublemakers? However, I gradually realized that to see Schoolboys and Troublemakers as fundamentally different was to make a grave mistake. As African American males, Schoolboys were always on the brink of being redefined into the Troublemaker category by the school. The pressures and dilemmas this group faced around race and gender identities from adults and peers were always palpable forces working against their maintaining a commitment to the school project. That is, of course, why schools across the nation witness the continual attrition of the ranks of the "schoolboys" as they join those of the "troublemakers."

All of the boys in the study lived in the neighborhood around the school. All except two of the Schoolboys were from low-income families eligible for the school lunch program.[15] The composition of these households varied greatly from family to family and affected resources available to them in significant ways. Of the Schoolboys, three came from families in which both mother and father lived in the household, four from mother-headed households, one lived with his grandmother, and one lived with both grandparents. Of the Troublemakers, two were living in families with both parents, four lived in mother-headed households, one was being raised by his father, two were in foster families, and one lived with his sister.[16]

I conducted a series of in-depth, unstructured interviews with the adults who had contact with the boys in the school: classroom teachers, principals, discipline staff, the district truant officer, school psychologists, social workers, school janitors. I also interviewed their parents or guardians—usually women, but in two cases fathers—as I explored the disciplinary systems outside of the school that the boys called on to make sense of interactions within the school. I came to know several of these families quite well as they drew me into their lives as a sympathetic ear, a sounding board, a person with resources and credibility in

15. About half of the kids in the school are eligible for the subsidized lunch program, while just over a third come from families that receive AFDC. Almost all of these students are from the Heartland (see note 7).

16. This pattern is replicated in the 1990 census data for the neighborhood in which a majority of the families are mother-headed households. This is in contrast to the children, mostly white, who are bused to the school from neighborhoods in which the vast majority of the families are two-parent households.

a community in which those currencies were often in short supply. In one instance, I became not just a friend or acquaintance, but was adopted as a member of the family.

Learning from Kids

Though I paid attention to the accounts of a variety of individuals and heard explanations and theories from numerous viewpoints, it is the perspective and the voices of the kids, mostly boys, whom I talked to that animate and bind this text together. I have spotlighted their voices not only because they are the most silenced and the most invalidated in discussions of school trouble and punishment, but also because they provide a critical view that augments significantly our knowledge about the contemporary crisis in education.

How I heard the voices of the boys whom I interviewed and how I listened to what they were saying changed qualitatively over the course of my research. I assumed at the start that I would learn *about* kids; but it was not long before I was obliged to question this premise and begin to learn *from* children. This enabled me to tell their story from a fresh viewpoint.

In my initial research design I had planned to learn about kids through "formal" interviews as well as through observation. My goal was to tape-record in my office at the university conversations about several topics including school, trouble and punishment, friends, heroes, adult careers. The venue of the interview was to set a tone of adult importance and serious business to the engagement that I hoped would have an effect on the quality of the responses that I got from the children.

I explained to the boys that I was writing a book about kids and school and that I wanted to tell the story from their perspective; that I needed their help, what they knew, in order to write something good. Word got around to their friends that I was writing a book, and a few approached me and asked if they could be in it. I was surprised at how savvy they were about the telling of life stories. For one thing, the favorite television program of almost all the kids was the *Oprah Winfrey Show*, which featured the telling of personal stories. One boy asked me what kind of cover the book would have; another seemed disappointed that I would not be using his real name. Most of the boys seemed gen-uinely pleased to discover that I wanted to talk about things that interested them. Two of them, however, were especially noncommittal during the interview. These two already had to deal with the criminal justice system. One boy had, in fact, been placed in a foster home for several days when his mother was arrested. Their demeanor was by no means hostile but extremely cautious, monosyllabic, noncommittal. After I interviewed each kid, he had a turn to be the interviewer and ask me whatever questions he wanted. Several took me up on the offer. I was asked about my work, my family, and what I spent my money on. Just the kind of questions I might get from social science researchers.

When the formal interviews were over, the reward for the boys was pizza and a visit to nearby video arcades, or a trip up to the lookout deck of the highest building at the university. I found that the spontaneous conversations that I had with them during these outings were often more informative about the topics that I was interested in than the actual interviews. The question-and-answer format, with me in control of the topic and them responding, was not the best one; in this form of dialogue, the kids responded to my questions, but carefully. Too carefully. On the other hand, rich stories of experience in and out of school, observations and theories, bits of advice, flowed out of the ad-lib, spontaneous conversations during the course of our "free" time together. I began to realize how imperative it was to rethink my interviewing strategies. "Free time" was the space in which the kids felt free to talk about what interested and impressed them. So, while I continued with the formal interviews, I began to understand that the time before and after the interviews was even more important.

When I decided to study a group of young people I did not think about how I would gain access to their meaning systems. I admit now with embarrassment that when I began the research my assumption was that my own knowledge and experience would give me the tools necessary to figure out what was going on in the lives of the boys I would interview and observe. I was required to provide a lengthy protocol for the Human Subjects Committee at the university. This procedure was couched in terms of "protecting children," so my efforts in composing the protocol were to assure the committee that my interview questions would not traumatize the "interviewees" in any way. At that point, my unexamined research common sense was that children were substantively different than adults; they were more transparent. They were "natural" subjects whose behavior I would interpret, rather than having to elicit interpretations from the kids themselves. I could

observe them in depth—almost as if they were animals in the labora-
tory—to make sense of what I perceived. They were somehow more
accessible because they were less social, more biologically determined.
They were not yet totally "human," but were humans-in-the-making.
It was me, not them, who was wise.

I was an "adult," beyond biology and development because fully
social, and would use my knowledge of the world to interpret what I
saw them do and what they told me of their lives. I did not even think
about whether the kids would choose to let me into their lives, tell me
their stories. They were on the surface: I would not have to plunge deep
into another world of experience, meaning, interpretation, learn
another language, unscramble new codes and symbols.

For one, I believed that I already knew a great deal about childhood. I am the mother of two sons; I have been a schoolteacher. From
these experiences, I assumed that children could be extremely good at
keeping, and highly motivated to keep, secrets, so that I would have to
work to put them at their ease with me. I planned to draw on the leg-
endary uncanny ability of mothers to ferret out information. But the
"omniscient mother" as interviewer kept me locked into a perspective,
into strategies of power from which I had to move away. This "extort-
ing information model" offered few surprises.

I had underestimated the enormous chasm of power that separated
grown-ups and young people. For one thing, question and answer is the
customary form of communicative exchange between powerful and
powerless, between adult and child. The young, especially, under the
circumstances of being interviewed by an outsider are guarded, cautious. They have been taught to be suspicious of strangers. They have
usually learned that almost anything they say can be the "wrong"
answer, can get them into trouble. Boys who were already marked as
troublesome were often anxious to present themselves in as positive a
light as possible. They wanted me to be aware that they knew what was
"right" and "wrong" in the context of school. In spite of my pledge
prior to the taped interview that what they said would be confidential,
they could not be absolutely sure that they could trust me. Why should
they? They were in the position of guarding not only themselves but
also families and friends from my scrutiny. The interview format also
contravened the code against "telling" that adults seek to undermine in
the name of "truth." As an interviewer, I too, was asking them to "tell."

Who and where I was in my own life acted both as a barrier and a facilitator to making meaning of their lives. I was an older black woman, not a youth, not male; yet, my life as a graduate student helped to freshen my memory of what it meant to be a "child" in a world of total and arbitrary "adult" power. To be a graduate student was to be "infantilized." I had returned to graduate school after years of working as a teacher, as a social worker, as a university administrator. I had mothered. But the hierarchy of knowledge in the university was one in which my accumulated knowledge counted for nothing; I was expected to start as if I were a blank slate on which would be written the theories, ways of understanding the world that were gleaned from "approved" texts. In seminars, I found that discussions of work, mothering, bureaucracy, and organizations deliberately excluded the personal experience of those around the table from what was considered appropriate, admissible data. Those students who drew on life experience in seminars quickly learned that scholarly discussion moved on over this offering as if it never occurred. I learned that experience was a shameful burden of knowledge acquired "practically," every day, rather than "theoretically" from a distance. This erasure of a particular form of knowing the world by the academy was one aspect of my present life that helped me to listen more respectfully to the children's talk than I might have otherwise. Moreover, it opened me up to consider how the knowledge, experience, and forms of expression that were brought into school by the group of kids that I was studying were excluded.

Research Assistance: Introducing Horace

But it was fundamentally through my relationship with twelve-year-old Horace that I began to be conscious that my research agenda was focused on learning about boys rather than from them. I was assigned to be Horace's tutor in the after-school program the first semester of my fieldwork. Though I wanted to get to know one of the boys "getting in trouble," I worried about whether I would be able to "handle" him. My anxiety had been raised by the reputation he had among school adults as a boy who was difficult and out of control. Horace's name had become the standard against which other children would be judged. For example, in a faculty meeting discussion of another African American boy at the school, Horace's name was invoked as the norm. The adult said, "That child's a problem, but he's not a Horace."

In spite of the bad press that he had gotten from the school adults and my anxiety about working with him, we got along well. I often found him exasperatingly determined to control the conditions of his after-school tutoring sessions. But I recognized that he was leaning on the side of "humanizing" our relationship, while I was bent on making our time together as "productive" as possible. I was out to "teach" him something. He was carefully laying out, testing, and undermining the original terms of our relationship, in which I had all the power and respect and he had none. With his help, I came to see kids not as humans-in-the-making but as resourceful social actors who took an active role in shaping their daily experiences. I began to recognize and appreciate the stresses and strains they faced and the strategies they devised for negotiating and maneuvering within structures of power.

Over the weeks and months that I got to know Horace, I pieced together a shifting portrait of how he was seen by others: his teachers, the student specialists, the principals, his mother and siblings; and how he saw himself. I also listened carefully to the stories Horace told me about what was going on in his life as well as his analysis of relationships in and out of school.

These stories and the time Horace and I spent together confirmed what I had suspected, had gotten glimpses of through observation in the school, through interviews with some of the boys' families. Those who were classified as lazy, belligerent, incorrigible at school could be respectful, diligent, and responsible in other contexts. Horace, who was characterized by school as "volatile," "insubordinate," was also described by others who knew him in different contexts as "a team player," "affectionate," "great with kids." From my observation of Horace, I could see that he tested, resisted, and defied the authority of certain adults. But it became clear that he was also conforming, obedient, and deeply focused in other contexts in school and out.

At the end of my first year of fieldwork at Rosa Parks, I asked Horace to be my research assistant during the summer vacation to help me put together the topics for my interviews with the other boys. He turned out to be an excellent guide to issues on young boys' minds with a remarkable "sociological eye." He saw patterns, relationships, contradictions, and disjunctures. Horace helped me decide—I might say he insisted—on the themes for the interviews I later conducted with the other boys. He was quick to let me know when he thought I was beating a topic to death or asking a question to which the answer seemed obvious. He interviewed *me* on issues such as mothering, school, and money.

Most important of all, he pointed out that I would learn nothing about his peers and himself if I didn't listen to their music. So I tuned in to their favorite radio station listening to the rap music, the DJ talk, the phone-in calls that weaved them together. I listened to the commercials, the advice, the attitudes that were being dished out. I began watching music videos. I became familiar with the names and works of contemporary popular rap artists such as Ice Cube, Ice T, Paris, Naughty by Nature, Pooh Man, Snoop Doggy Dog, Dr. Dre, Queen Latifah, Monie Love, Salt 'n' Pepa. I found that rap lyrics and the accompanying visual images, though sometimes offensive and shocking, and almost ritualistically misogynist, were also witty, ribald, catchy, and often sharpened by a measure of social criticism and political commentary. I was delighted to find that the lyrics articulated some of the very ironies and contradictions that I myself observed as a researcher. I have selected some examples of these as epigraphs to introduce and set the tone for several chapters of this book.

My introduction to this music opened up a cultural space to me that was far more rich and critically innovative than I had expected; it was more than the background noise and mindless escape of the music of my own youth that reproduced simple hegemonic notions of romance and power. Instead, I discovered a potent alternative site of knowledge for youth about bodies and beauty, sexuality, gender relationships, racial identification, authority, justice and injustice, loyalty and friendship, style and address, transmitted through a vehicle that simultaneously engaged pleasure and fantasy.

My brief and intense exposure to and growing familiarity with this cultural production was an indispensable element in alerting me to some key sources that the boys drew on for self-fashioning. Two of these are especially significant for this work. First, as I listened to the music, heard the lyrics, watched the images, I became conscious of the highly controversial, embattled figure of the "gangsta" in gangster rap. Rather than the stigmatized figure of the criminal feared by members of society, the gangster in rap music and videos was a heroic medium for articulating the tragic realities of urban poverty as well as the dangers, pleasures, and privileges of being male. This image led me to consider the multiple ways of incorporating authority figures, rules and laws, transgressive acts and consequences into a worldview. Second, I became aware that the alternative, critical discourse and heightened consciousness about race and racism that some kids brought to school was reflected in the lyrics and images of rap music.

Race Signifies

A structuring element of this text is an examination and analysis of the continuing significance of "race" as a system for organizing social difference and as a device for reproducing inequality in contemporary United States.[17] Race continues to be a ready-made filter for interpreting events, informing social interactions, and grounding identities and identification in school. One racial interpretation infusing several boys' accounts of the school day was that African American boys were singled out for punishment because of their race.

This claim was especially provocative because school adults were visibly uneasy about, and committed to, avoiding public discussions of race that went beyond a recitation of desegregation demographics. While several kids raised the issue of how race made a difference in their experience of school, the adults typically limited their talk about race to matters of numbers and distributions. Officially, race existed in school as the baseline category for classifying and distributing kids throughout the system and into classrooms, but beyond that the public consensus among adults was that distinctions of race were of no further significance. The working assumption was that racial discrimination had come to an end with school desegregation; that in its everyday operations school was race-blind to the differences that had led to the need for busing in the first place. In relation to this study, the position was that children were sent to the Punishing Room not because of who they were, but because of what they did. The institutional discourse was that getting in trouble was not about race but a matter of individual choice and personal responsibility: each child made a choice to be "good" or "bad." The homily "The Choice is Yours" was printed at the top of the list of school rules to emphasize this connection.

However, this discourse of "individual choice" was undercut by a more covert, secretive conversation about race that circulated primarily

17. I use the concept of race not to mark off essential, fixed differences between groups of humans but to refer to a socially constructed category of human difference and division whose boundaries and meanings have changed over time, but which always is a mechanism for the unequal distribution and allocation of social goods and status. This category, though a social fiction, because it is politically motivated has serious, real consequences for individuals and for social life.

among African American adults in the school that presumed race to be a continuing force in determining the outcome for children. In public, school people seemed to subscribe to explanations that the "at-riskness" of children was a consequence of apathetic or dysfunctional families; but in private conversations and interviews, black teachers and staff hinted that race, gender, and class made a significant difference in a child's experience of school. They suggested that certain boys got picked on because they were black and came from the neighborhood; that white teachers didn't know how to discipline black kids; that white teachers were "intimidated" by black boys; that some African American teachers had problems working with the neighborhood children, almost all of whom were black and poor. In several of these conversations, individuals seemed to be egging me on to pursue the saliency of race to the phenomena over which I was puzzling.

To jump to the conclusion that racism is a significant component of the problem is, in fact, not all that far-fetched. Up to 1968, when Arcadia schools were desegregated, the observation that black children were being treated differently from white children would have been a mere statement of fact. Racial discrimination sanctioned by law and by custom was the norm across the United States in every sphere. The Arcadia School District had, as did the vast majority of school districts across the United States, an official policy of racial segregation that applied not only to children, but to teachers as well.[18] Race made a vast difference in the treatment that was afforded to black and white students. Segregated schools were organized on the assumption that white students were entitled to a better education than black students. Black children were not being educated to compete with whites for jobs in the adult world of work. Memories of this injustice is still very much alive at Rosa Parks School among faculty and staff. Cyril Wilkins, the African American custodian at Rosa Parks, and a product of Arcadia schools, reminded me of this when he recalled applying for a job as a bus driver in Arcadia in the 1960s and having his application form crumpled up and tossed into a wastebasket right before his eyes by the white man in charge of hiring because those jobs were not open to black people.

Cyril Wilkins's personal experience is a vivid reminder of how the ways for maintaining racial hierarchies in the United States have

---

18. No black teacher taught in an Arcadia district white school until the late 1960s.

changed over the past generation as a result of political struggle. The marking of the boundaries of racial difference and the form that racism takes has varied according to the specific social relations and historical context in which they are embedded. Legal and open institutional endorsement of racial discrimination was dismantled as a consequence of the Civil Rights Movement that culminated in the 1960s. Disqualification on the basis of race in the blatant manner that Wilkins describes is now illegal. Yet, in spite of this profound legislative change, "race" continues to be a significant mode for the distribution of power in the society.[19]

For purposes of this study, we need to be aware of two ways that racial inequalities are reproduced today. One is through institutional practices, and the other is through cultural representations of racial difference. Both operate in a covert and informal manner. *Bad Boys* is a study of these two modes: how institutional norms and procedures in the field of education are used to maintain a racial order, and how images and racial myths frame how we see ourselves and others in a racial hierarchy.

Institutional practices continue to marginalize or exclude African Americans in the economy and society through the exercise of rules and purportedly objective standards by individuals who may consider themselves racially unbiased.[20] Punishment is a fruitful site for a close-up look at routine institutional practices, individual acts, and cultural

---

19. For examples of this in the realm of housing see Douglas S. Massey and Nancy A. Denton, *American Apartheid: Segregation and the Making of the Underclass* (Cambridge: Harvard University Press, 1993); in schooling see Kozol, *Savage Inequalities;* for an overview of some recent studies in business, see chapter 5 of Joe Feagin and Melvin Sikes, *Living with Racism: The Black Middle-Class Experience* (Boston: Beacon Press, 1994).

20. The concept of institutional racism as distinct from individual prejudice and bigotry was elaborated on by Stokely Carmichael and Charles V. Hamilton in *Black Power: The Politics of Liberation in America* (New York: Vintage Press, 1967). On page 5 they argued that "institutional racism relies on the active and pervasive operation of anti-black attitudes and practices. A sense of superior group position prevails: whites are 'better' than blacks; therefore blacks should be subordinated to whites. . . . 'Respectable' individuals can absolve themselves from individual blame: *they* would never plant a bomb in the church; *they* would never stone a black family. But they continue to support political officials and institutions that would and do perpetuate institutionally racist policies. Thus *acts* of overt, individual racism may not typify the society, but institutional racism does—with the support of covert, individual *attitudes* of racism." See also Thomas Pettigrew, ed., *Racial Discrimination in the United States* (New York: Harper and Row, 1975), x, for the following description: "racial discrimination is basically an institutional process of exclusion against an outgroup on largely ascribed and particularistic grounds of group membership rather than on achieved and universalistic grounds of merit."

sanctions that give life and power to racism in a school setting that not only produces massive despair and failure among black students, but that increasingly demonizes them.

In this contemporary racial formation the category of race has increasingly been defined through cultural rather than biological difference.[21] Relations of power and inequality are explained as the demonstrated consequence of superior or pathological cultural characteristics. Attitudes, values, behaviors, familial and community practices become the field from which social distinctions derive. Black people, in this form of racism, can only redress their condition by rejecting the cultural modes that make them "different." So, in the school setting, it is assumed that it is the cultural difference kids bring to school that produces the existing pattern of punishment rather than institutional operations themselves.[22] Since a good part of the ideological work of race is to fix meanings and relationships as natural and durable, the racialization of cultural forms and practices not only extracts behaviors and attitudes from the social matrix in which they are embedded but transforms them into immutable racially linked characteristics that produce poverty and bad citizens.

Two cultural images stigmatize black males in the United States today: one represents him as a criminal, and the other depicts him as an endangered species. I found that both of these images were commonly invoked at Rosa Parks School for identifying, classifying, and making punishment decisions by the adults responsible for disciplining the kids.

It is important that we understand human culture differently—not as a set of immutable characteristics that seem to be transmitted through the genes but as a practical, active, creative response to specific social and historical conditions. As such, culture can be a significant mode of defense, of succor, of resistance and recuperation for those

21. For discussion of historical changes in the racial formation in the United States see Michael Omi and Howard Winant, *Racial Formation in the United States: From the 1960s to the 1980s* (New York: Routledge and Kegan Paul, 1986). Paul Gilroy's work provides important parallels with racial formation in Britain. See, for example, Paul Gilroy, *Small Acts: Thoughts on the Politics of Black Culture* (New York: Serpent's Tail, 1993).

22. An example of this connection between race and culture and how it is used in understanding school trouble is found in the article about the Cincinnati schools by Hull, "Do Teachers Punish?" Teachers and administrators explained the disproportionate number of African Americans who were suspended by stating that "blacks tend to be more boisterous," "black students are much more trouble prone," and "some black males are more physical."

with few sources of power in society. A good illustration of this, which I elaborate on in the text, is the way that African American boys use language brought from home and community as a form of self-protection and asserting a group identification in opposition to school.

An example of the multiple meanings and contradictory uses of culture and of cultural representation developed in this study is the way in which a national event acts as a catalyst to both mark "otherness" and heighten racial self-definition. The videotaped beating of Rodney King by Los Angeles police, the trial and acquittal of the men charged with the attack, and the subsequent riots in Los Angeles occurred during my research. Students reacted visibly and vocally to the racism and public discourse emanating from the events. In this way race came into the school to create cultural and racial awareness. School adults, at the same time, drew on the spectacular events as a framework for evaluating the behavior of black kids. This national outpouring also made visible to me the way that traumatic and emotionally disturbing events outside of school directly contributed to children's anger and troubling behavior in school and how unwilling our society is to deal with issues of race as a real, divisive, social problem.

I have organized the text to reflect certain theoretical and methodological considerations of my research. One aim is to join the debate about the relative significance of social structure and personal agency in explaining human behavior.[23] As I was engaged in this project, I found stimulating and compelling arguments on both sides of this discussion.[24] I have found it rewarding to utilize both approaches to demonstrate the interplay between the determining effects of social structure

---

23. For an excellent summary of these positions see chapter 2 of Jay MacLeod, *Ain't No Making It: Leveled Aspirations in a Low-Income Neighborhood* (Boulder, Colo.: Westview Press, 1987); Stanley Aronowitz and Henry A. Giroux, *Education under Siege: The Conservative, Liberal, and Radical Debate over Schooling* (South Hadley, Mass.: Bergen and Garvey, 1985).

24. On the structural determinist side I found the following works most persuasive and insightful: Pierre Bourdieu and Jean-Claude Passeron, *Reproduction in Education, Society, and Culture,* trans. Richard Nice (Beverly Hills: Sage, 1977); Samuel Bowles and Herbert Gintis, *Schooling in Capitalist America: Educational Reform and the Contradictions of Economic Life* (New York: Basic Books, 1976). Some of the work that stressed personal agency and the creative insights and oppositional responses of subjects that I found important included that of Patricia Hill Collins and of John Ogbu. See for example, Patricia Hill Collins, *Black Feminist Thought: Knowledge, Consciousness, and the Politics of Empowerment* (Boston: Unwin Hyman, 1990); and John U. Ogbu, "Class Stratification, Racial Stratification, and Schooling," in *Class, Race, and Gender in American Educational Research: Toward a Nonsynchronous Parallelist Position,* ed. Lois Weis (Albany: State University of

and the creative response of individuals in everyday life that usually reproduces a status quo, but that sometimes produces change. Punishment is an especially fruitful site for this demonstration, as it is a space where educational structures clash with the resistance strategies of individual students. My conviction is, however, that the balance tilts heavily in favor of structural determinants.

The text is, therefore, designed to reveal this interaction between institutional and individual forces. There are two parts. The first part emphasizes structure. In this part I describe and analyze the disciplinary system of the school and the practices of labeling and categorization that construct the boys as individuals with behavioral problems. The second part foregrounds the meaningful actions of individuals as I present the school day from the youths' perspective. Here, I explore how kids recoup a sense of self as competent and worthy under extremely discouraging work conditions. Sadly, they do this by getting in trouble.

Another goal is to elaborate through practical application the theoretical work that challenges the use of the categories of race, class, and gender, as if they are isolated and independent social locations.[25] My analysis foregrounds the technologies of representation of subjects and the experience of subjectivity as a complex, dynamic interaction of race and gender. Sex is a powerful marker of difference as well as race. While the concept of intersecting social categories is a useful analytical device for formulating this convergence, in reality we presume to know each other instantly in a coherent, apparently seamless way. We do not experience individuals as bearers of separate identities, as gendered and then as raced or vice versa, but as both at once. The two are inextricably intertwined and circulate together in the representations of subjects

---

New York Press, 1988). The work that most inspired my own thinking in the early phases of my research was that which stressed the active cultural production of resistance and opposition: Paul Willis, *Learning to Labor: How Working Class Kids Get Working Class Jobs* (New York: Columbia University Press, 1977); and Paul Willis, "Cultural Production Is Different from Cultural Reproduction Is Different from Social Reproduction Is Different from Reproduction," *Interchange* 12, nos. 2–3 (1981).

25. For example, see Rose M. Brewer, "Theorizing Race, Class, and Gender: The New Scholarship of Black Feminist Intellectuals and Black Women's Labor," in *Theorizing Black Feminisms: The Visionary Pragmatism of Black Women,* ed. Stanlie M. James and Abena P. A. Busia (New York: Routledge, 1993). For a discussion and application of the concept of "intersectionality," see Kimberle Crenshaw, "Beyond Racism and Misogyny: Black Feminism and 2 Live Crew," in *Words That Wound: Critical Race Theory, Assaultive Speech, and the First Amendment,* ed. Mari J. Matsuda et al. (Boulder, Colo.: Westview Press, 1993).

and the experience of subjectivity. Though the racial etiquette of today's form of racism has sent a discourse of racial difference underground, it piggybacks on our beliefs about sex difference in the construction of images. I explore the specific way that black boys are constituted as different from boys-in-general by virtue of the sexing of racial meaning.

I have also structured the text along methodological lines to suggest the interplay between the "raw" form of the data that I collected and my own interpretive and analytical authorial work in framing the documentary evidence as one thing rather than another. Interspersed between the chapters is an example of the types of data that I drew on as I pulled together the strands that became this story: self-reflexive musings, transcriptions of interviews, primary source materials, field notes. These documents are, of course, not mere "examples," but are intentionally chosen to illustrate or to strengthen points that I make in the chapters themselves. Several of these seem to speak for themselves with the richly detailed, complex, often contradictory subjective voices that are the fabric out of which the ethnographer as storyteller tailors a coherent account. I have tried as much as possible to leave these complexities and contradictions in so that you, the reader, can more consciously participate in the critical work of interpretation.

He dragged me by the hand into his world one Saturday afternoon at the movies. On the afternoon that I crossed over, if ever so briefly, Horace and I were in one of those late-twentieth-century cinemas where half a dozen movies are simultaneously showing in theaters carved out of what used to be one big extravagant room. We were there to see the film of his choice, *The Last Boy Scout,* which I, primed by TV ads, had expected to be full of graphic scenes of violence and killing. Exactly the type of movie that I always carefully avoid. But I had rashly promised Horace this visit to the cinema as a reward for finishing a class project and I could not back down. I, the person who is about to go on an unexpected field trip guided by a twelve-year-old boy, am a black woman who is almost half a century old, the mother of two sons, a grandmother even, a wife, a daughter, a teacher. Horace and I do have some things in common. In spite of the enormous age difference, we are both students since I have recently returned to school to work on a Ph.D.

The Last Boy Scout had just opened at theaters and drive-ins everywhere and was expected to be so popular that it was being screened in not just one but two theaters in the complex. The particular screening we had come to see would not start for another thirty minutes, so I prepared to wait. But not Horace. He wanted to go in now. "But we'd see the end first," I said, "won't it spoil the movie for you?" It would for me; I hate ends before beginnings. But he didn't want to wait, and since this was supposed to be his outing I let him take the lead.

I reluctantly followed him through the closed door of the theater. He plunged into the darkness and I, feeling very responsible and more than a little guilty for aiding and abetting his consumption of violence, but fearing more than anything else to lose him, blindly followed. We squeezed by several sets of knees into seats that were in my estimation far too close to the front.

On the screen, the hero, popular actor Bruce Willis, is holding a large gun to the head of a girl who is about twelve years old, Horace's age. Willis is snarling at a visibly frightened man something like, "If you don't give me your car, I'm going to blow her head off." Willis looks mean enough to do just that. This movie was going to be far worse than I thought; just the type of film that I should never have brought this impressionable young boy to see.

Though Willis does not shoot the girl in the head, the violence of the scenes escalates. The hero gets blown up, blown away, burned, beaten, abused. The darkened theater becomes a roar of voices cheering him on and applauding when he hurts and kills. Horace is leaning toward the screen transfixed and excited. The climax takes place in a football stadium where the bad guy has his balls blown off in a foiled helicopter escape sequence.

The film has a happy ending. The twelve-year-old girl of the earlier scene had turned out to be Willis's resentful and disrespectful daughter, and the movie ends with him asserting his parental authority over an adoring, submissive girl. Willis's unfaithful wife is suitably chastened and adoring, and the black guy who reluctantly became his comrade-at-arms during the action is now his friend, and the soon-to-be partner in a detective agency. As the credits flash across the screen, our hero Willis has an admiring wife, a respectful daughter, a career, and a buddy.

I am rigid with horror at the violence, the antifemale patriarchal message, and the disturbing sexist qualities of the hero. I fully intend to have a discussion of the film with Horace later on to defuse the dangerous messages that he has received about masculinity, violence, and relationships with women.

As we walk out, I notice that the audience is almost entirely young men. The very few females all seem to be there in the company of men. One young man has a little boy and a little girl with him and I guess that this is his idea of baby-sitting.

I look at my watch. We have about an hour before the next full showing of *Boy Scout*. "Have you seen *My Girl*?" Horace asks as we stand in the hallway. This is one of the three films showing in the theater that afternoon. The other is *Hook*. Both of these films have "Family" ratings.

"You haven't? It's really good. It's hecka sad. Let's go!" He grabs me by the hand, tugs gently and then harder, pulling me in the direction of one of the other viewing rooms. "But we haven't bought tickets for *My Girl*," I counter. "Soooo?" he says looking at me impatiently. It occurs to me that this might be the way to avoid going back to the Willis film, so I stand my ground and begin to negotiate.

"Well if we do go to see this one, then we won't be able to go see the first part of *The Last Boy Scout*. We won't have time to do that and go get something to eat." So we fumble our way to two seats in the darkened room in which *My Girl* is showing.

My Girl is about a friendship between an adorably cute blonde boy who is about ten and a tomboyish white girl of the same age. The story is about family, about mothers and fathers, about love and a first kiss, about friendship, about death. It is about the tests and difficulties of becoming a boy. As we move into the final scenes, Horace leans over and hisses in my ear, "This part is hecka sad. Just wait." The boy hero dies in his attempt to recover a ring lost by the girl from a nest of hornets. He is stung to death.

The boy hero of the film is white, lives in a small town different and strange from the urban area that Horace and I live in. It is a place where children ride bicycles down sidewalks and bullies are vanquished. All the people who live in the town are white. The only danger comes from nature. We have escaped to that small town for forty minutes. For Horace it is like no place he has ever been or likely will be.

Unlike *Boy Scout*, masculinity can be soft and gentle. But in the final analysis, being masculine in this way is also mortally dangerous.

Our eyes glisten with tears as we leave the theater. I feel quenched. This movie has caught me, grabbed me, reminded me of so many things I could have said to my own children. Why does life have to be so sad, so complicated? Why can't we just honor each other, moment by moment?

By now, I'm finally in the spirit of the afternoon. We're both ready for *Hook*, which is showing in a theater upstairs. Together we fly up the stairs, dodging slow-moving adults in our impatience to get there as quickly as possible. I shove past knees and flop down gratefully into a cushiony seat. We are right up front and *Hook* is in progress. Beginning, middle, or end, what does it matter. This is heaven. Once again we are lost in a story about masculinity: gentle mothers, absent fathers, girls who get you into trouble, villains, tests of manhood. And the fight scene that inscribes masculinity.

I was never aware of the exact moment when I stopped being an adult. But somewhere between *My Girl* and *Hook,* I began to have a good time. A hecka good time at the movies. That was when the whole experience began to be transformed from the planned linear motion from beginning to end to a kaleidoscopic back-and-forth of sights, sounds, and tastes.

When *Hook* was over we headed for food, drink, and then back to *The Last Boy Scout.* We sat through the entire movie suffering and cheering. Horace turned the treat I had carefully planned for him unexpectedly into a shimmering afternoon of emotional ups and downs and adventures for both of us. As we went from theater to theater mixing up pathos, sentimentality, greed, violence, tears, screams, laughter, horror, fear, I glimpsed Horace in ways that I had not expected to. But I also recollected, experienced feelings, parts of myself that I did not even know I had lost: the experience of losing myself in a movie totally without the imperative to interpret, criticize, distance myself from plot, characters, and feelings. I lost my preoccupation with time and schedule. But this was not just about a shift in the way that I thought or felt, entirely about mental states; it was also about my body and how it began to grow more powerful and present. That body took me on a chase between theaters and up and down stairs. I swerved to avoid pedestrians and skidded to a halt rather than bump into or bowl over small kids and old people. I did not even think about how I must have appeared to observers as I dashed behind Horace, or sometimes ahead of him, from screening to screening.

When we finally emerged from the grip of the flickering screens, I felt tired and resentful knowing that I had to deal with time (it was growing dark, they expected us home hours before), adults (husbands, mothers) who expected us to slip back into the real world as if we had not traveled an exhausting journey through space and time; the shattering disappointment that unlike the movies all the problems out in the world were still unresolved, without visible cure. I felt sad, let down, and hungry. I was grumpy most of the rest of the evening and unwilling to hide this feeling of malaise from the other adult I lived with, who called me "a crab."

chapter two

the punishing room

Now, as I get to school, I hear the late bell ringing
Running through the hall, I hear the glee club singing
Get to the office, I can hardly speak
'Cause it's the third late pass that I got this week
So to my first class I run don't walk
All I hear are my sneakers and the scratching of chalk
And when I get to the room, I hear the teacher say
"Mr. Young, I'm happy that you could join us today."
I try to sit down so I can take some notes
But I can't read what the kid next to me wrote
And if that wasn't enough to make my morning complete
As I try to get up, I find there's gum on my seat
And with the seat stuck to me, I raise my hand
And say, "Excuse me, but can I go to the bathroom, ma'am."
The teacher got upset and she screamed out, "No
It's off to the principal's office you go."

—YOUNG MC, "PRINCIPAL'S OFFICE"

"This Is What Alain Wrote"

I can hear laughter from the Punishing Room before I get to the door. A crumpled ball of paper sails by my face in the direction of a wastebasket as I enter. Five children—four boys and a girl, all African American—are in the Punishing Room this morning. Two are sitting with books and papers spread in front of them. The three standing in one corner across the room from the wastebasket appear to be the players in the improvised game of hoops. There is a feeling of excitement that is quickly shushed as I enter the room. There are several wads of paper on the floor. Ten eyes fasten on me to see how I'm going to respond to the fact that they're out of their seats and not doing work.

The girl at the table decides to take charge and steer my attention to other matters. "Look what Alain did."

She directs my attention to the Formica-topped surface where something has been scribbled close by an open math book, some mimeographed worksheets, pencils, erasers, and lined notebook paper. As I fumble for my glasses in my purse, she begins to read aloud the words on the table. "Write 20 times. I will stop fucking 10 cent teachers and this five cent class. Fuck you. Ho! Ho! Yes Baby."

I have leaned over with a display of great interest to follow her finger as she traces the words penciled on the table in front of the boy. He is looking directly down onto his lap as she reads. The room is still as taboo words and deeds invade the silence. Five pairs of eyes filled with anticipation, awe, and suppressed giggles watch for my reaction. Now one of the boys takes over from her. Shaking his head in mock sorrow he begins to recite the words. I am saying, "Okay, okay, no need to repeat it. I can see for myself," when one of the student specialists enters the room. She is an older African American woman.

"Get to your seat," she orders the paper throwers, who quickly scramble to their places at the table. She turns to me. "You see the nasty words he wrote?" She scolds the seated boy who has been absolutely quiet since I came into the room. "You should be ashamed of yourself." He says nothing in response. He has a mournful expression on his face.

So the girl chimes in again, rapidly, with an expression of pure innocent indignation, to recite the boy's composition, this time by heart. The words and the girl's perfect act of righteousness cause all the children to start giggling. By the time she gets to "Ho! Ho! Yes Baby!" I am ready to howl with laughter myself.

The student specialist tells the girl to be quiet and get on with her work. But even she has a twinkle in her eye. She has brought another child into the Punishing Room with her, a boy who had clearly been crying on his way to the room, but who now seems to be cheering up considerably.

The student specialist moves over to the table and takes a seat at one of the child-sized chairs alongside the children. "I'm calling your parents," she says to the boy who has written the sentences on the table. To me she sighs, "What to do with these children nowadays!"

Now she proceeds to copy what the boy has written on the table onto a piece of blank paper. This paper will go into his file. As she does so, the children are whispering the phrases to each other. More admonitions to be quiet, more giggles.

The student specialist calls the boy's house. She has the father on the line. He must have asked what the boy has written because now we can all hear her repeating the words written on the table. From her remarks, the father is not happy to be called and I gather feels the school should deal with the matter. The boy who is the center of attention is looking stoic.

The student specialist hangs up. "Your father is coming to take you home." She orders the boy to wipe the words off the table with a wet paper towel. He makes them disappear. But the forbidden sentences are kept alive and passed from child to child, and repeated in classes and play areas throughout the day.

The Punishing Room is the name I have given to the place to which children are sent by adults when they get in trouble. The room is one of the smallest spaces at Rosa Parks School. Just two doors down from the school's main office, the sign on the door identifies the room as the Student Specialists' Office, a designation that though unfamiliar, seems promising, yet totally mystifying since it gives nothing away about the function of the room or the role of the people in it. The visitor passing down the hallway can see that it is a space like other spaces in the school inhabited by both children and adults. It is clearly an educational space, not an administrative space; children work in this room because the visitor can see them sitting at a table writing. I had been doing fieldwork in the school for several months before I actually went in and discovered for myself the place that the room occupied in the school.

Alain's composition and the events that marked it as memorable, made visible something that I had begun to suspect: getting into trouble in school did not necessarily arouse fear and shame in children, nor induce a resolve to turn over a new leaf and be good. Getting in trouble and making a trip to the Punishing Room was, for some children, also the occasion for escaping from classroom conditions of work, for self-expression, for making a name for yourself, having fun, for both actively contesting adult rules and power, as well as for the sly subversion of adult prohibitions. The Punishing Room was not the perfect site of surveillance and order that I had assumed, but a social hub, a space in which children put prohibited discourses into circulation and engaged adults in games of power in a series where wins and losses were chalked up on both sides.

Unlike the classroom where activity is routine, monotonous, highly predictable, and physically constrained, the Punishing Room is a place where the remarkable happens. It is never dull for long. In that space we witness major and minor dramas. Friends may be there or older children with "reputations" who you might never otherwise have a chance to sit next to. Note passing, bickering, whispering, and stories circulate around the table as children "do time" writing lines, copying the school rules, or finishing worksheets. As each new child enters and passes by to the inner office where the adults sit, the children acknowledge a potential new member with comments or a palpable silence. They openly eavesdrop to hear what has happened, standing with ears pressed to the closed door of the inner office, pulling up chairs to peer over the flimsy screening devices placed over the glass panels by staff as a gesture to confidentiality. They take advantage of the student specialist being fully occupied with the newcomer to play games, hurl accusations, and call each other names.

The Punishing Room is not a happy place of the type of creative activity that adults would like to think abound in schools; there is no pretense of that here. It is a place of drama, of tempers, of forbidden words, of witnessing others, both adult and child, behave outrageously, of scary enactment of adult power, of vivid tragedies with tears and of gut-wrenching comedy. For the children, it is a place of knowing that one is not alone. The child who gets in trouble is the norm. Identities and reputations are made and remade here. It is the space in the school in which everyone is like yourself—in trouble—and you are no longer different.

The Punishing Room is made up of a small rectangular antechamber with a door opening into a tiny office. The outer room is furnished with a low table flanked by child-sized chairs. The opposite wall is lined with shelves filled with the brightly colored uniforms and regalia of the children who act as the traffic guards before and after school. Children who have gotten in trouble as well as those who wear the colors of authority, who bear the symbols of order, find themselves in the same place. Many children in the school never pass into this small space at all.

The tiny inner office is the home of Faye and Rodney, the Punishing Room staff, or student specialists, their official job title. They are both African American. Faye, who is in her midfifties, has been working at this job for fifteen years. Rodney, in his first year at the school, is a man in his early thirties. He is tall and powerfully built as if he works out with weights on a regular basis. He has a loud, powerful voice. He provides an imposing male presence in the most stereotypical way that masculinity denotes power—through physique and voice. On the other hand, Faye plays out her side of the gender coin—she fusses, exhorts, despairs, and chides.

Enormous windows take up almost the entire wall at the end. Faye and Rodney have a view of the entire playground from the desk. A narrow bulletin board between the windows is covered with snapshots of children, all black, who have passed through the school. They have been put there by Faye. The beaming faces that shine down from the bulletin board make me think of happy, healthy, successful kids whose futures are bright with promise. There are two dingy but comfortable-looking chairs parked next to the door to the outer room.

Directly across from the desk is a green filing cabinet. The top drawer holds a file on each child who has been officially referred by a school adult. Some children, usually first-time offenders, come in with no record kept of the visit. During the year that I observed in the discipline office, the student specialists opened files and began accumulating evidence on 250 children, almost half the total number of kids in the school.

In the files are the data, the evidence, the material proof of wrongdoing that the adults carefully preserve. Some folders are chock full of official referral forms with comments by teachers, scraps of paper that contain forbidden words, crumpled worksheets demonstrating fits of temper, pictures drawn of parts of the body and acts that those body parts engage in that are determined to be obscene and pornographic by the adults in charge. I found drawings of mouths engaged in kissing with tongues prominently touching and remembered how deliciously terrifying and exciting even the words, much less the depiction of the act of, "French kissing" are at a certain age. One budding cartoonist had left behind a graphically funny replica of an "asshole" that was likened to a member of the discipline staff. There were a few letters of apology, all written by girls, declaring why what they had done was wrong and promising that they would never do it again. There were also signed confessions such as this one handwritten (in cursive) and signed by Marvin, a black boy in the sixth grade:

Last night at the scout meeting me claude, reds and tyrone went to the forth grade wing and we we [*sic*] saw some candy we took it and we whent downstairs and whent to the scout meeting and we was running in the hallway and that was it.

At the end of the school year, as I am going through the files, I find Alain's folder with the piece of paper on which the student specialist had copied the words he had written inserted as hard evidence of his misdemeanor. At the top of the page, Faye had added the following notation: "This is what Alain wrote about his teacher and class."

In one of the lower file drawers, all the contraband confiscated from the children during the year is kept. From the Viewmaster that had pornographic slides to an array of weapons: toy guns that look real, brightly colored water pistols, a rubber knife painted silver, a wooden sword, a slingshot, one genuine pocket knife, some dice. All the accoutrements of adult masculinity that are the socially sanctioned toys for boys. On a bookshelf behind the one desk in the room is the large tome that Rodney calls their Bible. This is the huge manual of state laws governing minors.

The Punishing Room is the first tier of the disciplinary apparatus of the school. Like the courtroom, it is the place where stories are told, truth is determined, and judgment is passed. The children who get off lightly in the sentencing process are detained in the outer room, writing lines or copying school rules as their penalty. Sometimes they lose their recreation time as well and have to sit on the bench at recess.

The Jailhouse

There is another room in the school whose sole purpose is the experience of punishment. The boys who I talked to call this room the "Jailhouse" among themselves. The Jailhouse is where you go for after-school detention. It is also the place where you spend time when you are given an in-house suspension. This means that you are banished from your class for a specified period of time—from half a day to three days—and enter a state of suspension.

The Jailhouse is the most invisible room in the school. The ordinary visitor to the school would never even know that such a room exists. It is not a part of the tour on Back to School night. Few teachers ever go in there, and the few that do are there for only a few moments.

It was not easy for me to find the room, which appears to be part of the wall of the building on the ground level. The one door opens from the playground, but it is rarely ajar. A large window looks out on the playground; while occupants can see out, it is extremely hard to see in. This is why the room's existence, what goes on inside, the activities of its occupants remain obscure and forgotten by the other adults and children in the school.

The room itself is tiny, the small space entirely taken up by an adult desk and chair, a round table with child-sized chairs, and two children's desks, both facing the wall of the room. There are six children, all African American, five boys and one girl, the day that I spend observing in the room. The space feels crowded and is made suffocatingly warm by the morning sun streaming in through the window. Mr. Sobers says that sometimes he has as many as a dozen children in the room at a time and I wonder how they all fit in.

Mr. Sobers is in charge of the room. He presides over after-school detention as well as the in-house suspension. He is a tall African American man, with a poker face and a soft voice that is deep and quite gentle. I find out that he was a professional baseball player, a pitcher, until an injury forced him to stop playing. At first, he is extremely suspicious of me. All that I learn about his life and work I must discover slowly as he begins to feel less antagonistic about my project.

Our first meeting was difficult. He made me very uncomfortable. Later I learn from Faye that Sobers wasn't very pleased with my request to observe in the suspension room. He wonders if I am working for the district office. Certainly concerns about outsiders coming in and evaluating his job at a time of budget cuts must be on his mind; Faye's as well, or she probably would not have brought the matter up. In fact, none of the adults was all that easy about my presence at first.

Sobers was skeptical of the nature of my research: "So they want to categorize the kids now." His face tells me nothing of what he's thinking, but his tone reveals the depths of his disapproval.

I explain to him that I am trying to understand why the vast majority of children that he saw in after-school detention and suspension were black and male. He laughed a bitter laugh. "I'd like to know the answer to that question myself." Pause. Then, "When you find out the answer to that question, what are you going to do with it?" he wanted to know. "People are always coming and studying black people and it never once made things better around here."

I answer, carefully, because this is clearly a home run or strikeout moment, that I want to write something that would be not only meaningful to the people that I was writing about, but useful. In order to do this I wanted to draw on the knowledge of the community of people who worked with the children on a daily basis as well as talk to the boys themselves.

I must have at least connected with the ball creditably because when I finish explaining who I am and what I am up to, Sobers begins to stipulate the conditions under which I could observe in his room. "People have different ideas about discipline," he tells me,

> and I don't want you coming in here and getting in the way of what I have to do. Don't come in and expect me to change my way of doing things. I come from the neighborhood, I know these kids and their families. I don't want someone leaning over my shoulder, observing me. That would make me very irritated.

I know without a doubt that Sobers is not a man that I would want to irritate and I am sure that the kids must sense this too. "Some days I'm going to be tense," he continues, "and not going to be as jovial as other times." I can't imagine what he would be like when jovial. He looks tough and pretty hard. But looking that way must certainly be the essential, though unwritten, requirement of his job description. I promise him that I will do none of the above but will help out with the kids—tutoring or just sitting quietly, whatever is needed. Later in the year, I asked Sobers if I could interview him. He refused me firmly. "Don't talk to me," he said.

> I have no power in this school at all. I just do what I'm told. Talk to Mr. Russell [the vice principal]. Talk to Joyce [the principal]. Talk to the teachers. Ask *them* why 99 percent of the kids that they send to me are black. Talk to the men who went to school with me who live around here who don't have any jobs. You could learn something from them. Not from me.

We learn about each other in a series of short conversations. I discover that he grew up in the neighborhood and attended Rosa Parks School with a number of the parents of the very children who he has to deal with in detention and in-house suspension. He is divorced, has a five-year-old daughter who lives with her mother and that he is so exhausted at the end of the school day that he goes home and falls asleep in front of the TV. I sense that he hates his job, but that it's reasonably secure. He also feels a commitment to the children of the neighborhood that he spends time with in his cramped room, day after day.

One of the things that I learn from Sobers is the importance of his mother in his life. "She's the one person I'm still afraid of. I knew that if I got in trouble that was it. She had the strongest backhand this side of the Mississippi. And you never knew when it was going to lash out and from where. The element of surprise was important. I give credit to her for what I am today."

Mothers and mothering in general, its present practice or as personal recollection, is an often-discussed topic in the ensemble of punishment rooms. In these discussions, mothers are key figures in the outcome of sons. The mothers of personal memories are credited with the successful attainment of manhood. The mothers of the boys who enter the room for punishment are blamed for their children's behavior.

Once I spend time in Sobers's domain, I realize that the minuscule size of the place, its physical layout, the nature of his job, and how this has structured his relationship with the children that he spends time with have provided concrete grounds for his stipulations to me. I can barely stand to spend the entire day in the room with Mr. Sobers and the six children who are there that day. The room is stuffy, airless, and we are all unceasingly in each other's presence. Unlike the classroom, unlike the Punishing Room upstairs, there is never a time or place for escaping surveillance through trips to the bathroom. There is no sociability, no relief from the boredom of schoolwork. The clichéd phrase, "Time seems to have stopped," becomes fresh with new meaning.

The timetable for the occupants of the room, both children and adults, for the punished and their keeper, is different than for the rest of the school. Our segregation from those who are good citizens is total. We have a recess and a lunch break, but at a different time than everyone else and for a much shorter period. We sit in the stifling room looking out at the playground wistfully. After the regular lunchtime is over, the children help clean tables in the cafeteria. This work is part of their punishment.

The children are supposed to do work assigned by their classroom teacher during suspension. On the day that I'm there, only one teacher comes in to check on a student. Jewelle, the only girl, is reading *Roll of Thunder*, which she informs me is boring. She doesn't like reading at all, she tells me emphatically. She spends a lot of time looking at the wall until Sobers tells her to come over and read to him. Jewelle has been suspended for fighting.

Michael, a fourth-grade African American boy, is the only one who volunteers when Sobers asks if anyone would like Mrs. Ferguson to help them. He has a whole page of long division to do. He has spent the first half hour of our time in the room looking from the blank paper to the math book, the wall, at Jewelle, and back. He has avoided eye contact with me. I am glad to help him if only to have something to do.

It becomes clear that he doesn't yet understand the concept of "remainders." He knows his multiplication tables and he can add and subtract, so we go through four or five problems step by step. I do not have his full attention. It is easy to be distracted in such close quarters and he is paying more attention to one of the boys reading aloud for Sobers. Sobers spots Michael chewing gum and orders him to go and spit it out in the wastebasket. Grateful to get up and stretch, he makes much of the short journey across the room and spits the wad into the basket. When he returns, we work on a problem dividing packs of chewing gum among different numbers of kids.

Sobers spends a lot of time haranguing, urging, threatening the kids to get on with their work. The most he has to threaten with is that they will have a shorter playtime. But this is also punishing for him as well, as he must surely look forward to stretching his legs outside the room while they run around for a few minutes. One of the boys whom I interviewed, a frequent visitor to detention, tells me that he feels sorry for Mr. Sobers because he has to spend the whole day locked up with all the bad kids.

An even more severe form of punishment is suspension from school. Children can be suspended for up to five days. The state limits to twenty the total number of days a child can be suspended before a hearing is held. The hearing involves parents, school personnel, and representatives from the district office. The few boys who approached the twenty-day limit began to be given longer stints of in-house suspensions to avoid these hearings. One was sent home every day for half the day because "that's all we can take of him," the principal told me. The most drastic action the school can take is of course expulsion, though for a variety of reasons they avoid taking this course.

If the Punishing Room is indeed a place where children come to occupy a "free space" with less surveillance than in the classroom, then full suspension has the potential to be the freest space of all that children can win in a state of punishment. Significantly, it is, as far as school goes, the most invisible form. One of the younger boys described it to me as "lonely because you don't have none of your friends. You watch TV." It did not stop him however, on one of the days he was suspended, from circling the school on his bike throughout the school day, much to the disgust of the school staff and the interest of the other children. In general, there is little expectation that any schoolwork will be done on the part of the school, no monitoring procedures, and plenty of TV watching. Suspension also provides a "freeing up" space for the classroom teachers who have, for a short time anyway, gotten rid of some of the children they consider the most difficult students in the room.

Whenever a child has to stay for after-school detention or is being suspended, the student specialist calls their home. The moment when mother, sister, grandmother, and in rare cases, father, comes in to pick up a child or to have a conference about a child's behavior is a traumatic one. Lamar's aunt, called away from work, shouted threats all the way down the hall and out the front door. I hear, "You know better than to call me from work. You want me to lose my job. You *know* it's going to be trouble now." An older sister, bringing her own baby in a stroller, rebuked and exhorted Tyrone for his suspension when she came to pick him up. Tyrone had brought a "look-alike" gun to school—the kind of toy gun that can be purchased at any toy store—and had been caught. Having even a toy gun at school, I discovered then and there, was grounds for expulsion. The boy looks scared and pinched as he huddles beside his sister, waiting for the principal. The sister is saying to Tyrone over and over, "What is grandma going to do with you? She doing her damn best for you and look what you carrying on with. You want to kill her?"

The principal comes into the antechamber of the Punishing Room where we are sitting. She says that just a few weeks ago Tyrone had brought another toy gun to school and at that time she had talked to the district office and managed to get just a five-day suspension for him. This is the second time so she doesn't know if she can do anything. She'll have to call and see.

The principal is an Asian American woman who is always elegantly dressed. She is unsmudged by childish hands and unwrinkled by events such as this. She has an unfriendly demeanor and a brisk manner. Sympathy is not one of her favorite expressions, and she doesn't show it now.

Tyrone looks bereft. The sister looks impassive but ready to hear the worst. She looks like she's only a few years older than Tyrone herself. She sits waiting with her young baby, Tyrone at her side. This is the day that I discover that a sixth-grader could be expelled from school. "What happens to him then? Where will he go? What will they do?" I ask Faye, who is looking grim. "Well, his family have to try and enroll him in a school in another district." In the end, Tyrone does not get expelled but is suspended for another five days at home.

Punishing Room as a Window

The Punishing Room is a window onto the disciplinary system of the school in which I am doing fieldwork, a lens through which to examine how the race/gender identities of preadolescent African American boys are constituted through punishment. It is a location from which to investigate the ways that contemporary discourses about black masculinity become authoritative resources for school adults in the construction of school identities of "bad" boys. The Punishing Room is also a site to explore how these boys negotiate individual identities and life histories in the collective experience of race/gender.

The disciplinary system comprises the physical spaces I have described, and the adults and children who come into them. It includes the rules, codes, rewards, and punishments prescribed by state laws, by custom, and by written and unwritten standards of social interaction. It embraces the manners and politeness that govern the relationships of adults and children. It is a key element backstage in the presentation of the educational process as a smoothly functioning machine. This view from inside gave me an insight into some of the more concealed, less presentable mechanisms and functions of schooling.

In the Punishing Room, school identities and reputations are constituted, negotiated, challenged, confirmed for African American youth in a process of categorization, reward and punishment, humiliation, and banishment. Children passing through the system are marked and categorized as they encounter state laws, school rules, tests and exams, psychological remedies, screening committees, penalties and punishments, rewards and praise. Identities as worthy, hardworking, devious, or dangerous are proffered, assumed, or rejected.

The punishing system is supported by nothing less than the moral order of society—the prevailing ideology—which simultaneously produces and imposes a consensus about a broad spectrum of societal values, manners, presentation of self including style of dress, ways of standing, sitting, tone of voice, mode of eye contact, range of facial expressions. It is also assumed that the rules, codes, social relations, and behaviors adjudicated by a school's discipline system are about the transmission and enactment of a moral authority from adults, who are empowered to transmit and enact, to children, who are seen as lacking the essential values, social skills, and morality required of citizens. The state laws and the school rules that put them into effect are treated as if they are universal truths, blind and neutral to differences of class, race and gender among groups of children. They are part of our common-sense knowledge of young people: who they are and what they must be taught. Teachers and school administrators speak of discipline as the essential prior condition for any learning to take place.

However, adults and children, parents and relatives, teachers, custodians, and student specialists come into the Punishing Room as self-identified and identifiable members of different social categories of class, race, and gender. They bring with them theories, commonsense knowledge, readily available explanations, to give meaning to the everyday occurrences in these rooms. So, the Punishment Room is a focal point of intersecting and contradictory ideas of how and why so many African American boys are found in spaces like this one all across the nation. The dominant theory that I heard expressed was that the problem was one of dysfunctional families. This explanation is grounded in a gender discourse that identifies females, as mothers and as teachers, as "incompetent" or inadequate socializers of masculinity.

Notions of family, in general, come in as relatives are called up, called in, or more rarely, come on their own volition to challenge the school's assessments. They enter this classificatory system as a credit or a debit to the child. School adults call upon images, representations, beliefs about family to theorize away school dilemmas and difficulties in dealing with youth: troublesome children come from troubled or troublemaking families. School adults have families and family histories and bring in these concepts to inform the truths they hold about family in general.

Children bring parents, grandparents, and guardians into the room as they come for punishment. They come with the baggage of family knowledge and history, warnings, daily practices, family admonitions about how to handle oneself in the face of confrontations with authority. And they especially bring in all the mannerisms of speech, laughter, and emotional expressions that echo in the household.

Punishment practices are mapped on assumptions about "essential" differences. The apparent consensus underlying the discipline system is fractured by the racial and gender meanings of social relations and of power brought in by children and adults. For example, some adults in the school privately disagree with the changes in discipline and punishment procedures that have been made in the last decade. This disagreement crystallizes around claims that there are different racial styles in disciplining children, a "white" style and a "black" one, and that this difference affects the knowledge and expectations that adults and children bring to school. Several black teachers, for example, described the present mode at Rosa Parks School as representing a "white" style that was confusing to black children, who were used to more direct and clear-cut authority relations and practices in black households. A frequently cited example was that the white style disguises what are really commands in the form of suggestions or requests, thus causing black children to misinterpret the nature of the relationship with the consequence of getting in trouble.

School rules also seem to be specifically designed to control, manage, and channel the "natural" behavior of boys, who are said to be more physical, aggressive, sexual. Girls are believed to be more naturally agreeable, tractable, and able to tolerate the controlled atmosphere. Several adults and many of the boys I interviewed claimed that girls got off more lightly than boys under school rules; classroom structures and organization, it was argued, are more suited to girls. African American girls are expected to "get in trouble" in ways that damage their own life chances, rather than make trouble for others like the boys do.

There is the assumption that the gender of the adult authority figure and that of the child's is important in shaping adult-child interactions in disciplinary moments. Men bring a certain authority to the interaction by virtue of what being male means in the world in general. It is not by chance that three of the four punishing jobs in the school are held by African American men (race relations are significant here as well), nor that these men have imposing physiques. Furthermore, the male adult's interaction with girls is constrained and complicated by sexual overtones, making touching or contact between adult male and female child bodies suspect and dangerous. The chastising relationships between the two are therefore more likely to be at arm's length and verbal. On the other hand, male adults do not hesitate to grab boys by the shoulder, by ears, or to push and shove them in body contact.

Our construction of femininity from the earliest age as victimizable and requiring protection, as well as sexualized, makes body contact volatile, while for boys physicality and the active development of a defense system against encroachments from others becomes something admirable. Masculinity is constructed as the practice of power plays and brinkmanship. Boys are expected to learn how to take body contact in stride, to handle situations independently, and to not get ruffled by them.

For some of the boys, the route from the Punishment Room leads to another series of rooms where psychological counseling is offered in order to teach them "impulse control" and how to get along better with their peers. So troublemaking acts become transformed into "troubled" children, with pathological personalities and character flaws that must be documented and treated. This psychologization of "troublesome" behavior is linked with a discourse about the nature of the problem as an individual disorder rather than one that is social and systemic.

The punishment rooms are workplaces, reflecting a division of labor that draws on race and gender relations in the world outside the school in order to function effectively. The actual punishing work is experienced by the African American adults in conflicting and troublesome ways that directly involve their knowledge of the community they live and work in, their own life history, the conditions of their work, their feelings about what their job should be versus what it is, the pressures from the system to accomplish goals that may or may not conflict with their own image of the job. One of the systemic pressures making for more oppressive, punitive relations for African American children is the fear that white middle-class families will increasingly pull their children out of the public school and send them to private schools. Pressure is felt by the student specialist and "Jailhouse Keeper" to contain, suppress, and conceal damaging behavior that could contribute to the school's reputation as a hostile environment.

But the Punishing Room is not just a space in which identities are conferred and taken up by children, a field in which power is exercised

My first impressions of the children and their families came from the school: from what teachers and administrators said, from school records and test scores. It was a powerful, seamless story that reinforced a "natural" connection between certain groups of children and certain outcomes. The following piece is my regurgitation of the institutional narrative with its litany of "commonsense" correlations.

According to the statistics, the best-behaved children in the school are also the brightest, the most gifted. They score high on tests and participate in the program for Gifted and Talented children. A very tiny percentage of these best-behaved children are classified within school records as black. But most often, these children are racially classified white, live in nice neighborhoods, and come from homes that have separate, quiet places for them to do their homework. They arrive at the school in a bus. At recess, they mostly hang out with each other. From time to time, they are naughty in childlike ways. Occasionally, one of the boys gets into a fight or talks back and has to stay for detention. The girls, however, are models of good behavior, and no trace is found in the record of them breaking a single rule or getting out of line. All in all, these are children who resolve disagreements with others in socially appropriate ways.

According to the school people, the best-behaved children in the school, some of whom are "average achievers," come ready to work; they know what they're there for. When it's time for them to listen, they listen, they raise their hand, they wait their turn. They are responsible for themselves and they get down to work. They know what is expected of them. They have a language for their feelings. Most important of all, they have self-control and can sit and listen and learn from the teacher.

According to the school people, these children are well behaved because they have parents who care about their education and oversee their homework. They have total support from home. Not only do these adults want their children to succeed, but they are role models for this success. Fathers are strong but they can show their emotions as well. They spend quality time with their sons so they can learn what it means to be a man. Daughters are encouraged to develop all their talents and potentials. The mothers of these well-behaved children are active in school in a helpful, supportive way. They raise money for special programs, attend meetings, go on field trips, make sure the homework gets done. They respect their children's rights, but they treat them as children.

According to the statistics, the worst-behaved children in the school are black and male, and when they take tests they score way below their grade level. They eat candy, refuse to work, fight, gamble, chase, hit, instigate, cut class, cut school, cut hair. They are defiant, disruptive, disrespectful, profane. These black males fondle girls, draw obscene pictures, make lewd comments, intimidate others, and call teachers names. They are banished from the classroom to the hall, to the discipline office, to the suspension room, to the streets so that others can learn. They are suspended from one to five days. Separate files are kept recording their misdemeanors and accumulating the objects that have been confiscated from them as evidence: scraps of paper with obscene drawings of penises and tongues meeting in kisses. The drawers are crammed with the forbidden objects which these boys have brought into the school: neon pink and green water pistols, slingshots, pairs of dice, cigars.

According to the statistics, black girls are misbehaving too, though not at the same exaggerated rate. They also fight, steal, talk back to teachers, eat candy, cut class, instigate, damage school property, act disrespectful, and call other children names. But if they have the same sexual yearnings, they do not appear recorded in the statistics. They do not fondle, fantasize, or engage in sexual horseplay; though sometimes they fight with boys and get in trouble.

All of these boys and girls come from the local neighborhood and walk to school most days. That their neighborhood is not a good one is made obvious by the signs on many street corners telling drug dealers and their customers to beware because their license number is being taken.

According to the statistics, black children in the school rarely make it into the ranks of Gifted and Talented programs but are in the compensatory education or special day classes or working with resource specialists. They have poor impulse control and attention disorders. They need psychological counseling.

According to the school, these black kids need special treatment because they lack attention at home and are always demanding it in the classroom. Their parents do not care about their education. Many live with grandparents or other relatives. Some even live in foster care. Sometimes they have fathers, but mostly not. In any case, they have no male role models. In fact they have no role models at all and efforts must be made to create relationships for them with total strangers who can teach them how to become responsible men and women. You can smell alcohol on their mothers' breath at parent conferences, relatives get belligerent on the phone, most talk a good line but never follow through. They don't show up for evening meetings, even when they are scheduled especially for their convenience. These families are always blaming others and never taking the responsibility for their own actions. The children learn this habit of blaming others, bring it to school and never take responsibility for their own behavior or failure there. Both children and parents are in need of special training programs; parents need to learn how to parent, how to discipline their kids, what to do and what not to do. Children need to learn to recognize what they are feeling and deal with those feelings in ways that involve only themselves and does not endanger others.

chapter three
school rules

This is the "banking" concept of education, in which the
scope of action allowed to the students extends only as far as
receiving, filing, and storing the deposits. They do, it is true,
have the opportunity to become collectors or cataloguers of
the things they store. But in the last analysis, it is men themselves who are filed away through the lack of creativity, trans-
formation, and knowledge in this (at best) misguided system.
For apart from inquiry, apart from praxis, men cannot be
truly human. Knowledge emerges only through invention and
reinvention, through the restless, impatient, continuing,
hopeful inquiry men pursue in the world, with the world, and
with each other.

—PAULO FREIRE, *Pedagogy of the Oppressed*

I am in school to learn.
I pledge to accept responsibility
for myself and my school work.
I pledge to accept responsibility
for my actions toward parents,
teachers, and my schoolmates.

—ROSA PARKS SCHOOL PLEDGE

School as a Sorting System

School rules govern and regulate children's bodily, linguistic, and emotional expression. They are an essential element of the sorting and ranking technologies of an educational system that is organized around the
search for and establishment of a ranked difference among children.
This system is designed to produce a hierarchy: a few individuals who

are valorized as "gifted" at the top and a large number who are stigma-tized as failures at the bottom. School rules operate along with other elements of the formal curriculum such as standardized tests and grades to produce this ordered difference among children.

Since this is not the prevailing assumption about the goal of edu-cation in our society, we must turn to alternative views of schooling for a theoretical explanation of the process of how social difference is cre-ated and reproduced in schools. One view is that of "radical schooling" theorists, and the other is that of the poststructuralist Michel Foucault. In contrast to the widely held liberal belief that schools are meritocratic and that through them individuals regardless of their social, economic, or ethnic background are able to realize their potential and achieve eco-nomic and social mobility, these alternative perspectives presume schooling to be a system for sorting and ranking students to take a par-ticular place in the existing social hierarchy.

Radical Schooling Theory

The radical perspective assumes that educational institutions are orga-nized around and reflect the interests of dominant groups in the soci-ety; that the function of school is to reproduce the current inequities of our social, political, and economic system. It proposes that the crucial element for creating and reproducing social inequality is a "hidden cur-riculum" that includes such taken-for-granted components of instruc-tion as differences in modes of social control and the regulation of rela-tions of authority,[1] and the valorization of certain forms of linguistic and cultural expression.[2] This hidden curriculum reflects the "cultural hegemony" of the dominant class and works to reinforce and reproduce that dominance by exacerbating and multiplying—rather than dimin-ishing or eliminating—the "inequalities" children bring from home and neighborhood to school.

Pierre Bourdieu is representative of this school of thought. He argues that schools embody the class interests and ideology of the dom-inant class, which has the power to impose its views, standards, and cul-tural forms—its "cultural capital"—as superior. Thus the ruling class is

---

1. Bowles and Gintis, *Schooling in Capitalist America.*
2. Bourdieu and Passeron, *Reproduction;* Basil Bernstein, *Towards a Theory of Educa-tional Transmission,* vol. 3 of *Class, Codes, and Control* (London: Routledge and Kegan Paul, 1974).

able to systematically enforce the social distinctions of its own lifestyle and tastes as superior standards to be universally aspired to. This imposition is effected through the exercise of "symbolic violence," the painful, damaging, mortal wounds inflicted by the wielding of words, symbols, standards.

Bourdieu's concept of "symbolic violence" is particularly useful for an examination of punishment practices as symbolic enforcers of a cultural hegemony in the hidden curriculum. He directs our attention to the manner in which this type of violence operates through taken-for-granted notions of the form and content of "proper" behavior overlooked by liberal notions of schooling. For example, "politeness," in his view, "contains a politics, a practical immediate recognition of social classifications and of hierarchies between the sexes, the generations, the classes, etc."[3] This example of the politics of politeness is one I will develop to demonstrate the way the social hierarchy of society is recreated by the school: how manners, style, body language, and oral expressiveness influence the application of school rules and ultimately come to define and label African American students and condemn them to the bottom rung of the social order.

Foucault's Theory of Disciplinary Power

Foucault's concepts of normalization and of normalizing judgments are also fruitful theoretical starting points for grounding the discussion of how power works through punishment. Though schooling is at the center of a vast social science investigation of socialization processes, most studies focus on classroom organization and interaction, on curriculum or on analysis of texts. In cases where discipline is the subject of inquiry, the salient issue typically becomes one of effective classroom management and style of social control for children.[4] Punishment as a mechanism in a process of social differentiation is generally neglected in this research.

One reason for this emphasis is the role that school discipline is assumed to play in the learning process. Conformity to rules is treated by school adults as the essential prior condition for any classroom

---

3. Pierre Bourdieu, "The Economics of Linguistic Exchanges," *Social Science Information* 26, no. 6 (1977): 646.

4. See, for example, Delwyn Tattum, ed., *Management of Disruptive Pupil Behavior in Schools* (New York: John Wiley and Sons, 1986).

learning to take place. Furthermore, rules bear the weight of moral authority. Rules governing children are seen as the basis of order, the bedrock of respect on which that order stands. Rules are spoken about as inherently neutral, impartially exercised, and impervious to individual feelings and personal responses. The question of how order is obtained, at whose expense, the messages this "order" bears, and the role that it plays in the regulation and production of social identities is rarely addressed.

Foucault provides an alternative approach to the function of discipline in institutions like schools. He conceptualizes discipline broadly as the mechanism for a new mode of domination that constitutes us as *individuals* with a specific perception of our identity and potential that appears natural rather than the product of relations of power. The disciplinary techniques of the school actively produce individual social identities of "good," "bad," "gifted," "having potential," "troubled," and "troublesome," rather than ferret them out and reveal them as they "naturally" exist. The objective of this mode of power is the production of people who are docile workers, self-regulating and self-disciplined.

Foucault asserts that normalizing judgments made through the allocation of reward and punishment are the most powerful instruments of this disciplinary power, whose function is not to suppress unwanted behavior or to reform it, but to

> refer individual actions to a whole that is at once a field of comparison, a space of differentiation. . . . It measures in quantitative terms and hierarchizes in terms of value the abilities, the level, the "nature" of individuals. It introduces through this "value-giving" measure, the constraint of a conformity that must be achieved. Lastly, it traces the limit that will define difference in relation to all other differences, the external frontier of the abnormal. . . . [It] compares, differentiates, hierarchizes, homogenizes, excludes. In short, it *normalizes.*[5]

So, school rules operate as instruments of normalization. Children are sorted, evaluated, ranked, compared on the basis of (mis)behavior: what they do that violates, conforms to, school rules.

---

5. Michel Foucault, *Discipline and Punish,* translated from the French by Alan Sheridan (New York: Vintage, 1979), 183.

Foucault argues that disciplinary control is a modern mode of power that comes into existence with the formation of the bourgeois democratic state as a technique of regulation particularly suited to a form of governance predicated on the idea of formal equality. Under this type of regime, our status in a hierarchical system is no longer formally ascribed by birth but appears to be derived from how we measure up with regard to institutionally generated norms. "Each individual receives as his status his own individuality, in which he is linked by his status to the features, the measurements, the gaps, the 'marks' that characterize him and make him a 'case.'"[6] We come to know who we are in the world, and we are known by others, through our socially constituted "individual" difference rather than through an ascribed status such as class or race. In contemporary United States, disciplinary power becomes a particularly relevant technique of regulation and identity formation in a desegregated school system in which status once ascribed on the basis of racial superiority and inferiority is no longer legitimate grounds for granting or denying access to resources or attainment of skills.

Individualization is accomplished in institutions through a proliferation of surveillance and assessment techniques. In school, routine practices of classification, the ranking of academic performance through tests and grades, psychological screening measures, the distribution of rewards and punishment construct the "truth" of who we are.

We turn now to look at some of the mechanisms of the school that classify, compare, evaluate, and rank children through standardized tests and scores based on the official, academic curriculum. Though the official curriculum is not the subject of this study, I offer a brief overview because, as I will argue, there is a strong relationship between the hidden curriculum and the formal academic one, between a teacher's subjective evaluations of students' character and behavior and the kinds of classrooms they end up in. A disproportionate number of the kids who are in the remedial, low-track classrooms are those getting in trouble. A number of studies indicate that the placement of kids in high- or low-track groups or classrooms within schools is not simply the result of test scores of student achievement but is influenced by such things as teachers' perceptions of student appearance, behavior,

---

6. Ibid., 192.

and social background.[7] My objective is to suggest several ways in which to look at the interaction between objective standards and subjective modes of interpretation.

The Official Curriculum

Within Rosa Parks School, children are formally classified and sorted into classrooms on the basis of age (grade level) and on the basis of race or ethnicity. The official explanation for this sorting is that it is to maintain a racial balance in classrooms and in the system in general. This racial balance, however, is not replicated in the special pullout programs for kids who deviate from the academic norms of the school system.

Children at Rosa Parks are sorted and ranked on the basis of tests of academic and psychological "capacity" as well as through the discipline system of the school. They are rank-ordered in relation to each other and to national norms on the basis of tests. At one end of this range of potential, ability, and talent are those who fall into the category of Gifted and Talented (GATE), the vast majority of whom are white. At the other end of the spectrum are students who are below average, failing, "at risk." The overwhelming majority are poor and black. In the final analysis, low-skill classrooms and supplementary programs like PALS are the place in school occupied by blacks, while enriched, innovative programs are largely the province of white kids.

These observations support Hochschild's findings that classrooms in schools with official desegregation policies are more racially segregated than schools in general, suggesting the existence of inequitable disciplinary practices and the segregation of blacks and whites into different "tracks."[8] She argues that for this reason it is important to look behind the official accounting of racial equity in school districts and follow sorting practices into the classrooms. There we find students who have been labeled "at risk" being pulled out from their regular classroom during the day to attend special classes tailored to treat or

---

7. For example, David H. Hargreaves, Stephen K. Hester, and Frank J. Mellor, eds., *Deviance in Classrooms* (London: Routledge and Kegan Paul, 1975); Perry Gilmore, "'Gimme Room': School Resistance, Attitude, and Access to Literacy," *Journal of Education* 167, no. 1 (1985); Helen Gouldner, *Teachers' Pets, Troublemakers, and Nobodies: Black Children in Elementary School* (Westport, Conn.: Greenwood Press, 1978).

8. Jennifer L. Hochschild, *The New American Dilemma: Liberal Democracy and School Desegregation* (New Haven: Yale University Press, 1984), 31.

"compensate" for the specific deficiency for which they have been diagnosed. Here I briefly describe some of the methods of categorizing, ranking, and resegregating students and what this means for the actual quality of education they get, before turning my full attention to the valuation of children through punishment.

Individualizing Instruction

A student is placed in compensatory education, or "comp. ed.," classes at Rosa Parks for two hours a week if they score lower than the thirty-seventh percentile on the California Test of Basic Skills (CTBS). The funding for these classes comes from federal allocations for poor and minority children to compensate for the "deprivation" in their home environments that they bring into the school. This remedy emanates from the prevailing perspective that black children and their families are "culturally disadvantaged"; it takes for granted the superiority of the white, middle-class culture of the school and the inferior nature of the values, life experience, knowledge that black students bring.

The CTBS ranks each child on a scale in relation to every other child in the state and in the nation. This test is considered an achievement test measuring what you already know and, according to my teacher informant, "ignores potential." Every student in the state is supposed to take this test, and the score of each is compared to the national norm in reading and math. Schools, school districts, cities, and states are also ranked according to the test results that are published in the newspapers. This ranking is taken very seriously: teachers' performance within school is monitored according to their pupils' performance on the test, and the ranking enters into real estate values and a "calculus of community livability" across the United States. The CTBS score is put in each child's file as part of the identifying material that follows them as a place marker from school to school.

Black students in the Arcadia School District placed below the national norm in reading, language, and mathematics in all grades, while whites placed above the national norm in all grades. So the overwhelming majority of children in the compensatory education program at Rosa Parks School are African American.

What is the approach being used to address this lack of achievement? When I observed the reading/language arts component of the program, I noticed two significant differences from the regular classroom. First, the special classes had two adults to ten children in the room, while the teacher-student ratio was one to thirty in the regular classroom. Second, the entire system of instruction in the compensatory education class was based on computerized software, so that each pupil interacted mainly with a computer terminal.

My initial response was to be heartened by these differences, which seemed to provide the groundwork for some exciting educational possibilities for those who needed to catch up in terms of basic skills. By the end of the session, however, I was deeply discouraged. Even though the teacher-pupil ratio and the technology appeared to be at a level that allowed for a more challenging, individualized learning experience, the actual educational process in the special class was even more routinized and mechanical than in the regular classroom. It was, in fact, a system of instruction that kept the children locked into the same level of learning, and the low student-to-teacher ratio, rather than increasing the amount of time that pupils had to interact with a teacher, instead increased the level of surveillance and control that adults had over each child. Here is an extract from my field notes:

This was my second visit to observe in the comp. ed. room. I observed two different fifth-grade classes at work. There are six girls and three boys in one and three girls and seven boys in the other. Out of a total of nineteen, two are white, four are Asians. All the rest are African American. The teacher, Mrs. Smythe is white and her aide, Miss Alvaro is Filipino.

The classroom has a long table down the center. Big sunny windows face out on the street. Two rows of ten computers sit on the table back to back. All of the kids sitting at the terminals are either black, Hispanic, or Asian. This year one hundred seventy-nine children are in comp. ed. One hundred thirty-four of them are African American. Most of the others in the program speak English as a second language and need to practice English language skills.

On each computer is a paper cup with a number written on the cup. When children come into the room, they take a folder from Miss Alvaro and sit in front of a computer terminal. Each program is personalized so that each child is greeted at the terminal by name when they log on and at the end of each exercise is given their score by name. But this individualization is more apparent than real since the children are all pretty much kept working in the same program and at the same level.

Mrs. Smythe generally has the kids start with "games" and with typing instructions. The typing program has exercises designated as accuracy and speed builders which are followed by accuracy and speed building tests. One boy, working on speed building, was typing rows of sas sas sas sas. Mrs. Smythe tells the group how valuable learning to type is because it is a way that they can earn some money later. This is the first and only time in my observation in the school that I hear a teacher connect a classroom activity with something tangible such as paid work.

Then Mrs. Smythe moves on to a reading exercise which teaches how to "get the main idea" from a paragraph. Kids read a short paragraph out of a booklet and then have to pick the correct answer from a multiple choice list. If kids don't know how to pronounce a particular word or are having trouble with reading then they ask one of the adults for help. As I glance through the paragraphs, I notice that most are either about "nature" or about Indians. One paragraph is about how Indians made fishhooks. Another is about how they made the color red using plants. Indians are always presented as museum pieces, as if they live today the kind of life that they lived before the Europeans came to America.

I find the exercise frustrating because often more than one sentence could be the "right" answer. I have to check in the teacher's book to make sure. Mrs. Smythe says she has the same problem. But the point to be learned here by the children is that there is only *one correct answer* and there is no discussion of why one answer is more right than another.

Children are admonished over and over not to read ahead. If they finish reading before the others they are encouraged to turn over their sheets and doodle on the back until the group is finished. Unlike the classroom, there is no incentive for working fast. Unlike the regular classroom, there are tangible rewards. Kids who get the answer right get a bean dropped in the paper cup on top of the computer. Mrs. Smythe tells the children that this exercise will help them do better on the CTBS.

When I return to observe a few weeks later, I was not surprised that the kids who read faster than others or who get all correct answers are still working in the same group.

The class also works on a series of exercises called sequencing. This is the most routinized and simplistic in a series of programs that seem to encourage the most rudimentary level of thinking rather than any creative effort on the part of the kids whatsoever. The graphic on the screen is a train made up of engine, car, and caboose. When you put three random sentences into proper order then the train moves off. The sentences in the sequencing exercise included the following sets of three: put on shoes, tie shoes, put on socks; pitch the ball, hit the ball, catch the ball; pick flower, plant seed, water seed; untie shoes, take off shoes, take off socks; find pencil, write letter, mail letter; wash apple, take a big bite, pick an apple; give present, buy present, wrap present. Fifth-grade kids who I already know from other places in the school as highly intelligent are working on stringing these sentences into the proper sequential order. I notice that kids play around with the sequences to get different responses from the computer.

The classes also work on a "logic" program. The graphic on the terminal screen consists of two tanks which hold different amounts of oil and pipes leading from the tanks into an oil truck. Each round of the game, the program gives a specific amount which must be taken from the tanks and put in the truck. The kids have to move the amounts back and forth between the tanks to get just the right amount into the truck. The material they are moving back and forth have cute names like funny fluff, odd oil, and jolly juice. The aim is to find the most efficient way of getting the tanker truck filled. Most of the kids are fairly attentive to the monitor screens as these problems are harder than the sequencing.

At the end of each exercise, one of the adults drops a bean in the cup by each child's terminal. These are counted up at the end and a stamp is placed on a sheet of paper in the kid's folder. Mrs. Smythe tells me that these stamps accumulate and can be cashed in for small prizes such as stickers, colored pencils, and prizes such as pizza parties.

The interaction between teacher and pupils is highly programmed. The level of control is intense. The movement between seats and activities that I observed in the regular classroom that was often initiated by the kids themselves rarely occur. There is no excuse to sharpen a pencil, get materials. Children sit and stare

diligently occupied with the graphics and movements on the computer screen for the entire period.

My observations in the compensatory education classroom confirmed the argument of radical schooling theorists that low-income and
minority kids will be schooled to take their place in the bottom rungs
of the class structure. My findings also corroborated those of Oakes
that students placed in low-track and remedial classes are exposed to a
severely restricted knowledge base requiring the most rudimentary
learning processes. In a national study of secondary school tracking,
Oakes found that learning in the low tracks rarely inculcated the
knowledge and thought processes requisite for moving into a higher
track; instead, it ensured that participants would remain at the lowest
level, falling increasingly behind. She found that students were being
trained to follow directions, to conform, to be passive, to take standardized tests rather than to think creatively and independently.[9]

A second technique for sorting students at Rosa Parks is through
what used to be called special education classes. These are for children
working at two grade levels below their capacity. More euphemistic
names have been devised for these programs because "special education" classes came under heavy criticism in the 1960s for being a popular dumping ground for black students. As a result, a process was put in
place to ensure that schools could not place a child in a special education program without going through a series of formal steps. A meeting
between a team from the school and a parent or guardian takes place
culminating in an instructional plan drawn up by the school psycholo-
gist based on a series of tests that "identify specific cognitive problems"
that determines the child's placement.[10]

The instructional plan will involve one of two options that exist
under the umbrella of "special education": a Resource Specialist Program (RSP) that pulls the child out of the regular room for one or two
periods a day for individual instruction in a small group, or the Special

---

9. Jeannie Oakes, *Keeping Track: How Schools Structure Inequality* (New Haven:
Yale University Press, 1985), 85.

10. For an excellent discussion of institutional practices for classifying students and
placing them in categories such as "learning disabled" or educationally handicapped by
committees such as these, see Hugh Mehan, Alma Hertweck, and J. Lee Miehls, *Handicapping the Handicapped: Decision-Making in Student's Educational Careers* (Stanford: Stanford University Press, 1986).

Day Class (SDC) that is either a whole or a half day in a separate class-room. The object of RSP, according to one of its instructors, is to teach the children in ways that suit different learning styles. The SDC is reserved for students who "have such a severe learning or emotional" disability that it interferes with their ability to learn in the regular class-room. Several teaching positions and some administrative positions are paid for through compensatory and special education funding.

I participated as a reading tutor for two months in the SDC room. I found an incongruous mix of children, all but two of whom were black: some had "severe learning disabilities," while others were there because they had been "acting up" and so had been defined as having an emotional disability. The kids who were pointed out to me as "emo-tionally disturbed" were all African American and predominately male.

There is a pullout program of a different type at Rosa Parks School. It is the program for the Gifted and Talented (GATE), the vast major-ity of whom are white. GATE children are pulled out of class and bused to another school where they have the hands-on, interactive learning experience that, as one of the teachers put it, most kids could benefit from in every classroom. Children in GATE are identified through a test given in the third grade. Unlike the CTBS, which is required for all kids, only those identified by teachers as having potentially gifted qual-ities are eligible for this test. It is worth speculating on the role that cul-tural capital plays here, on how different perceptions of what a "gifted" child looks and sounds like might determine who is given the opportu-nity to take this test. Perhaps as a result of such speculation, an African American teacher at Rosa Parks took the initiative to organize a pro-gram for minority students who show promise of going on for a higher education. These children meet twice a week with the teacher before and after school to work on science and math.

Several of the Troublemakers as well as some of the Schoolboys were in the "remedial" programs. Since these rooms involved more rou-tinized work and a heightened surveillance rather than an enriching compensatory program, it seemed unlikely that they would develop the skills to catch up with the "norm" for their age grade. The exercises and drills they provided might help the kids perform better on the stan-dardized tests, but it was likely that overall they would fall increasingly behind. However, the programs provide the institution with funds for several teachers and aides as well as expensive computer technology.

Now let us return to the subject of trouble and punishment, keeping in mind the inference that there is an uneasy connection between the subjective and objective modes of evaluation of worthiness and potential in school. Both of these modes draw on and reflect hegemonic cultural forms and values.

Breaking the Rules

What do kids do that gets them into trouble in school? Referral forms disclose the following categories of offense: cutting class, tardiness, misbehavior, defiance, disrespect, disruption, profanity, gambling, obscenity, fighting. The forms typically contained descriptions of the interactions and events that led up to infractions as well as the severity of the punishment. A brief description of some of these suggests the array of behaviors that might contravene the rules through any school day. Some like cutting and tardiness are predictable and self-explanatory; we know what they entail. Other categories such as gambling seem out of place in an elementary school. The few official actions taken against gamblers that I found usually documented the incident in vague language: "gambling with dimes"; "gambling in the cafeteria." This last, involving one of the Troublemakers, was punished by two days in the Jailhouse.

The category of "misbehavior" on the referral form covers a range of possible acts from minor misdeeds that were punished by benching during recess to more grave acts that result in doing time in the Jailhouse. Examples of these offenses gleaned from the files include the following charges: eating candy, chewing gum, littering, spitting, not lining up properly, shooting rubber bands, chasing and running in the halls, goofing off, messing around. All have to do with the maintenance of a general atmosphere of order, cleanliness, comportment in the school. These infractions often contravene the "right time, right place" principle. Over the course of the school year 70 percent of those referred and punished for misbehavior were boys and 30 percent were girls.

Getting in Trouble: The Wrong Time and the Wrong Place

It is easy for a kid to get in trouble in school. It can happen at any time and any place during the school day. Rules encode the pervasive, all-encompassing power of adults over the movement of children's bodies through the space of the day and the physical regions of the school. One school rule captures this pervasiveness graphically: "Students will be in the right place at the right time."

The right place at the right time is the subject of the timetable and the spaces in which activities are allowed. All movement in school is regulated, organized, and monitored by adults. Let us look at some of the different sites as children navigate in and out of trouble through the space and time of the school day, when children are supposed to be in classrooms doing work, on their way to other rooms in which work takes place, in the cafeteria, or on the playground at recess.

In the classroom, the teacher controls movement of bodies through time and space. The teacher decides when tasks begin, how long they last, when they end, and where they can be carried out. In the classroom, pupils must be doing tasks set by the teacher. The vast majority of work involves individuals sitting and listening or writing. So kids create endless excuses for moving around. This movement can lead to breaking the "right time, right place" rule. Children can get into trouble in classrooms if they move too slowly from one task to the next or if they move too quickly from one part of the room to another. Foot-dragging, slowing the pace down between tasks, is a frequently used form of resistance.

Playing in the classroom is against the rules. Play is supposed to be confined to the schoolyard in the periods of time allotted for the two recesses of the day. Otherwise, the yard is used as the instruction space for the physical education classes. At playtime, children stream out of the building and for twenty minutes in the morning and fifty minutes at lunchtime are ostensibly free to move from space to space within the yard, which is surrounded by a high chain-link fence.[11]

During recess, children must either be on the playground or in the school cafeteria. All entrances to the building are guarded by play-ground aides who also patrol the bathrooms that, in the case of the boys, are a potential trouble zone. The adults complain that the boys go into the bathroom and urinate on the walls in various competitions.

Because the cafeteria is too small to accommodate the whole

---

11. Movement into spaces on the yard, however, is constrained within gendered and racialized distributions created and monitored by the children. My observation in a racially mixed school was that groups were overwhelmingly racially homogeneous. For a rich ethnographic account of the gender patterns of play, see Barrie Thorne, *Gender Play: Girls and Boys in School* (New Brunswick, N.J.: Rutgers University Press, 1993).

school, each grade has an assigned time for lunch. When that time is up, the children must leave the cafeteria for the yard, in order to make room for the next group.

Children hurry through their lunch in order to go out and play. One result of this organization of eating is that they often get in trouble for having food in the classroom after lunch. Having and eating food, candy, or chewing gum in class is against the rules except during authorized parties and the numerous candy drives initiated by teachers to earn money for class projects. This food rule seemed to affect boys more. One of them explained why this was so: he and his friends often didn't want to waste time eating at recess because they had to go out and reserve a place on the football field for their team; he didn't want to miss being picked for one of the teams. Older boys, who ate in the last shift, do not want to interrupt the game in order to eat. Girls rarely play team sports during recess; they walk around with friends or jump rope or play spontaneous games of catch that they organize themselves and do not have to hurry as much to compete for playground space.

In the yard, children run, shout, jump rope, throw balls, push, shove, hold hands, hang upside down until the bell rings. Those who want to spend recess indoors must request a pass from an adult to go into the library. A few teachers stay in the classroom at recess and kids stay in and play board games, chat, or take care of the classroom pets. It is interesting that this was the one space in the school day when I saw kids voluntarily interacting across race and gender lines. However, this space only opened up if a teacher was willing to give up lunchtime.

The auditorium is a space of institutionally organized cultural productions. It exists between pleasure, play, and classroom educational activity. The events that take place in that space are called assemblies. Some are about entertainment: plays, music, school productions as well as visiting artists. Very rarely are the programs produced and organized by the children themselves with adults playing only minor roles.

Assembly is where children learn how to be an audience: when to be quiet, look, and listen; when to laugh; when to clap; when to stop clapping. Children sit with their class on the hardwood floor of the auditorium cross-legged or with legs stuck straight out in front, often for long periods of time. They fidget, wiggle, touch others with legs or hands or elbows. Teachers sit in chairs at the end of each class row. A continual surveillance, weeding out, picking off of children who are whispering, giggling, laughing more obviously than the others or who are just unlucky enough to get caught or who are known as "trouble-makers" and "ringleaders."

Children must have authorized passes or be accompanied by an adult in order to move from one space to another in the school. They have no automatic "right" to be anywhere in school though by law they are required to be *in* school. Children must have adult permission to make trips to the bathroom. They are sent from class, referral slip in hand, to the Punishing Room. They are also sent on errands by teachers.

These transitions between spaces are a glorious opportunity for children to gain free time and reduce the hours spent doing work. Passage down the halls without a teacher offers a myriad of pleasures. To be alone for even a moment is a pleasure, to meet other children making similar journeys, to pass the open doors of classrooms and meet the gaze of others happy for some diversion no matter how small. Dragging out a trip from one space to another is a fine art, but one that holds the danger of being too protracted through making too many stops, lingering in front of too many bulletin boards, and arriving late for class. This breaks the "right time, right place" rule and gets you into trouble.[12]

The public spaces of the halls are fraught with potential trouble. The right to be in such a place and *how* to be there is the province of adults. A child in the hall is open to challenge by any adult and must have a good excuse for not having a pass. Sometimes even a pass or a good excuse is not enough; just the fact of being forced to come up with an explanation for one's presence is the precursor of trouble. What happened to Keisha, a fourth-grade girl, is a good example from my field notes of this vulnerability when one is not under the protection of the classroom teacher.

> I am standing on the landing with the vice principal, Mr. Russell, when I observe how small misdeeds can escalate into bigger infractions bearing larger consequences or punishments in the course of any interaction. The bell had rung and children are moving between classes. We can hear some children chattering excitedly as they are coming up the stairs. They are not loud or unrestrained.

---

12. Some children feel sick and have to go and lie down in the room, which serves as staff mailroom, copy center, and dispensary. Sickness as a ploy to get out of work did not seem to be used much by the kids at the school as an escape since the sickbed is right under the eye of many adults.

As they get to the top, they see us and fall silent. One little girl, very engrossed in the telling of a story, goes on talking after she glances at us.

Mr. Russell stops her. "Is that how you're supposed to behave in the halls?" The other two girls who have been quiet, scuttle down the hall and Mr. Russell tells Keisha to go back and come up the stairs properly. She obediently walks back down the steps in the direction she had come from and then returns making a silent, demure entrance. But there is the barest hint of parody in her primness which Russell does not miss. She is acting the part of ladylike decorum rather than sincerely expressing it. He calls her over and begins giving her a proper dressing down. She stands there shifting from foot to foot, looking him in the eye. This seems to me the correct stance since when children don't look adults in the eye but stare at the ground, the adult is likely to bark, "Look at me when I'm talking to you." He tells her to stand still, which she does. But now she is standing still on one leg. So he orders her to stand straight. She puts her feet together, beginning a slight shuffling little dance from foot to foot almost as if to keep her balance. At the same time she is looking Russell dead in the eye. He says, "Stop that dancing." Though her feet become still, her body sways ever so slightly. He has had enough. "Okay, you can spend the day in my office. Go and tell Mrs. Tyler [the class she is going to] that you're going to be with me today."

Adults not only regulate the passage through the time and space of the school day of individual children but, as we see in the case of Keisha, police their bodies and presentation of self. The right to this policing is hidden behind the bland, reasonable facade expressed by another school rule: "Children will be courteous, cooperative, and show respect for self, others and their surroundings."

Getting in Trouble: Regulating the Self

Body Trouble

Adults constantly monitor what the body of the child is saying to them, using the grammar of demeanor, posture, proper gesture. A certain humbling of the body, a certain expression of submission, a certain obeisance toward power must be displayed in order to get off without a penalty or, next best, to get the minimum. Movements of eyes, head, placement of arms, hands, and feet can be the cause of the escalation of trouble. Face to face with adult power, children's bodies should not jiggle, jounce, rock back and forth, twist, slouch, shrug shoulders, or turn away. In interactions with school adults, children are expected to make and maintain eye contact. Looking away, down at the ground, or off in the distance is considered a sign of insubordination. Hands must be held at the side hanging down loosely, limply, not on hips (an expression of aggression) or in pockets (a sign of insolence and disrespect). A certain fearfulness is desirable, but must be displayed with sincerity, without any cockiness. Bodies have to actively express respect for adult authority: if they are too rigid they give off a sign rebelliousness or insincerity. Any one or any combination of those movements could violate the "Be courteous, cooperative" rule.

In the classroom, teachers demand bodies be arranged in certain positions before work can begin: sit up straight, both feet on the floor, hands off the desk, eyes in front toward teacher, or down on the desk. Bodies must be properly arranged both individually and as a group before they can erupt from the classroom to play. They must organize themselves into neat lines before they can enter or exit from classrooms, though lines become raggedy as soon as teachers move ahead or lag behind.

Bodies can move too fast or too slow. Running in the hallway is forbidden. Moving too slowly in the classroom from task to task can get you in trouble, so can opening one's desk and getting out the required textbook in slow motion, or going over to the pencil sharpener and taking too long to sharpen the pencil. These things in themselves do not call for disciplinary action, but become the occasion for an intervention by the teacher that can escalate into real trouble.

Adult bodies physically symbolize power in the school. For one, difference in body size between adults and most elementary school kids is still enormous. Adult bodies loom over children in moments of trouble. Most disturbing, however, is the way that this embodiment of fearsome power is specifically signaled by the presence of the adult black men in the school; their size and appearance speak volumes in punishment. The bodies of the adult black men come to stand in for the physical power that lies behind the verbal reprimands to which school authority is limited. Three of the five African American men working with children in the school are responsible for discipline. Each has impressive physiques, as if body size is a part of the job description. The figure whose job it is to strike fear in the hearts of children in school is epitomized by the intimidating physical presence of the African American male. Yet, these same men, guardians of law and order in the school, may become suspicious, dangerous characters in the eyes of ordinary citizens on the streets outside. The constant here is the fixing of meaning in the connection between black male bodies and fear.

Trouble and Emotion: "Attitude"

Whether the emotional expressions of children are proper displays of feeling or punishable acts is a matter of adult interpretation. Expressions of anger, outbursts of temper, tears of disappointment, while not against the rules, are potential moments of trouble. Many of the infractions coded as disruption, defiance, or disrespect—or sometimes as all three—seemed to emanate from the display of emotions by children, the performance of self in this relation of power described by the popular expression *attitude.* These generally involved interactions where children are seen as challenging adult authority and power. Girls committed approximately 40 percent of these infractions to boys' 60 percent; the vast majority were African American.

Adult descriptions of infractions on the referrals often invoked their reading of the tone of the exchange as expressed through children's body language and nonverbal forms of communication. Here is how a teacher documented one incident of defiance: "James was doing math, so I asked him to return Lashawn's geography book. The third time I asked he did it, but gave me a look that said, 'you bitch . . .' I cannot let this sort of action pass unnoticed." James's punishment was a cooling-off period in the Punishing Room. This was also the consequence for a girl who "responded very disrespectfully. Tone of voice, words used, body language, unwilling to acknowledge misbehavior, shoves blame back on teacher." Another girl got detention because, as the student specialist wrote, "She was 'moving' her mouth while P.E. teacher was talking." Another girl received after-school detention for a "sassy mouth, standing with attitude, walking away when I called to her in the 6th grade line at lunch." The same girl got two days of in-house detention for "disruption in class. disrespectual [*sic*] and defiant when spoken to. Mouthy and had an attitude." A white girl was sent to cool off in the Punishing Room after she was charged with "defiance; flapping & pouting; slamming drawers, called Sharon a bitch."

What is most significant for us here is that readings of "defiant attitude" are often deciphered through a racialized key. Gilmore's study of literacy achievement in predominately low-income, urban black elementary school students corroborates this point.[13] He found that many of the most crucial social interactions in school settings were highly charged with emotion and regularly interpreted by teachers in terms of students' "attitude."[14] He documents how African American pupils' expression of feeling in confrontations with authority figures in school often involved a bodily display of "stylized sulking" as a face-saving device. For girls, this included a sound such as "humpf" followed by chin held high, closed eyelids, and movement of the head upward and to the side. For boys, the display involved hands crossed at the chest, legs spread wide, head down, and gestures such as a desk pushed away. Both black and white teachers perceive these displays as threatening, as denoting a specifically black communicative style that they interpreted as showing a "bad attitude" by demonstrating the child's refusal to align himself with the school's standards, choosing instead to identify with what they considered a black lower-class style. Gilmore found that teachers used these displays as a measure of students' academic potential and that teacher judgments about this kind of "attitude" weighed heavily when decisions about placement in special honors classes were being made, even outweighing more "objective" measures such as demonstrated academic achievement.[15]

Whether these ways of displaying emotion do or do not conform to the acceptable rules for comportment in school is not the main issue here. What I want to foreground with this example is the exercise of symbolic violence and the relationship between a hidden or noncognitive form of assessment and an official one. Cultural modes of emotional display by kids become significant factors in decisions by adults about their academic potential and influence decisions teachers make about the kinds of academic programs in which they will be placed. These are the kind of emotional displays, for example, that can also be the basis for placement in Special Day Classes or for denying access to enrichment classes.

---

13. Gilmore, "Gimme Room."
14. Ibid., 114.
15. Ibid., 112.

Moments of discipline are also occasions when adults act emotionally, when the appearance of distance and control slips. I observed the way the adults' need to act the part of outrage or shock with the body seemed to stir up real expressions of feeling in them. This performance is something slightly shameful that must be guarded, kept private, protected from too much outside observation. Later, I was especially aware of how these displays entered into early considerations about allowing me to observe in the relatively private, hidden, space of the Punishing Room.

The Troublemakers almost by definition were characterized by school adults as defiant and disrespectful. At the same time, the boys are conscious of how adults often let go and lose control in moments of discipline. They charged that the teachers treated kids rudely, with no respect. They expressed strong feelings of resentment of the asymmetrical power relations that existed between the adults and themselves. They pointed to the different rules of demeanor and "attitude" that apply to the teachers.

TREY: You see the teachers talk about us having an attitude problem, but then they do have one too.

ANN: The teachers do? How?

TREY: They think that just because we're younger than them, they're older—they can have attitude with us or something. They think it's all right to treat us anyway they want.

ANN: An example?

TREY: The way they talk to us. Like they yelling up in your face and pointing at you—and you want to do that back and you get in trouble. But they don't want that done to them. *No!* They think they're *it.*

Horace told a story that for him exemplified the one-sidedness of the respect exchange:

The math teacher kept calling me by my last name but everybody else by their first name. He was getting on my nerves. [Horace's last name is Budd, so calling him by his last name did have a special twist.] I asked him about five times to stop doing it but he just kept on. He also called people names like *retard.* Then he was writing on the board—we was all laughing because he had a "murphy" [his pants were caught in the back of his crotch]. Everyone was laughing but the teacher said, "Budd, you're going to be the first one out of this class. Get out right now." Then I just stayed out of the classroom till the whole second period was over.

Trey's observation that adults are rude to kids in school and Horace's example are not a distortion of reality in order to cast their own behavior in a good light. I witnessed the discourteous, harassing treatment of pupils by some of the school adults. This verbal disparagement and the harsh dressing-down of kids was carried out in the name of school discipline required by certain kinds of children; it was seen as an essential weapon, given the circumstances, in the creation and maintenance of order. It was typically unleashed against children who were black, poor, and already labeled as trouble; students whose parents had little power or credibility, who would come in and complain about how their kids were being treated.

For Troublemakers, this lack of reciprocity of respect and display of "attitude" on the part of the teachers is an important structuring element of the conditions of schoolwork that has consequences both for their interactions with adults as well as with their peers. I discovered that other research investigating teacher-student relations documented the way that pupils' feelings about disrespectful behavior on the part of teachers prompted reciprocation on their part: teachers who were uncivil were treated in kind.[16]

While the relations of power and the lack of respect for pupils by school adults was articulated as a source of real anger and emotion by the Troublemakers, the sense of resentment was not echoed by the Schoolboys, who generally did not engage in power struggles with the teachers. The Schoolboys, however, were conscious of the "work" they do to produce an identity that was unimpeachable. Though they

<hr/>

16. P. Marsh, E. Rosser, and R. Harre, *The Rules of Disorder* (London: Routledge and Kegan Paul, 1978). This disregard on the part of adults also had an effect on interaction between peers. Ray Rist observed that kindergarten children identified by the teacher as high achievers began to model their own relationship with the children identified as lows after that of the teacher. He recorded a number of interchanges in the classroom in which the highs belittled the lows. For example: "When I asked Lilly [low group] what it was she was drawing, she replied, 'A parachute.' Frank [high group] interrupted and said, 'Lilly can't draw nothin'.'" Ray C. Rist, *The Urban School: A Factory for Failure, a Study of Education in American Society* (Cambridge: MIT Press, 1973), 174.

described behavior that they engaged in that was technically rule breaking, they conform to the teacher's description of the ideal pupil who
follows orders without argument or questions. They talked about the
work they do to stay out of trouble. The performance of obedience and
management of impression is a key element in this work. Martin, one
of the Schoolboys, talked about the enactment of obedience. When I
asked him how he managed to stay away from the Punishing Room, he
replied: "Just kinda like what the teacher says—I just do it real quick."
Martin knows that it is more than merely following orders. Keisha,
after all, was following orders when she got in trouble in the hallway.
Orders must be followed "real quick" without hesitation and sincerely
played. It is not just doing what one is told but the visible commitment
to the idea of following orders that is important. Martin understands
that the speed of compliance demonstrates the unthinking impulse to
obey; hesitation implies that perhaps a decision is being taken about
whether to obey or not and is seen as a clear challenge to relations of
power.

Clothes, Language, and Identities

The school has unwritten rules about clothing that remain informal so
that they can deal as required with the coming and going of youth style.
The policing of clothing at Rosa Parks is most vigilant around boys'
style of dress. Certain articles of clothing have become identified by
school as signals of rebellion, uncontrollability, of gang membership.
The school reads male expression through clothing as the harbinger of
more dangerous expressions, as if the representation of the thing is the
thing itself.

Baseball caps, especially worn back to front and slightly angled, are
a particularly powerful object in the contest of power between adults
and children in the school. The unwritten rule is that caps are allowed
before and after school and during the recesses. Many teachers ignore
the rule as petty but call it into action at some point as an instrument
of asserting dominance. This illustration from my field notes is an
example of what I mean.

I have come to talk to Jamal's teacher at recess. He is going out the
door, football in hand as I enter, but the teacher calls him back
because I am there. He is wearing his cap pulled low on his fore-

head. He looks dismayed at the delay and asks how long it will be. The teacher seems furious at this question. "Don't you ever dare ask me how long I'm going to keep you or you'll be in here for the whole lunch period." He slouches into a seat. She continues to harangue: "Take that hat off! I want to see your eyes." He pulls it off slowly.

Some of the fundamental aspects of presentation and performance of self, such as language, as well as some of the more changeable and passing, such as style, can get a child in trouble. Language, like bodies, is important in conveying sincerity and deference. Style of address is a signal for adults to either escalate the demand for obedience or permit safe passage. For example, a "yeah" rather than "Yes, Mr. or Mrs. ——" is considered cheeky. Mumbling in response to something an adult asks is also taken as possible insubordination and is usually followed with further interrogation to ascertain the intention.

The use of Black English, the mother's tongue, rather than "standard" English will get an African American child in trouble. This is true at the level of the formal curriculum as well as in terms of more subjective judgments about how its usage reflects on individual intelligence and cultural deficiency. All the reading, all tests, all communications with and of power are supposed to take place in Standard English. The whole lexicon of home and street, the way the children tell their lives to themselves and others must be squeezed into this standard. When you create yourself through words, the official language of power must be used in order to be rewarded directly or indirectly.

A defiant, challenging, oppositional body; dramatic, emotional expressions; a rich, complex nonstandard vocabulary establish the "outer limits" in a field of comparison in which the desired norm is a docile bodily presence and the intonation and homogeneous syntax of Standard English. This outer limit is exemplified by the black child: the closer to whiteness, to the norm of bodies, language, emotion, the more these children *are* self-disciplined and acceptable members of the institution.

I have been looking at relations of power in this discussion of school rules as if the only axis along which these operate is that of adult and child: adult policing of the boundaries and children's incursions into the territory and privileges of being "grown up." It is easy to run afoul of the rules, to get in trouble. The rules govern not just the surfaces of the time and spaces of school but also deep, personal structures: self-expression and the proper display of feeling. It is clear that there is an enormous amount of interpretation, of reading of the meaning of personal, as well as cultural, forms of communication, that takes place in exchanges between adults and children.

I have only briefly mentioned how race might make a difference in the exercise of rules. Yet the statistics that I have presented suggest that though all children may be up to their eyeballs in this sea of adult rules, the overwhelming majority of those who get in trouble in school are African American males.

How race is used as a filter in the interpretive work of making judgments about the implications of children's behavior is the subject of chapter 4. I will examine the racialized images, beliefs, and expectations that frame teacher appraisals of black children, in general, and African American boys, in particular. It is crucial to emphasize here that I am not concerned with investigating *individual* teacher's racial attitudes, but institutional discourses and practices. As a whole, teachers at Rosa Parks School seemed genuinely convinced of the racially blind, impartial nature of their practices. Schoolwide there were efforts made to infuse assemblies, classroom, and curriculum with "multicultural" programs. This is one reason why it seems imperative to lay out the processes by which well-intentioned individuals actually and actively reproduce systems of oppression through institutional practices and symbolic forms of violence.

field note
SELF-DESCRIPTION

Ann asks, "How would you describe yourself. What words would you use?"

OLIVER, FIFTH-GRADE BOY: Hyper. Like if I eat sugar I end up practicing my football moves inside the house. I collide with the chair and the chair goes back and forth and I collide with the furniture. Sometimes kind. Because I like to do things for people. Like my sister this morning, she was trying to get the braids out of her hair—so I was helping her get her hair out for her. I'm helpful. And intelligent.

TERRENCE, SIXTH-GRADE BOY: Tall, playful, handsome, kind. My timing is impeccable. It's like this morning I have a poster of Michael Jordan that's in a glass [frame] and it started to fall but I caught it. It still broke. So that's how I got cut. [Shows me a cut on his hand.] That's why I was kinda mad 'cause I only got it last month.

DONTE, FIFTH-GRADE BOY: I'm [long hesitation, then very decisively] sensitive, 'cause I hate when people around like start annoying me. It makes me mad. Makes me want to start bumping against them and stuff.

MARTIN, SIXTH-GRADE BOY: I don't know. [Thinks. Then quietly, so quietly I have to ask him to repeat what he said,] Middle.
ANN: Tell me what that means. Sounds fascinating.
MARTIN: Like sometimes you bad. Sometimes you good. Not one thing or another.

EDDIE, SIXTH-GRADE BOY: Tall. Nice *and* mean person. I be nice when I'm playing with my friends but when somebody hit me or something, I be all angry and mean. But I like the nice part of me better.

ADAM, SIXTH-GRADE BOY: Funny, fast, smart, intelligent, that's it.

MALEK, SIXTH-GRADE BOY: Nobody really knows me. Well, probably one person or two. But nobody *knows* me. I'm the only person that knows myself. The teachers, they might think that—he's this or that. But really I just be acting so they'll think I'm like that—just acting.

HORACE, SIXTH-GRADE BOY: She [referring to teacher] thinks that I could do the work and I could do above the work, but I don't because sometimes I'm lazy. Sometimes I don't want to think.

DONEL, FIFTH-GRADE BOY: Kind of depends on what neighborhood you raise up your kid. But not all that much. Because some kids are just plain bad. Some kids are good.
MARCUS, FIFTH-GRADE BOY: Unnnhnnn. Nobody's bad! Nobody!
DONEL: I know people that won't change their ways.
MARCUS: In this world right now, the reason why people is like this is because TV is setting people a bad example for us and they want to follow them. But nobody's *bad,* though.

naughty by nature

What are little boys made of?
What are little boys made of?
Frogs and snails
And puppy-dogs' tails,
That's what little boys are made of.

—*Oxford Dictionary of Nursery Rhymes*

What makes the presence and control of the police tolerable
for the population, if not fear of the criminal?

—MICHEL FOUCAULT, *Power/Knowledge*

In order for me to live, I decided very early that some mistake
had been made somewhere. I was not a "nigger" even though
you called me one. . . . I had to realize when I was very young
that I was none of those things that I was told I was. I was
not, for example, happy. I never touched a watermelon for all
kinds of reasons. I had been invented by white people, and I
knew enough about life by this time to understand that whatever you invent, whatever you project, that is you! So where
we are now is that a whole country of people believe I'm a
"nigger" and I don't.

—JAMES BALDWIN, "A TALK TO TEACHERS"

Two representations of black masculinity are widespread in society and
school today. They are the images of the African American male as a
criminal and as an endangered species. These images are routinely used
as resources to interpret and explain behavior by teachers at Rosa Parks
School when they make punishment decisions. An ensemble of historical meanings and their social effects is contained within these images.

The image of the black male criminal is more familiar because of its prevalence in the print and electronic media as well as in scholarly work. The headlines of newspaper articles and magazines sound the alarm dramatically as the presence of black males in public spaces has come to signify danger and a threat to personal safety. But this is not just media hype. Bleak statistics give substance to the figure of the criminal. Black males are disproportionately in jails: they make up 6 percent of the population of the United States, but 45 percent of the inmates in state and federal prisons; they are imprisoned at six times the rate of whites.[1] In the state of California, one-third of African American men in their twenties are in prison, on parole, or on probation, in contrast to 5 percent of white males in the same age group. This is nearly five times the number who attend four-year colleges in the state.[2] The mortality rate for African American boys fourteen years of age and under is approximately 50 percent higher than for the comparable group of white male youth, with the leading cause of death being homicide.[3]

The second image, that of the black male as an endangered species, is one which has largely emanated from African American social scientists and journalists who are deeply concerned about the criminalization and high mortality rate among African American youth.[4] It represents him as being marginalized to the point of oblivion. While this discourse emanates from a sympathetic perspective, in the final analysis the focus is all too often on individual maladaptive behavior and black mothering practices as the problem rather than on the social structure in which this endangerment occurs.

These two cultural representations are rooted in actual material conditions and reflect existing social conditions and relations that they appear to sum up for us. They are lodged in theories, in commonsense understandings of self in relation to others in the world as well as in popular culture and the media. But they are condensations, extrapola-

---

1. *New York Times,* September 13, 1994, 1.

2. *Los Angeles Times,* November 2, 1990, 3.

3. G. Jaynes and R. Williams Jr., eds., *A Common Destiny: Blacks in American Society* (Washington, D.C.: National Academic Press, 1989), 405, 498.

4. See, for example, Jewelle Taylor Gibbs, "Young Black Males in America: Endangered, Embittered, and Embattled," in Jewelle Taylor Gibbs et al., *Young, Black, and Male in America: An Endangered Species* (New York: Auburn House, 1988); Richard Majors and Janet Mancini Billson, *Cool Pose: The Dilemmas of Black Manhood in America* (New York: Lexington Press, 1992); Jawanza Kunjufu, *Countering the Conspiracy to Destroy Black Boys,* 2 vols. (Chicago: African American Images, 1985).

tions, that emphasize certain elements and gloss over others. They represent a narrow selection from the multiplicity, the heterogeneity of actual relations in society.

Since both of these images come to be used for identifying, classification, and decision making by teachers at Rosa Parks School, it is necessary to analyze the manner in which these images, or cultural representations of difference, are produced through a racial discursive formation. Then we can explain how they are utilized by teachers in the exercise of school rules to produce a context in which African American boys become more visible, more culpable as "rule-breakers."

A central element of a racist discursive formation is the production of subjects as essentially different by virtue of their "race." Historically, the circulation of images that represent this difference has been a powerful technique in this production.[5] Specifically, blacks have been represented as essentially different from whites, as the constitutive Other that regulates and confirms "whiteness." Images of Africans as savage, animalistic, subhuman without history or culture—the diametric opposite of that of Europeans—rationalized and perpetuated a system of slavery. After slavery was abolished, images of people of African descent as hypersexual, shiftless, lazy, and of inferior intellect, legitimated a system that continued to deny rights of citizenship to blacks on the basis of race difference. This regime of truth about race was articulated through scientific experiments and "discoveries," law, social custom, popular culture, folklore, and common sense. And for three hundred years, from the seventeenth century to the middle of the twentieth century, this racial distinction was policed through open and unrestrained physical violence. The enforcement of race difference was conscious, overt, and institutionalized.

In the contemporary period, the production of a racial Other and the constitution and regulation of racial difference has worked increasingly through mass-produced images that are omnipresent in our lives.

5. See, for example, W. E. B. Du Bois, *Souls of Black Folk* (1903; reprint, New York: Bantam, 1989); Frantz Fanon, *Black Skins, White Masks,* trans. Charles Lam Markmann (New York: Grove Press, 1967); Stuart Hall, "The Rediscovery of 'Ideology': Return of the Repressed in Media Studies," in *Culture, Society, and the Media,* ed. Michael Gurevitch et al. (New York: Methuen, 1982); Leith Mullings, "Images, Ideology, and Women of Color," in *Women of Color in U.S. Society,* ed. Maxine Baca Zinn and Bonnie Thornton Dill (Philadelphia: Temple University Press, 1994); Edward Said, *Orientalism* (New York: Vintage, 1978).

At this moment in time it is through culture—or culturalism[6]—that difference is primarily asserted. This modern-day form for producing racism specifically operates through symbolic violence and representations of Blackness that circulate through the mass media, cinematic images and popular music, rather than through the legal forms of the past. The representational becomes a potent vehicle for the transmission of racial meanings that reproduce relations of difference, of division, and of power. These "controlling images" make "racism, sexism, and poverty appear to be natural, normal, and an inevitable part of everyday life."[7]

Cultural Representations of "Difference"

The behavior of African American boys in school is perceived by adults at Rosa Parks School through a filter of overlapping representations of three socially invented categories of "difference": age, gender, and race. These are grounded in the commonsense, taken-for-granted notion that existing social divisions reflect biological and natural dispositional differences among humans: so children are essentially different from adults, males from females, blacks from whites.[8] At the intersection of this complex of subject positions are African American boys who are doubly displaced: as black children, they are not seen as childlike but adultified; as black males, they are denied the masculine dispensation constituting white males as being "naturally naughty" and are discerned as willfully bad. Let us look more closely at this displacement.

The dominant cultural representation of childhood is as closer to nature, as less social, less human. Childhood is assumed to be a stage of development; culture, morality, sociability is written on children in an unfolding process by adults (who are seen as fully "developed," made by culture not nature) in institutions like family and school. On the one hand, children are assumed to be dissembling, devious, because they are more egocentric. On the other hand, there is an attribution of inno-

---

6. Gilroy, *Small Acts,* 24, argues that "the culturalism of the new racism has gone hand in hand with a definition of race as a matter of difference rather than a question of hierarchy."

7. Collins, *Black Feminist Thought,* 68.

8. While many of the staff at Rosa Parks School would agree at an abstract level that social divisions of gender and race are culturally and historically produced, their actual talk about these social distinctions as well as their everyday expectations, perceptions, and interactions affirm the notion that these categories reflect intrinsic, *real* differences.

cence to their wrongdoing. In both cases, this is understood to be a temporary condition, a stage prior to maturity. So they must be socialized to fully understand the meaning of their acts.

The language used to describe "children in general" by educators illustrates this paradox. At one districtwide workshop for adult school volunteers that I attended, children were described by the classroom teacher running the workshop as being "like little plants, they need attention, they gobble it up." Later in the session, the same presenter invoked the other dominant representation of children as devious, manipulative, and powerful. "They'll run a number on you. They're little lawyers, con artists, manipulators—and they usually win. They're good at it. Their strategy is to get you off task. They pull you into their whirlwind."

These two versions of childhood express the contradictory qualities that adults map onto their interactions with children in general. The first description of children as "little plants," childhood as identical with nature, is embedded in the ideology of childhood. The second version that presents children as powerful, as self-centered, with an agenda and purpose of their own, arises out of the experience adults have exercising authority over children. In actual relations of power, in a twist, as children become the objects of control, they become devious "con artists" and adults become innocent, pristine in relation to them. In both instances, childhood has been constructed as different in essence from adulthood, as a phase of biological, psychological, and social development with predictable attributes.

Even though we treat it this way, the category "child" does not describe and contain a homogeneous and naturally occurring group of individuals at a certain stage of human development. The social meaning of childhood has changed profoundly over time.[9] What it means to be a child varies dramatically by virtue of location in cross-cutting categories of class, gender, and race.[10]

Historically, the existence of African American children has been constituted differently through economic practices, the law, social policy, and visual imagery. This difference has been projected in an ensemble of images of black youth as not childlike. In the early decades of this century, representations of black children as pickaninnies depicted

9. See, for example, Phillipe Ariès, *Centuries of Childhood: A Social History of Family Life* (New York: Vintage, 1962).

10. Thorne, *Gender Play;* and Valerie Polakow, *Lives on the Edge: Single Mothers and Their Children in the Other America* (Chicago: University of Chicago Press, 1993).

them as verminlike, voracious, dirty, grinning, animal-like savages. They were also depicted as the laugh-provoking butt of aggressive, predatory behavior; natural victims, therefore victimizable. An example of this was their depiction in popular lore as "alligator bait." Objects such as postcards, souvenir spoons, letter-openers and cigar-box labels were decorated with figures of half-naked black children vainly attempting to escape the open toothy jaws of hungry alligators.[11]

Today's representations of black children still bear traces of these earlier depictions. The media demonization of very young black boys who are charged with committing serious crimes is one example. In these cases there is rarely the collective soul-searching for answers to the question of how "kids like this" could have committed these acts that occurs when white kids are involved. Rather, the answer to the question seems to be inherent in the disposition of the kids themselves.[12] The image of the young black male as an endangered species revitalizes the animalistic trope. Positioned as part of nature, his essence is described through language otherwise reserved for wildlife that has been decimated to the point of extinction. Characterized as a "species," they are cut off from other members of family and community and isolated as a form of prey.

There is continuity, but there is a significant new twist to the image. The endangered species and the criminal are mirror images. Either as criminal perpetrator or as endangered victim, contemporary imagery proclaims black males to be responsible for their fate. The discourse of individual choice and responsibility elides the social and economic context and locates predation as coming from within. It is their own maladaptive and inappropriate behavior that causes African Amer-

---

11. Patricia Turner, *Ceramic Uncles and Celluloid Mammies: Black Images and Their Influence on Culture* (New York: Anchor, 1994), 36.

12. A particularly racist and pernicious example of this was the statement by the administrator of the Alcohol, Drug Abuse, and Mental Health Administration, Dr. Frederick K. Goodwin, who stated without any qualms: "If you look, for example, at male monkeys, especially in the wild, roughly half of them survive to adulthood. The other half die by violence. That is the natural way of it for males, to knock each other off and, in fact, there are some interesting evolutionary implications. . . . The same hyper aggressive monkeys who kill each other are also hyper sexual, so they copulate more and therefore they reproduce more to offset the fact that half of them are dying." He then drew an analogy with the "high impact [of] inner city areas with the loss of some of the civilizing evolutionary things that we have built up. . . . Maybe it isn't just the careless use of the word when people call certain areas of certain cities, jungles." Quoted in Jerome G. Miller, *Search and Destroy: African American Males in the Criminal Justice System* (New York: Cambridge University Press, 1996), 212–13.

icans to self-destruct. As an endangered species, they are stuck in an obsolete stage of social evolution, unable to adapt to the present. As criminals, they are a threat to themselves, to each other, as well as to society in general.

As black children's behavior is refracted through the lens of these two cultural images, it is "adultified." By this I mean their transgressions are made to take on a sinister, intentional, fully conscious tone that is stripped of any element of childish naïveté. The discourse of childhood as an unfolding developmental stage in the life cycle is displaced in this mode of framing school trouble. Adultification is visible in the way African American elementary school pupils are talked about by school adults.

One of the teachers, a white woman who prided herself on the multicultural emphasis in her classroom, invoked the image of African American children as "looters" in lamenting the disappearance of books from the class library. This characterization is especially meaningful because her statement, which was made at the end of the school year that had included the riots in Los Angeles, invoked that event as a framework for making children's behavior intelligible.

> I've lost so many library books this term. There are quite a few kids who don't have any books at home, so I let them borrow them. I didn't sign them out because I thought I could trust the kids. I sent a letter home to parents asking them to look for them and turn them in. But none have come in. I just don't feel the same. *It's just like the looting in Los Angeles.*

By identifying those who don't have books at home as "looters," the teacher has excluded the white children in the class, who all come from more middle-class backgrounds so, it is assumed, "have books at home." In the case of the African American kids, what might be interpreted as the careless behavior of children is displaced by images of adult acts of theft that conjure up violence and mayhem. The African American children in this teacher's classroom and their families are seen not in relation to images of childhood, but in relation to the television images of crowds rampaging through South Central Los Angeles in the aftermath of the verdict of the police officers who beat Rodney King. Through this frame, the children embody a willful, destructive, and irrational disregard for property rather than simple carelessness. Racial difference is mediated through culturalism: blacks are understood as a group undifferentiated by age or status with the proclivity and values to disregard the rights and welfare of others.

Adultification is a central mechanism in the interpretive framing of gender roles. African American girls are constituted as different through this process. A notion of sexual passivity and innocence that prevails for white female children is displaced by the image of African American females as sexual beings: as immanent mothers, girlfriends, and sexual partners of the boys in the room.[13] Though these girls may be strong, assertive, or troublesome, teachers evaluate their potential in ways that attribute to them an inevitable, potent sexuality that flares up early and that, according to one teacher, lets them permit men to run all over them, to take advantage of them. An incident in the Punishing Room that I recorded in my field notes made visible the way that adult perceptions of youthful behavior were filtered through racial representations. African American boys and girls who misbehaved were not just breaking a rule out of high spirits and needing to be chastised for the act, but were adultified, gendered figures whose futures were already inscribed and foreclosed within a racial order:

---

13. The consensus among teachers in the school about educational inequity focuses on sexism. Many of the teachers speak seriously and openly about their concern that girls are being treated differently than boys in school: girls are neglected in the curriculum, over-looked in classrooms, underencouraged academically, and harassed by boys. A number of recent studies support the concern that even the well-intentioned teacher tends to spend less classroom time with girls because boys demand so much of their attention. These studies generally gloss over racial difference as well as make the assumption that *quantity* rather than *quality* of attention is the key factor in fostering positive sense of self in academic setting. See, for example, Myra Sadker and David Sadker, *Failing at Fairness: How America's Schools Cheat Girls* (New York: C. Scribner's Sons, 1994). Linda Grant looks at both race and gender as she examines the roles that first- and second-grade African American girls play in desegregated classrooms. She finds that African American girls and white girls are positioned quite differently vis-à-vis teachers. In the classrooms she observed, white girls were called upon to play an academic role in comparison with African American girls, who were cast in the role of teacher's helpers, in monitoring and controlling other kids in the room, and as intermediaries between peers. She concluded that black girls were encouraged in stereotypical female adult roles that stress service and nurture, while white girls were encouraged to press toward high academic achievement. Most important for this study, Grant mentions in passing that black boys in the room receive the most consistent negative attention and were assessed as having a lower academic ability than any other group by teachers. See Linda Grant, "Helpers, Enforcers, and Go-Betweens: Black Females in Elementary School Classrooms," in *Women of Color in U.S. Society,* ed. Maxine Baca Zinn and Bonnie Thornton Dill (Philadelphia: University of Pennsylvania Press, 1994).

Two girls, Adila and a friend, burst into the room followed by Miss Benton a black sixth-grade teacher and a group of five African American boys from her class. Miss Benton is yelling at the girls because they have been jumping in the hallway and one has knocked down part of a display on the bulletin board which she and her class put up the day before. She is yelling at the two girls about how they're wasting time. This is what she says: "You're doing exactly what they want you to do. You're playing into their hands. Look at me! Next year they're going to be tracking you."

One of the girls asks her rather sullenly who "they" is.

Miss Benton is furious. "Society, that's who. You should be leading the class, not fooling around jumping around in the hallway. Someone has to give pride to the community. All the black men are on drugs, or in jail, or killing each other. Someone has got to hold it together. And the women have to do it. And you're jumping up and down in the hallway."

I wonder what the black boys who have followed in the wake of the drama make of this assessment of their future, seemingly already etched in stone. The teacher's words to the girls are supposed to inspire them to leadership. The message for the boys is a dispiriting one.

Tracks have already been laid down for sixth-grade girls toward a specifically feminized responsibility (and, what is more prevalent, blame) for the welfare of the community, while males are bound for jail as a consequence of their own socially and self-destructive acts.

There is a second displacement from the norm in the representation of black males. The hegemonic, cultural image of the essential "nature" of males is that they are different from females in the meaning of their acts. Boys will be boys: they are mischievous, they get into trouble, they can stand up for themselves. This vision of masculinity is rooted in the notion of an essential sex difference based on biology, hormones, uncontrollable urges, true personalities. Boys are naturally more physical, more active. Boys are naughty by *nature*. There is something suspect about the boy who is "too docile," "like a girl." As a result, rule breaking on the part of boys is looked at as something-they-can't-help, a natural expression of masculinity in a civilizing process.

This incitement of boys to be "boylike" is deeply inscribed in our mainstream culture, winning hearts and stirring imaginations in the way that the pale counterpart, the obedient boy, does not. Fiedler, in an examination of textual representations of iconic childhood figures in U.S. literature, registers the "Good Bad Boy" and the "Good Good Boy" as cultural tropes of masculinities:

> What then is the difference between the Good Good Boy and the Good Bad Boy, between Sid Sawyer, let us say, and Tom? The Good Good Boy does what his mother must pretend that she wants him to do: obey, conform; the Good Bad Boy does what she really wants him to do: deceive, break her heart a little, be forgiven.[14]

An example of this celebration of Good Bad Boy behavior, even when at the risk of order, is the way that one of the student specialists at Rosa Parks School introduced a group of boys in his classroom to a new student:

TEACHER: Hey, they're thugs! Hoodlums! Hooligans! Gangsters! Stay away from these guys.
BOY (ACTING TOUGH):   Yeah, we're tough.
TEACHER (REALLY HAVING FUN):   You ain't as tough as a slice of wet white bread!
BOY (SIDLING UP TO THE TEACHER CHEST PUFFED OUT):   I'm tougher than you.
TEACHER: Okay! Go on! These are a bunch of great guys.

The newcomer looks at home.

African American boys are not accorded the masculine dispensation of being "naturally" naughty. Instead the school reads their expression and display of masculine naughtiness as a sign of an inherent vicious, insubordinate nature that as a threat to order must be controlled. Consequently, school adults view any display of masculine mettle on the part of these boys through body language or verbal rejoinders as a sign of insubordination. In confrontation with adults, what is

---

14. Leslie A. Fiedler, *Love and Death in the American Novel* (New York: Criterion, 1960), 267.

required from them is a performance of absolute docility that goes against the grain of masculinity. Black boys are expected to internalize a ritual obeisance in such exchanges so that the performance of docility appears to come naturally. According to the vice principal, "These children have to learn not to talk back. They must know that if the adult says you're wrong, then you're wrong. They must not resist, must go along with it, and take their punishment," he says.

This is not a lesson that all children are required to learn, however. The disciplining of the body within school rules has specific race and gender overtones. For black boys, the enactment of docility is a preparation for adult racialized survival rituals of which the African American adults in the school are especially cognizant. For African American boys bodily forms of expressiveness have repercussions in the world outside the chain-link fence of the school. The body must be taught to endure humiliation in preparation for future enactments of submission. The vice principal articulated the racialized texture of decorum when he deplored one of the Troublemakers, Lamar's, propensity to talk back and argue with teachers.

Lamar had been late getting into line at the end of recess, and the teacher had taken away his football. Lamar argued and so the teacher gave him detention. Mr. Russell spelled out what an African American male needed to learn about confrontations with power.

> Look, I've told him before about getting into these show-down situations—where he either has to show off to save face, then if he doesn't get his way then he goes wild. He won't get away with it in this school. Not with me, not with Mr. Harmon. But I know he's going to try it somewhere outside and it's going to get him in *real* trouble. He has to learn to ignore, to walk away, not to get into power struggles.

Mr. Russell's objective is to hammer into Lamar's head what he believes is the essential lesson for young black males to learn if they are to get anywhere in life: to act out obeisance is to survive. The specter of the Rodney King beating by the Los Angeles Police Department provided the backdrop for this conversation, as the trial of the police officers had just begun. The defense lawyer for the LAPD was arguing that Rodney King could have stopped the beating at any time if he had chosen.

This apprehension of black boys as inherently different both in terms of character and of their place in the social order is a crucial factor in teacher disciplinary practices.

Normalizing Judgments and Teacher Practices

Teacher enforcement of rules results in differential treatment for children in general. Teachers must weigh immediate practical considerations about classroom management as well as more abstract imperatives of imparting social values and standards of interaction as they define the actions of a child as rule breaking.

A teacher decides whether to "notice" the behavior at all. Each time a child breaks a written or unwritten rule, the teacher has to make a decision about whether to take the time for disciplinary action. Another important consideration is the larger effect that this action might have on spectators in the public arena of the school.[15]

Hargreaves, Hester, and Mellor, in a study of how teachers come to label some children as deviant, analyze the function that rules play in these labeling practices. They identify two principles of rules by which teachers decide to intervene.[16] The first is a "moral" principle grounded in the belief that rules teach children values. The second, a "pragmatic" principle, recognizes rules as an efficient and effective way for imposing order and affirming teacher authority. The researchers also found that when and whether these principles came into play were highly dependent on the perception that the teacher had of a pupil. Teachers not

---

15. Teachers are also held in the grip of rules. One important consideration is the teacher's own presentation of self as a competent teacher. Teachers are assessed according to how well they control children and keep classroom order. Teachers, as well as children, are expected to show a respect for the rules, to be consistent in enforcing them. Adult conformity to the rules, their allegiance to them, is never taken for granted, as unproblematic, but must be publicly affirmed over and over. Just to be an adult, to occupy that status, is not enough. At one of the in-service workshops dealing with school discipline, several teachers blamed school discipline problems on the fact that some teachers did not wholeheartedly support the rules: "It doesn't help when some people just let the kids do whatever, just ignore some of the rules when they don't agree with them. I've been making my kids keep their caps off in the classroom, then when we go to assembly there are other classes where the kids are wearing their caps, which makes it impossible for me. I end up looking like the bad guy. We've all got to agree to the rules and then we've all got to stick by them."

16. Hargreaves, Hester, and Mellor, *Deviance in Classrooms,* 222.

only ranked rules according to their significance, but ranked individual pupils according to an evaluation of their culpability: what was tolerated in some pupils might be punished in others.[17] Most significant for this study is that the researchers found that the criteria used for determining hierarchies of culpability were highly subjective, including elements such as facial appearance, physical size, likability, friends, and style of presentation of self.

Teacher perceptions of students are grounded in their own location in social categories of race, class, and gender. They make sense of their interactions with pupils and the conditions of their work from these social locations.[18] Teachers bring different experiences and knowledge of racial structures into school that provide a framework from which to interpret, to organize information, to act. These factor into the creation of hierarchies of culpability of rule-breakers.

In the case of African American boys, misbehavior is likely to be interpreted as symptomatic of ominous criminal proclivities. Because of this, teachers are more likely to pay attention to and punish rule breaking, as "moral" and "pragmatic" reasons for acting converge with criteria of culpability. On the basis of "moral" reasons, teachers use troublemakers as exemplars to mark boundaries of transgressive behavior; this also has practical effects on general classroom order.

Black teachers are especially likely to advocate and enforce ways of presenting self in the world, strategies of camouflage, that will allow African American children not only to blend into and become a part of the dominant culture, but have survival value in the real world. Black boys must learn to hide "attitude" and learn to exorcise defiance. Thus they argue for the importance of instilling fear and respect for authority.

There are real consequences in terms of the form and severity of punishment of these social fictions. The exemption of black males from

---

17. Ibid., 227.

18. A substantial body of studies on teacher expectations have demonstrated that gender, class, and race have considerable influence over assumptions teachers have about students. For examples of gender bias, see Sadker and Sadker, *Failing at Fairness;* for class and ethnicity, see Ursula Casanova, "Rashomon in the Classroom: Multiple Perspectives of Teachers, Parents, and Students," in *Children at Risk: Poverty, Minority Status, and Other Issues in Educational Equity,* ed. Andres Barona and Eugene E. Garcia (Washington, D.C.: National Association of School Psychologists, 1990); for class, see Ray C. Rist, "Student Social Class and Teacher Expectations: The Self-Fulfilling Prophecy in Ghetto Education," *Harvard Educational Review* 40, no. 3 (1970).

the dispensations granted the "child" and the "boy" through the process of adultification justifies harsher, more punitive responses to rule-breaking behavior. As "not-children," their behavior is understood not as something to be molded and shaped over time, but as the intentional, fully cognizant actions of an adult. This means there is already a dispositional pattern set, that their behavior is incorrigible, irremediable. Therefore, the treatment required for infractions is one that punishes through example and exclusion rather than through persuasion and edification, as is practiced with young white males in the school.

The point must be made here that the power of the images to affect teachers' beliefs and behavior is greatly exacerbated because of their lack of knowledge about the black children in their classrooms. None of the teachers at Rosa Parks School were a part of the community in which they taught; only the custodians and the "Jailhouse Keeper" were resident in the neighborhood. Teachers rarely visited children and families in their homes. Though school adults had many stories to tell me about the families of the boys I was interviewing, these were typically horror stories. Sad, shocking tales of one family's situation would become emblematic of "those families."

As a result of these stories, I was at first anxious about going into homes that were described as "not safe." After visiting with several families, I began to realize that school people had never stepped into any of the children's homes and knew nothing about the real circumstances in which they lived. This distance, this absence of substantive knowledge, further contributed to their adultification of the children and the fear that tinged their interactions with them.

Let us examine now more closely some widespread modes of categorizing African American boys, the normalizing judgments that they circulate, and the consequences these have on disciplinary intervention and punishment.

Being "At-Risk": Identifying Practice

The range of normalizing judgments for African American males is bounded by the image of the ideal pupil at one end of the spectrum and the unsalvageable student who is criminally inclined at the other end. The ideal type of student is characterized here by a white sixth-grade teacher:

Well, it consists of, first of all, to be able to follow directions. Any direction that I give. Whether it's get this out, whether it's put this away, whether it's turn to this page or whatever, they follow it, and they come in and they're ready to work. It doesn't matter high skill or low skill, they're ready to work and they know that's what they're here for. Behaviorally, they're appropriate all day long. When it's time for them to listen, they listen. The way I see it, by sixth grade, the ideal student is one that can sit and listen and learn from me—work with their peers, and take responsibility on themselves and understand what is next, what is expected of them.

This teacher, however, drew on the image of the Good Bad Boy when she described the qualities of her "ideal" male student, a white boy in her class. Here the docility of the generic ideal student becomes the essentially naughty-by-nature male:

He's not really Goody Two-shoes, you know. He's not quiet and perfect. He'll take risks. He'll say the wrong answer. He'll fool around and have to be reprimanded in class. There's a nice balance to him.

The modal category for African American boys is "at-risk" of failure. The concept of "at-riskness" is central to a discourse about the contemporary crisis in urban schools in America that explains children's failure as largely the consequence of their attitudes and behaviors as well as those of their families. In early stages of schooling they are identified as "at-risk" of failing, as "at-risk" of being school drop-outs. The category has been invested with enormous power to identify, explain, and predict futures. For example, a white fifth-grade teacher told me with sincere concern that as she looked around at her class, she could feel certain that about only four out of the twenty-one students would eventually graduate from high school. Each year, she said, it seemed to get worse.

Images of family play a strong role in teacher assessments and decisions about at-risk children. These enter into the evaluative process to confirm an original judgment. Families of at-risk children are said to lack parental skills; they do not give their children the kind of support that would build "self-esteem" necessary for school achievement. But this knowledge of family is superficial, inflamed by cultural representations and distorted through a rumor mill.

The children themselves are supposed to betray the lack of love and attention at home through their own "needy" behavior in the classroom. According to the teachers, these are pupils who are always demanding attention and will work well only in one-to-one or small-group situations because of this neglect at home. They take up more than their share of time and space. Donel, one of the African American boys who has been identified as at-risk by the school, is described by his teacher:

> He's a boy with a lot of energy and usually uncontrolled energy. He's very loud in the classroom, very inappropriate in the class. He has a great sense of humor, but again its inappropriate. I would say most of the time that his mouth is open, it's inappropriate, it's too loud, it's disrupting. But other than that [dry laugh] he's a great kid. You know if I didn't have to teach him, if it was a recreational setting, it would be fine.

So Donel is marked as "inappropriate" through the very configuration of self that school rules regulate: bodies, language, presentation of self. The stringent exercise of what is deemed appropriate as an instrument of assessment of at-riskness governs how the behavior of a child is understood. The notion of appropriate behavior in describing the ideal pupil earlier, and here as a way of characterizing a Troublemaker, reveals the broad latitude for interpretation and cultural framing of events. For one boy, "fooling around" behavior provides the balance between being a "real" boy and being a "goody-goody," while for the other, the conduct is seen through a different lens as "inappropriate," "loud," "disruptive."

Once a child is labeled "at-risk," he becomes more visible within the classroom, more likely to be singled out and punished for rule-breaking activity. An outburst by an African American boy already labeled as "at-risk" was the occasion for him to be singled out and made an example of the consequences of bad behavior before an audience of his peers; this was an occasion for a teacher to (re)mark the identity of a boy as disruptive. It was also one of those moments, recorded in my field notes, in which I observed the rewards that children might actually gain from getting into trouble.

This incident takes place in a second-grade classroom in another school which I am visiting in order to observe Gary, who has been identified as "at-risk" by the school and eligible for a special after-school program. The teacher, Miss Lyew, is an Asian woman with a loud, forceful voice. Twenty-five children are sitting in groups of three or four at tables as she goes over the recipe for making "a volcano erupt"—they do this together—she on the blackboard, they on sheets of paper in front of them. Miss Lyew has said she will call on people who have their hands raised. Lots of hands waving in the air and children vying for the right answer. There are always several possible answers for the next step, but only one that is "right." Children are not supposed to shout out the answer, but must wait to be called on. Sometimes, however, a child says the answer before being called on. Sometimes Miss Lyew ignores this, at other times she scolds the student.

It soon becomes clear that Gary is one of those she notices when he calls out. He gets a warning. The next time, Gary raises his hand and simultaneously calls out. She stops the class discussion of volcanoes and for the first time a kind of democracy enters the room. She turns to Gary's peers and asks what punishment Gary should get the next time he calls out an answer.

Now children are waving hands held high to suggest various forms of punishment: send him to the office, take points away from him, call his mother, send him home, send him to stand outside the room, wash his mouth out. There is no end to the various forms of punishment the children can think of. Gary himself gets into the act, he proposes that they take all the points away from his table. This is a punishment that Miss Lyew herself has threatened to use earlier in the day.

Miss Lyew looks indignant, then asks the class if this would be fair. How would the other children at the table feel? They would be punished for something they didn't do. The teacher then asks the children to vote on which one of the punishments they feel Gary should face if he should call out again. The voting begins. I notice that all the girls, but only a few boys, vote, as sympathy breaks down along gender lines. The teacher urges, "Everyone has a vote." It is an amazing and fascinating display because the classroom has suddenly for the first (and for the only time during my observation) taken on the semblance of a democratic operation with children actually getting to "choose" how something should be done.

Gary sits dispassionately calm, almost serene. He is the eye of the storm. He has shaped the direction of class activity in a powerful way. The teacher presses the issue so that everyone finally raises their hand in some kind of vote. Finally, it has been decided, if Gary answers out of turn again he will be sent out of the room and the next time his mother will be called. Gary does not look anxious, he does not look humiliated.

The class returns to the study of classifying inanimate objects. They are working on shapes. The answers are supposed to be, "It is a cube. It is a rectangular prism," etc. I notice that several other kids call out of turn and Miss Lyew does not pay attention. Enough time has been spent on *that* lesson. In fact, one of the children reminds her about the punishment when someone else calls out of turn, but she does not refocus on the misdeed.

Gary is positioned as an "at-risk" black male in the room. From the teacher's perspective, this carries with it powerful received meanings of who the "at-risk" child is and what he needs to learn in order to succeed. She believes, for one, that boys like Gary need to learn impulse control; that they need to learn respect for authority, self-discipline, to be appropriate, to keep their mouths shut. Gary is not only more visible because of the label, but the recipient of a series of specific remedies and prescriptions about what he needs. That Gary knows the answer and is bursting with the excitement of this knowledge is not as significant here as the fact that in his case conformity to the rule must be enforced.

Most important, moments of public punishment are powerful learning experiences about social location and worthiness for everyone involved. These cultural spectacles signal profound meanings of "racial" difference through a performance that engages audience as well as actors in a reenactment of social roles within relations of power. In these spectacles, the singling out, the naming, the displaying of that which is "bad" affirms the institutional power to stigmatize. Gary becomes a lesson to other children in the room about what it means to be caught in the spotlight of disciplinary power. The spectators learn that to get in trouble with authority is to risk becoming the example, the spectacle for the consumption of others. It is to risk, not mere momentary humiliation, but the separation from one's peers as different.

Gary is made the object of a lesson. But he uses different strategies to recuperate his sense of self. He tries to reenter the group by proposing a punishment that the teacher in fact uses herself—to punish the whole table by taking away the group points—but he's pushed farther to the margins. Now he is not just someone who is disrupting the order of the room but would drag others down with him as well. For a second-grade boy like Gary, already labeled, the classroom is potentially a place of shame and humiliation in the marginalizing activity of the teacher.

However, the moment is a complex experience. For several minutes Gary is the focus of the entire room. In this moment of trouble and punishment, he has become the counterauthority. The teacher occupies one leadership pole and he another. He proposes his own punishment and he does not protest when a decision is finally made. He is the epitome of grace under pressure.

I, the adult observer, am impressed by his fortitude, his presence. By the end of the confrontation, it is clear to all the children, including Gary, that he receives special treatment, is marked for special attention. His exposure of the arbitrary nature of punishment captivates me.

Getting a Reputation

Children are sorted into categories of "educability" as they get a reputation among the adults as troubled, troubling, or troublemakers. They are not only identified as problems, as "at-risk" by the classroom teacher, but gain schoolwide reputations as stories about their exploits are publicly shared by school adults in the staff room, at staff meetings, and at in-service training sessions. Horror stories circulate through the school adult network so that children's reputations precede them into classrooms and follow them from school to school. I pointed out earlier how Horace's name was invoked at a staff meeting as a benchmark of misbehavior against which other boys would be judged. As in: "That child's a problem. But he's not a Horace."

Once a reputation has been established, the boy's behavior is usually refigured within a framework that is no longer about childish misdemeanors but comes to be an ominous portent of things to come.

They are tagged with futures: "He's on the fast track to San Quentin Prison," and "That one has a jail-cell with his name on it." For several reasons, these boys are more likely to be singled out and punished than other children. They are more closely watched. They are more likely to be seen as intentionally doing wrong than a boy who is considered to be a Good Bad Boy. Teachers are more likely to use the "moral principle" in determining whether to call attention to misdemeanors because "at-risk" children need discipline, but also as an example to the group, especially to other African American boys who are "endangered." The possibility of contagion must be eliminated. Those with reputations must be isolated, kept away from the others. Kids are told to stay away from them: "You know what will happen if you go over there." In the case of boys with reputations, minor infractions are more likely to escalate into major punishments.

Unsalvageable Students

In the range of normalizing judgments, there is a group of African American boys identified by school personnel as, in the words of a teacher, "unsalvageable." This term and the condition it speaks to is specifically about masculinity. School personnel argue over whether these unsalvageable boys should be given access even to the special programs designed for those who are failing in school. Should resources, defined as scarce, be wasted on these boys for whom there is no hope? Should energy and money be put instead into children who can be saved? I have heard teachers argue on both sides of the question. These "boys for whom there is no hope" get caught up in the school's punishment system: surveillance, isolation, detention, and ever more severe punishment.

These are children who are not children. These are boys who are already men. So a discourse that positions masculinity as "naturally" naughty is reframed for African American boys around racialized representations of gendered subjects. They come to stand as if already adult, bearers of adult fates inscribed within a racial order.

a shift in perspective

The material presented up to now has documented the institutional practices that produce social identities of "at-risk," troublemakers, "unsalvageables." From this point on, I turn to look at the meaning of getting in trouble from the kids' perspective. We change from a standpoint that features the school's identifying practices to one where the school day is viewed from the point of view of the pupils themselves.

Children's work of subjective identification and disidentification with school will be examined. By disidentification I mean how and why many African American boys actively distance and separate themselves from school as a desirable and authoritative object of identification while simultaneously embracing alternative subject positions as a means for becoming visible and gaining recognition in the social world.

We will explore how Schoolboys and Troublemakers actively configure self through two social identities, race and gender, to provide the social, psychic, and emotional resources for recouping a sense of self as competent and admirable in an institutional setting where they have been categorized as problems or as failures. These identities are not just arbitrarily chosen modalities of identification for self-fashioning, but are already an integral part of their lived and imaginary world that structures, constrains, and makes intelligible every facet of social life.

With this shift of focus from that of school to that of students, two aspects of this new perspective are featured. The first is what kids know and how this affects the meaning of rules and getting in trouble. Children are highly knowledgeable about teachers' identifying practices and assessments. They are sophisticated participant observers themselves, skilled interpreters and astute analysts of social interactions, cognizant of a variety of cues that signal teachers' expectations of children. They are aware not only of the institution's ranking and labeling system, but of their own and other children's position within that system. This knowledge has a marked effect on concomitant self-fashioning within school.[1] Kids know who is deemed troubled, troubling, or troublemaking. They are influenced by these labels, but they also have their own critical perspective on the process itself.

My awareness of the acutely perceptive observational work of the children whom I interviewed has been corroborated in a series of studies that ask elementary school students for their own interpretation of classroom interactions.[2] They find that children as early as the first grade are conscious that there is a disparity in teachers' interactions with students. The kids recognize that teachers treat "high achievers" differently than they do those they perceive as low achievers. They notice, for instance, that low achievers receive more negative feedback and more rule-oriented behavior from teachers. Children draw on a range of verbal and nonverbal cues to make these inferences. For example, they conclude that when and how teachers called on children in class sends an implicit message about the expected performance: kids who were seen as smart were called on for the right answers because teachers expected them to know more, while low achievers were not called on often "because she knows they don't know the answer," or were called on to "give them a chance," or because "they goof off."[3]

I found that Troublemakers and Schoolboys also drew on an additional body of information to make judgments about what they observed. This is the local knowledge that comes from family and neighborhood to function as an interpretive screen through which the events of the school day are filtered. This knowledge is the generative matrix for an oppositional discourse about the contrasting treatment they observe and experience. It challenges the school's version of trouble as a matter of individual behavior and personal choice.

The second feature that will be systematically reviewed in the chapters to follow is the complex interaction between rule breaking and

---

1. Studies that examine children's internalization of teacher expectations include Casanova, "Rashomon in the Classroom"; Rist, *The Urban School;* and United States Commission on Civil Rights, *Teachers and Students: Differences in Teacher Intervention with Mexican American and Anglo Students* (Washington, D.C.: U.S. Government Printing Office, 1973).

2. See, for example, Donna Eder, "Ability Grouping and Students' Academic Self-Concepts: A Case Study," *Elementary School Journal* 84, no. 2 (1983); N. N. Filby and B. G. Barnett, "Student Perceptions of 'Better Readers' in Elementary Classrooms," *Elementary School Journal* 82, no. 5 (1982); Rhonda Strasberg Weinstein and Susan E. Middlestadt, "Student Perceptions of Teacher Interactions with Male High and Low Achievers," *Journal of Educational Psychology* 71, no. 1 (1979).

3. Weinstein and Middlestadt, "Student Perceptions."

processes of identification. For the Troublemakers, already categorized as prison material, academic achievement and conforming behavior as the basis for a constitution of self as smart, promising, worthy is already foreclosed. So they disidentify with school in a process that Kohl describes as "active not-learning," the conscious effort of obviously intelligent students to expend their time and energy in the classroom actively distancing themselves from schoolwork, thereby short-circuiting the trajectory of school failure altogether.[4] This takes place when a student has to cope with

> unavoidable challenges to her or his personal and family loyalties, integrity, and identity. In such situations there are forced choices and no apparent middle ground. To agree to learn from a stranger who does not respect your integrity causes a major loss of self. The only alternative is to not-learn and reject the stranger's world. . . . [These students are] engaged in a struggle of wills with authority, and what seemed to be at stake for them was nothing less than their pride and integrity. Most of them did not believe that they were failures or that they were inferior to students who succeeded on the school's terms.[5]

I will elaborate on the role that racial and gender identification play in "not-learning" as Schoolboys and Troublemakers in the classrooms at Rosa Parks School confront circumstances that assault and violate family and communal bonds as well as the configuration of selfhood. We will find that a hegemonic masculinity provides the resource for refashioning a sense of self through body practices in enactments of gender power. Simultaneously, racial identification with Blackness becomes the source for a subversive, reverse discourse to recoup personal esteem.

---

4. Herbert Kohl, *I Won't Learn from You: The Role of Assent in Learning,* (Minneapolis: Milkweed Editions, 1991).

5. Ibid., 16–17.

chapter five
the real world

It's like a jungle sometimes, it makes me wonder
How I keep from going under
It's like a jungle sometimes, it makes me wonder
How I keep from going under

Broken glass everywhere
People pissing on the stairs
You know they just don't care
I can't take the smell, can't take the noise
Got no money to move out, I guess I got no choice
Rats in the front room, roaches in the back
Junkies in the alley with a baseball bat
I tried to get away but I couldn't get far
'Cause the man with the tow truck repossessed my car.

Don't push me 'cause I'm close to the edge
I'm trying not to lose my head.
Ah huh huh huh huh
It's like a jungle sometimes, it make me wonder
How I keep from going under.

—GRANDMASTER FLASH AND THE FURIOUS FIVE, "THE MESSAGE"

It was candy, sweet, chewy, a pink and white swirl on a stick, glossy and fragrant from a big jar and offered to me for sale by a fourth-grade girl that got me thinking seriously about the meaning of rules for different groups of children in the school. Until that moment, school rules were really only words written on a piece of paper. Myelisha, a pupil in the after-school tutoring program, had pulled the jar of candy out of her backpack and asked me to buy one.

"Do you have a quarter?" she asked. "They're cheap." I looked over my shoulder furtively. Candy in school was against the rules, and as tempted as I was by the lollipop I realized that it might be trouble for me if I was seen giving money to a fourth-grader in exchange for candy. My own approach to rule breaking, I discovered, was fearful, shifty behavior.

"Here. If you don't have the money today, I'll give you one," Myelisha was saying, pulling out something wrapped in red and yellow paper. "Pay me later," she said grandly.

"Careful, Myelisha, having candy is against the school rules. You should put that away until later." I could see teachers moving around at other tables. I was afraid that one of them might dart over at any moment and seize the contraband.

"Hush, Ann," Myelisha was teasing me now in a singsong voice a smile on her face. "The teachers was the one started selling candy first. So there!"

We were both right. I in the legalistic sense, paying attention to the authority of the written, the codified. One of the most concrete, straightforward of the rules listed on the poster that hung on the wall of every classroom was that no candy was allowed in school. At the same time candy was everywhere. Kids had candy in their desks, in their school packs, in their pockets. I had observed several of them ordered to spit out "whatever that is you're eating," followed by a ball of sugar, well-sculpted by a tongue, plummeting into the nearest waste-basket. One day, one of the boys in Mrs. Deane's class was sent to the office because he took up too much class time as he moved from his desk to the wastebasket. Candy, having it, sharing it, eating it, and sell-ing it, was prohibited in school.

Yet for the past week, as both Myelisha and I had observed, chil-dren in various classrooms had been toting boxes of candy around and selling openly. This sales drive had been initiated by the teachers to raise money for class activities. While children were supposed to take the candy home and sell it to relatives, friends, and neighbors, teachers were ignoring efforts to make sales at school. Our tutoring sessions had been disrupted by kids pressing adults to buy, to make change, and by the banking of substantial amounts of money. The rule about candy in school had not been overturned but was being overlooked for the time being. The sale of authorized candy was now permitted, which allowed individual entrepreneurs to display their wares.

Myelisha's profits were also for a worthy cause. She informed me that *she* was selling candy in order to put on a birthday party for her mother. She wanted to buy a present and get a nice cake. Other children were coming over to our table and after handing over pennies, nickels, and dimes were being allowed to put their hand in the jar and make a selection. Myelisha was letting no one but me have candy on credit. Even a girl I had come to know as one of her good friends was turned down decisively. "Try and get it from Somika," she suggests as she refuses to let her friend take a handful of Tootsie Rolls now and bring the money tomorrow.

Nor is this the end of Myelisha's entrepreneurial career. Several weeks later, during the school day, I find her wandering around in the hallway. I have noticed that she is often in the hallway when classes are in session. No one ever seems to notice her there—judging from the absence of her name on referrals for being tardy or cutting. "Hey Ann!" she hails me. "I'm selling Santa cups, wanta buy one?"

I try to put her off. "Aren't you in class now? Maybe later."

"No, wait." She ducks in and out of her classroom in no time, and comes back bearing a brightly painted mug molded with a Santa Claus face and filled with candy. "It's three dollars. I'm going to buy my mom a Christmas present. Take it now and you can give me the money later." My credit is always good with her.

Later, when I am paying off my debt, I discover that the candy in the mug has been culled from the Halloween candy that Myelisha and her older sister collected several weeks before when they were out trick or treating.

There is a thriving informal economy in the school. The adult focus on contraband has been on the possibility of kids bringing drugs to school. While no child was ever caught with possession or sale of drugs during the period that I was a participant observer, a number of children were caught selling things to eat.

Jamar, one of the Troublemakers, brought his lunch in a plastic shopping bag. He often had several apples, oranges, bananas, as well as a sandwich. After recess, I would notice him tossing an orange to one of his classmates, an apple to another. I was puzzled by his "sharing," since often the kids who were receiving the fruit were not members of the group he spent time with at recess. I discovered that he was selling the fruit one day when, as he tossed an orange to one of the boys, his teacher warned him that she knew what was going on and he had better stop bringing food to school to sell or she would send him to the principal.

Myelisha and Jamar live in the neighborhood around Rosa Parks School. They are both African American children and their families are poor. They are among the 50 percent of the children in the school eligible for the free lunch program. When Myelisha and Jamar sell food or candy in school, they are working to earn money. They are also breaking the rules.

The purpose of these anecdotes is to point to two features of what kids know and believe about school rules and getting in trouble: first, children are highly aware that rules are arbitrarily applied, often flagrantly ignored, by the adults; second, the rules and relative cost of getting into trouble for breaking them have different meanings for different groups of children in the school. The candy example is an obvious one: for some children the small amount of money that is earned through food sales makes a difference in the cash available to a family living on the economic edge. From this perspective, choosing to break the rule makes sense. A simple rule like the ban on candy means something different to children from low-income families than it does to the children of the affluent. This mix of marginal poverty and relative affluence is exactly the combination of pupils at Rosa Parks School. At the same time, race differences mirror class divisions in the school. The vast majority of the children from low-income families are African American, while the middle-class children are predominately white. Childhood is constituted within a social order divided sharply along class and race lines.

This condition of racialized poverty is the matrix for the reverse discourse and the use of local "popular" knowledge that Myelisha, the Troublemakers, and the Schoolboys bring to school to make sense of the rules, of relationships with peers and adults, and of work and play. The choice to abide by the rules is not an individual matter at all but influenced and constrained by one's social class location and the access to the material and cultural capital that this position provides.

What I am referring to here as popular knowledge is what is described by Foucault as "local, discontinuous, disqualified, illegitimate knowledges" that serve as a source for a critical stance toward institutional knowledge and power.[1] This form of knowledge confronts

---

1. Michel Foucault, *Power/Knowledge: Selected Interviews and Other Writings, 1972–1977,* ed. and trans. Colin Gordon (New York: Pantheon, 1980), 82.

institutional practices with a distinct, competing set of theories and methods of knowing the world. It relies heavily but not solely on observation and experience; the data gathered by the senses and the emotions is taken seriously and valued over book learning. Folk and popular culture are important vehicles for this knowledge. It is the form of knowledge that the individualizing, dispersing, hierarchizing strategies of school seeks to eradicate.

Popular knowledge is rooted in a particular social and geographic space, the neighborhood. Embedded in the local, it draws on lore that is orally transmitted through family histories, forms of music and song, cautionary tales as story and rumor.

Now let us follow Troublemakers and Schoolboys out of school to the neighborhoods in which they live to examine the familial and public space where their identification is rooted and to pinpoint the elements of popular knowledge generated in family and neighborhood. This excursion reveals how class location and mobility strategies as well as race and gender identities shape what African American boys learn about dealing with power and authority. It uncovers several interrelated aspects of popular knowledge that directly affect how the boys deal with school: observation and experience as a method of knowing; a critical and oppositional stance to authority; and a collective rather than individualized explanatory frame that constitutes black masculinity in a context of social terror.

Neighborhood

The notion of neighborhood came up in conversation as several of the boys asked me whether I lived in or had grown up in "a good neighborhood" or "bad neighborhood." They were trying to figure me out. They wanted to know if I had the experiential knowledge to appreciate what they were telling me. They assumed that where you lived shaped the knowledge base that generated different modes of being in the world. For example, Eddie asked me, "Were you raised up in a bad neighborhood? If you were raised up in a bad area then you have to know how to defend yourself."

The assessment of their neighborhood as "bad" by the boys is neither a figment of their imagination nor an exaggeration. The components of a "bad" neighborhood include both objective indicators as well as the subjective feelings of the people who live there. At a first glance, the neighborhood around the school where most of the boys live appears deceptively quiet and stable. When I first drove around the area surrounding the school I was pleasantly surprised to see streets lined with small houses and apartment buildings that seemed peaceful and quiet, yards that were neat. The area did not fit the image I had of a low-income urban environment as physically unkempt and rundown. A closer look, however, revealed the evidence of problems. The most visible of these were street signs warning drug dealers and their customers that they were being watched. Drug dealing is symptomatic of an ensemble of other social ills: unemployment, theft, guns, homicide, police brutality and harassment. Since the highest percentage of murders in Arcadia occur in this precinct, the neighborhood is, indeed, one of the most dangerous in the city.

What is the likely life-world for children living in this neighborhood? They are likely to come from female-headed households that must worry about money for basic necessities.[2] Whether a child grows up in a household that is headed by a single female or a married couple or is multigenerational has profound effects on the family environment and budget. The more adults that families can muster to help with child minding, laundry, cooking, cleaning, and shopping, the better. In the past, low-income African American families typically lived in multigenerational households, and family networks provided the physical and material backup support for single mothers.[3] The fairly recent breakup of this kind of household means the physical and emotional work of child rearing and housework has to be shouldered by single women, many of whom often already work for a wage outside the home.[4] Funding for public social services has also been disappearing, so organized recreation and after-school programs for children that might have offset some of this burden have not been extended to fill the gap.

There is now an all-pervasive fear that families will lose their children to the "bad" elements of the neighborhood. This influences the child-rearing practices of adults and colors the experience and meaning of childhood in and out of school for families in the neighborhood.

---

2. U.S. Census, 1990.

3. Carol B. Stack, *All Our Kin: Strategies for Survival in a Black Community* (New York: Harper and Row, 1974).

4. Niara Sudarkasa, "African-American Families and Family Values," in *Black Families,* ed. Harriette Pipes McAdoo (Thousand Oaks, Calif.: Sage, 1997).

Family Lessons

Families talked to me about what they believe is vital knowledge for the boys to have when they go, as they put it, out into "the real world." This means life outside the relative security of home. While these family precepts included the general messages that parents pass on to kids, they also emphasized the special instructions that were a matter of life and death for young black males. The adults are filled with dread about what might happen when their sons leave their house every day. They especially worry that the boys will do something that will entangle them in "the system," the shorthand reference to the criminal justice system.

At this stage, kids are still young enough that parents feel they have some control over their social development as well as their physical comings and goings, their social relationships. They feel an urgency to inculcate strategies in the boys for dealing with the humiliating and often dangerous situations in which they are likely to find themselves. These guidelines are conveyed through exhortation and modeling, cautionary tales of personal experience, and through object lessons drawn from witnessing public racial spectacles. Embedded in these life-lessons is wisdom about the meaning of Blackness and its special dangers for males in contemporary America.

Many of these precepts and the underlying assumptions of family life-lessons came to light in interviews that are worth recounting. I have made selections from the family interviews that typify the two prevailing survival strategies in the neighborhood. The first anticipates upward mobility for their sons through school achievement. These prescribe strategies of "racelessness" in the presentation of self and avoidance to deal with racism. The second strategy is found in poor families who feel unable to protect their kids from the exigencies of the real world. Their kids must learn how to stand up for themselves and play more adult roles. It is not feasible for these parents to advocate avoidance, nor do they have the cultural capital to promote racelessness.

The Norton family pursues a strategy of racelessness and avoidance. The family includes Terrence, one of the Schoolboys, and his mother and father, Arlene and Desmond. Both adults have relatively well paid jobs. Terrence's father is a mechanic at a local car dealership; his mother is a nurse. With their two incomes they can afford to live a middle-class lifestyle. They have bought an older home and remodeled it, doing most of the work themselves. Terrence is their only child and they want to make sure that he has the best education, so they sent him to a private school for his first four years of education. Their growing concern that he was learning little about the real world in that setting made them decide to enroll him in public school. He is now in his second year at Rosa Parks.

Terrence's parents believe there are some essential things that every African American boy must learn about the real world. These range from what to wear and how to conduct oneself in public, to relationships with other human beings, and the proper performance of masculinity. It seems like fairly typical elements of parental advice. However, their instructions about styles of self-presentation are specifically designed to prepare him for a life in which he will be a target for verbal and physical assaults from strangers as well as acquaintances because of his race. As a way of warding off these types of encounters, they give him tools to downplay his Blackness, to camouflage himself through a careful selection of clothing, mode of self-deportment and style. The most important aspect of these is how to derace himself, make himself visibly different from the prevailing image of black males as poor, lawless, and dangerous. Terrence must learn how to demonstrate through a variety of symbolic gestures that he is harmless.

His father, Desmond, describes how significant the choice of clothing is in this presentation of self:

> It doesn't make any difference where you are or how much money you have because you don't want to dress like you a Fortune 500 company everyday. . . . You might just want to go to the store in your torn pants looking all raggedy and everything and walk around and not buy nothing. Which is supposed to be okay. But for some people it's not okay. You just can't go to the department store and just hang out.

Terrence's father knows that if you are black and male you do not have the freedom to wear whatever you like, whatever you are comfortable in, when you go into public. He teaches his son that he must select clothing carefully; not based on individual preference, but as a protective layer for psychic even physical survival. Terrence cannot take for granted the permission to linger and loiter in the public space, especially if he is not dressed to look like a person of means and status.

Black males who want to avoid humiliating encounters must dress so they can be seen as purposeful, conservative, not threatening.

Demeanor is important, so is the ability to produce money as physical evidence of one's value. Desmond assumes that this surface presentation of self will help to stave off harassment:

> Even at his age, he knows prejudice exists. He knows people some-time aren't informed as he is. That he's polite—for whatever reason people might look at him and he might go to a store y'know. He told me last week he went to a store with his cousins, and that is something I really don't allow him to do go around a store and browse around because people will follow him around just because he's a little black kid. Figure that they come in and steal something. I as a parent, anytime that Terrence is gone I tell him that he make sure that he has at least a couple of dollars in his pocket just so people can realize he's not going around stealing anything. He has a little money in his pocket. He can buy little knickknacks if he goes to the store or anywhere.

Desmond presents racism as stemming from individual prejudice and ignorance rather than institutional practice and power. Arlene, Terrence's mother, speaks about racism as a more generalized phenomenon. Both ground their cautionary tales about presentation of self in the world in experience. Desmond has been stopped and interrogated by the police when he was on his way home one night for no apparent reason. He was questioned at length about where he was going and where he was coming from. Arlene described how the incident was used to teach Terrence about the real world:

> My husband has had experiences since we've lived in this house where he has had interaction with the police that hasn't been favor-able or that have been precipitated largely because he's black. Being in the wrong place at the wrong time. Those experiences he's shared with Terrence. I think that they are very important for our son to learn about the real world. No matter how we like to think the world is today.

Arlene believes that it is crucial to teach her son that dominant representations of Blackness will determine how people see him. The only way to mitigate this stereotyping is through proving your difference from the racial image. She sees education and putting forward a 100 percent effort as the only way to do this:

> It is important that black male children or even black children period are taught to be prepared. Prepare yourself the best way you possibly can. That means doing well in school academically. Doing your best at everything you attempt to do. To be your best—'cause there's one thing that's never going to change about you—and that's your skin color and you can't change people's perceptions based on that. Even as a black professional, my colleagues, their perception of me doesn't change just because I'm educated. Constantly you have to prove who you are or that you're worthy, if you choose to do so. It's a constant thing. Racial attitudes are embedded in the person and there's really not a heck of a lot that the individual who's subjected to the negative racial attitudes can do about it other than to be the very best that you can be at anything you desire to be. . . . And I think that kids need to learn that.

She draws on her own experience as a professional who still has to prove her "worth" because she is always and already seen through a racial lens as "inferior." She feels pressure to demonstrate that she is different from her colleagues' preconception of her. Her own move for inclusion is to work at being "worthy."

Terrence had his own direct experience with racism when one of the white kids in the neighborhood called him "nigger." Desmond described their reaction to the incident:

> She [points to Arlene] blew up and wanted to do something about it. But I didn't. I told him it's not the first time that someone's going to call you a nigger and it won't be the last time, and I asked him, I said, "How many times have you called your friends at school a nigger?" And he said [laughing], "A lot of times." So I said, "Well, see, its okay for a black person to call a black person a nigger." I guess its like a Mexican calling a Mexican a "chollo" as long as it's in your family. But when it comes outside of your family it'll pinch you.

Arlene's response is to act; Desmond's is to use this event as a way of inuring the boy to the inevitable. He is preparing Terrence for damaging assaults on his personhood by giving the boy a strategy, both practical and emotional, for dealing with the injury. He prepares Terrence for the emotional "pinch," the psychic pain of racism. The owning of the word *nigger* as a symbol of camaraderie, of an in-group, to which the white boy is an outsider, is intended to remove some of the sting. Desmond invokes their membership in a larger undifferentiated black community even when the overall family project is for members to differentiate themselves from the vernacular culture that has reclaimed the word *nigger* as a proud part of black male identity.

The parents have differences about the strategic responses and actions for Terrence in the face of power. Both emphasize a strategy of individuation by setting oneself apart from the group. Being different from Blackness means behaving and being excellent, worthy. They have internalized the belief that a good part of the problem of black urban youth and their families lies with lack of individual effort. These assumptions emerge from their upwardly mobile, middle-class orientation:

> I tell my son, the best thing you to do is to stay out of trouble. I think that's the best thing any black kid can do, because once you get in trouble, once you get into their tracking system which is the courts, the penal institution, then you're trapped, they know everything about you. Long as you can stay out of that system you pretty much can go.

Desmond's attitude is that it is essential for Terrence to swallow his anger. This fits with the school's position that individual "bad" behavior is what brings punishment down on your head. He subscribes to the notion that confrontations can be avoided and that fighting back is what gets you in trouble in the first place. The knowledge he imparts to his son is specifically targeted to the likelihood of encounters with the police. Terrence's work here is to perform a self that cannot be construed as threatening. Otherwise he is responsible for the consequences:

> I think that the most important thing to teach any black man if they come in contact with the police—especially if they're white police, is to be as courteous as possible. The more courteous you are, the quicker you going to resolve whatever situation there is. If for any reason that you start smart-mouthing or acting tough, they going to look at you and say oh, okay, here we go again, another

threat. And they going to come down a lot harder. When it happens, you just have to roll with the punches and do what they ask you to do. Lay on the ground. They going to tell you to get on the ground, put your hands up. They going to humiliate you. Once you get past that, it's okay.

Desmond requires that Terrence as a rule practice an enactment of self as nonthreatening and avoiding physical confrontation. Arlene disagrees with this approach. She offers a stance that is more in keeping with the notion that you have to learn how to take care of yourself:

He's so afraid of what his father might do if he gets into a fight that he doesn't. He says the kids are always testing him. "Mom, what should I do?" And I tell him, I say, "If someone hits you, you smack him as hard as you can and they're not going to do it again." But my husband is saying, "No, I don't want you to fight." But on the other hand, from where I'm standing, kids are going to fight and I don't want my kid to be perceived as a big wimp!

She argues the importance of Terrence standing up for himself and fighting back. When he comes to her for advice about dealing with his peers who challenge him to fight, she urges him to give as good or better than he gets. This is both about the construction of self as well as appraisal by others. Arlene is afraid her son will not be perceived by others as sufficiently masculine, but also that he will not have developed the necessary accoutrements of masculinity. She is concerned that training for passive submission to symbolic or physical violence will hinder his move into manhood; that not only will he be characterized as ineffectual, but that he will be ineffectual.

Eddy, one of the Troublemakers, is also prepared for dealing with racism by his father, Karl, who uses a different approach than Arlene and Desmond. Eddy lives with Karl, who is black, his stepmother, Sheryl, who is white, and his younger bother and sister. Karl is on disability insurance because of a back injury, and Sheryl describes herself as a homemaker. She is on welfare. Karl has raised Eddy and his brother since they were small.

Karl is convinced that it is crucial for black kids to learn how to take care of themselves. "I try to teach them, you go out of my door, reality hits. I'm not going to baby you up in here because life is not goin'ta baby you out that door." He warns his son: "I tell Eddy, you going to be filled with prejudice in your life. Prepare yourself. There's no way around it." Eddy's family does not have the resources to shield him in the world. His father reiterates the message that Eddy should strive to be the best, but seems to have given up on school as a route to success. He sees baseball, which is what the twelve-year-old is good at, as the route to the boy's adult achievement. The family attends all of Eddy's games and speaks enthusiastically about the boy's prowess.

Karl talked about preparing Eddy for inevitable and perilous encounters with the police. He drew on his own experience to make a connection with the national spectacle of the Rodney King beating by Los Angeles police:

> Personally I have some real messed-up instances with the police in which I was definitely the victim and I really got messed up feelings. Like that thing with Rodney King. I was one of them. It still bothers me. They beat me, they beat me. They didn't have no proper cause whatsoever. It was about twelve o'clock at night. I seen three guys dart out there with some guns. By the time I run I hear, "Police, police!" So my mind is clicking. So I stop. They come round that corner, they stomp me. They beat me till I couldn't walk.

Karl explained how the police took him to jail, held him overnight. When he went before the judge the next day, he was released without being charged. He frames his encounter not as an isolated incident, but contextualized through the Rodney King beating. He sees his own experience not as a consequence of his own behavior, but as part of a much larger pattern of police treatment of black men. This assumption on his part is supported by a 1993 study carried out by the California State Assembly's Commission on the Status of African-American Males that finds that 92 percent of the black men arrested by police on drug charges were subsequently released for lack of evidence or inadmissible evidence.[5] Karl does not suggest to Eddy that there are things Karl might have done that created the situation. His, he teaches, was a collective, not an individual, experience.

Horace, the Troublemaker who became my research assistant, has

5. Cited in Miller, *Search and Destroy*, 8.

learned strategies for dealing with the world through direct observation and emulation as well as from family. He is a fighter, both verbally and physically. This gets him into trouble in school. As I get to know his mother, Helene, I realize that he has learned from this tiny white woman how to stand up for himself and how to challenge people who have power over you. He is conscious of this model because he describes his mother as the person he most respects:

> I know she be real mad at me when I get in trouble in school, but I know she'll go to the school board, right to the very top to protest if she thinks it's unfair how they treat me. I don't know how she does it. She's little [he pauses thoughtfully], but she makes people listen to her.

Horace and his two siblings live with their mother in a shabby apartment building about a mile away from the school. There are many drawbacks to living there. The building is rat-infested, hot in the summer and cold in the winter. Helene's fantasy is to be able to move out of the city to the suburbs, where she will have nice neighbors and her children won't have so many "negative influences in the schools."

The chances of this happening, however, are slight. The family is barely surviving on her income as a nurse's aide. The rent is relatively low because it is regulated by the rent control laws of the city. Helene is in a continuing battle with the building's owner, Mrs. Kwon, to hold her to her legal obligations to keep the building in good repair. She is convinced that Mrs. Kwon would like to find an excuse to evict her so she could renovate the building and raise the rents. I discover all this one day when Helene shows me documents from a bulging file that are letters back and forth between herself, the owner, and the city rent board. She asks if I will come and be "moral support" for her at mediation hearings that are being held because she has refused to pay rent for several months until repairs agreed upon previously have been completed. The landlord is demanding she pay up or be evicted.

I have included the following account of the rent board hearings in part because they illustrate the anxieties about basic necessities that are a part of the real world some children experience and that shadow their school day, but also because the hearings emphasized so dramatically for me a number of observations that I had already made about power and trouble. First was the power of institutional language and form to disable oppositional voices as unreasonable, out of control, illegitimate. Second was the fact that a boy who might be a Troublemaker in the context of school could be identified as an exemplary figure in other contexts and act accordingly. Finally, the struggle to procure and maintain basic necessities such as a roof over one's head makes troublemaking essential for survival.

Horace is there at the hearings as "moral support" too. Helene has chosen him as the family member to act as witness to some of the claims and counterclaims that are being made. She describes Horace as "the one I can depend on. More than any of my other kids."

The rent board hearings go on for a couple of hours. I find the proceedings frustrating and disheartening. I had expected a procedure similar to the conflict resolution process at the school in which each side tells their story with the mediator acting as facilitator. Perhaps this is how it might have worked if the owner's lawyer had not been there. The lawyer, however, manages to dominate the meeting. Using the language of the law to rule on what is "admissible evidence," he determines what is said, when it is said, and by whom it is said. The city's mediator is no match for him; he is a petty bureaucrat without the tools to take charge. Sometimes I suspect him of being in cahoots with the landlord, sometimes I assume that he is just ineffective. This is the operation of institutional power at its most visible. I am stunned as the lawyer virtually blocks Helene's story down every avenue she takes to tell it. She is made to look like a hysterical woman who is, in fact, obstructing the repair work. Mrs. Kwon, the owner, appears eager to do everything she can to make the place livable if only her crazy, obstructive tenant would allow her.

The lawyer does worse than silence Helene. She is made to seem disruptive, out of control, wasting the precious time of everyone else sitting around the table. Her attempt to tell her side is continually framed as irrelevant or out of order. On the other hand, he skillfully manages to talk almost all the time; he is able to interrupt her with impunity. When I finally point this out, I, too, am silenced because I, too, have spoken out of turn.

Horace looks glum. He sits quietly, intensely taking it all in. He has been asked to testify a couple of times by his mother. He is the only one of the three of us at the hearing who has in fact not gotten in trouble, not spoken "out of turn." His side has not made much of a showing. Horace is a witness for his mother, but he also witnesses her humiliation in this setting of institutional power. Formal, specialized language and knowledge systems hold sway; we do not have the words, the phrasing, to command respect. Someone else makes, knows, and adjudicates the rules. Helene and I are like children in the classroom, silenced or disruptive because we cannot speak the "language" of the courtroom. In the final analysis, however, Helene scores a small temporary victory. The landlord agrees again to make certain repairs after which the back rent as well as an increase in rent will be paid.

For Horace and his mother the possibility of eviction from a seedy apartment is an ever-looming reality. Horace cannot be shielded from that possibility. He must act as witness on behalf of his mother. He observes what they are up against when he sits with her through the rent board hearing. He observes that she must engage in tactics that are "impolite," disruptive, in order to be heard and to win even small concessions.

The Haven of Childhood

The boys are alerted by family to the dangers of "the real world" for black males through admonitions, object lessons from direct personal experience, and electrifying moments such as watching the videotape of Rodney King being beaten senseless by the police. The constant reiteration of this danger and the need to be on guard or to handle dreadful encounters themselves saturates their daily journeys through school and neighborhood. Throughout my interviews and conversations with them, I heard the strong undercurrent of fear flowing beneath their talk. The very boys who were being constituted in school and in the media as demonic, terrifying, and unsalvageable were themselves fearful.

What I mean by fear is not the individualized, psychological anxieties that stem out of a personal trauma. Though expressed individually, this fear is a reflection of the social terror that arises out of a group condition. It is the emotional space C. Wright Mills describes as the intersection of "the personal troubles of milieu" and "the public issues of social structure."[6] This social terror permeates the daily life of which the school day is a part. It constitutes the feeling component of the popular, illegitimate knowledge that the boys bring into school, which

6. C. Wright Mills, *The Sociological Imagination* (New York: Oxford University Press, 1959), 8.

informs their practices, their relationships, what they accept as truth, what they shut out, suspect, question, or challenge. Young African American males who are a scary alien presence for adults on the street, whose very presence signals not only that you are in a "bad" neighborhood, but who actually are among the elements that define a bad neighborhood, are also terrorized.

Donte, a fifth-grade "Troublemaker," powerfully evoked for me his consciousness of the vulnerability of childhood. He is one of the African American boys who was being redefined into the category of "unsalvageable" as his teacher assessed which of the children in her classroom would most benefit from her limited time and energy. Donte's teacher describes him this way:

> There were other children in the classroom who seemed like if they had a little bit of attention they would take off. So I thought, okay, maybe I should give them that little bit of attention. And in those cases it's really working. Because Donte is going to be more of a full-time job to really sit there, see that he follows through, be there the next day to see that he turns it in, and be there to reinforce the good or reinforce the negative. But it is a choice that he is making not to work.

She rationalizes her own dilemma under conditions of triage by placing the onus on Donte—he made the choice, not she—rather than on the conditions of work for both adult and child that have forced the choice on both of them.

During my conversations with Donte, his voice was soft, his answers hesitant. He seemed shy, afraid of talking to me at first. His answers were monosyllabic "uhnns" or "yeses." The only time he lost his shyness and the words came without hesitation was when he described his concern about "the lost children." His neighborhood, he tells me, is a bad neighborhood with a lot of bad people. Maybe one of those people has kidnapped one of the lost children and they are living close by. When I ask him who the "lost children" are, he reminds me of the faces of missing children that I have seen on the side of milk cartons, the posters at bus shelters, the warnings on the side of grocery bags.

Donte believes that if someone pays attention to the faces of the children who are lost they have a better chance of being found. He cuts the pictures of the children out, one by one, from the milk cartons and puts them up on his refrigerator with tape. He memorizes their faces just in case he might see them one day. He would recognize the child and rescue him or her. He tells me that sometimes he worries that he could be kidnapped just like one of those kids, but he notices that most of them are white. He spends time imagining ways he would escape if he got snatched away by some strangers.

In the "bad" neighborhood context, learning to take care of yourself, to stand up for your needs, to dodge, hide, and protect yourself is paramount. But in collecting the pictures of "lost" children, Donte is pinpointing something that is more than a local condition; the photographs of the missing children make a global connection between youth. A warning to be careful, for adults are dangerous. This is the vulnerability and fear of even the most protected children living in "good" neighborhoods. But for children like Donte, who regularly witness the inability of the adults in their lives to provide safe havens, to successfully champion their cause in school, their vulnerability to a horde of powerful and terrifying adults looms ominously.

The prevailing image in our society of childhood is that it is a separate and distinct phase from adulthood when one is shielded from adult worries about survival. Children, in this ideological construction, are afraid of monsters, of the dark, but these fears are chimeras born out of the active, creative imaginations of childhood. In this scenario the role of adults is to assure them that they will be protected, that their fears are groundless. There are no monsters, no dangers lurk in the dark. Donte's mother, Mariana, lamented the fact that her son and daughter were unable to be "children" in this way. Growing up in a "bad" neighborhood means that the idealized image of childhood as a carefree stage of life is an unattainable condition. She deplores the fears that her children feel when they have no money:

> And they look at me like—what you going to do, Mom? But when they worry, I worry. Because I can tell when they feel *fear*. I tell them it's okay, Momma's going to take care of it. I don't know how, but—I let them know not to worry. Let me carry the burden, don't do this to yourself, you're young.

Mariana, who has a part-time job and some public assistance while she studies for her GED, still fantasizes the possibility of playing out idealized roles in the family where adults free children from everyday worry. In her circumstances, however, she does not have the money to shield her three children from her always-present anxieties over basic necessities.

A childhood constituted within this context of vulnerability also anticipates adulthood in a different way. I heard over and over the fear of growing up expressed in the most tangible symbol of moving toward adulthood: going to junior high school. Adults as well as kids repeated the belief that things would be very different when kids entered junior high school; that kids were being given a lot of leeway in elementary school, which was like a dress rehearsal for the real performance that was for keeps. In junior high, rather than the special dispensation they presently got, the consequences of their work would be "real."

I heard this worry for the first time from Horace's mother. She was paying for her son to go to a private after-school tutoring program because she worried that he would be lost when he got to junior high, when tracking began in earnest.

I heard the warning issued by Mrs. Deane, Horace's teacher, one day when the three of us were having a conference about how I could best help Horace as a tutor. Mrs. Deane explained to me that any improvement was up to Horace. She asks him how he did on the math test that day. He says, "Not so good." She searches for a copy of his test on the table where all the children have turned in their work. He has not handed his in. Reluctantly he fishes it out of his desk where he has hidden it from the light, folded up in a small square.

Once unfolded, the test makes clear why he has hidden the work away. Horace has done very few problems. The teacher turns to me as if Horace is not sitting right next to both of us.

TEACHER: Next year Horace will be in seventh grade. I worry for him in seventh grade. If you didn't turn a test in like this in seventh grade, no one would be giving you a second chance. What would you have gotten in seventh grade, Horace?

HORACE (VERY SOFTLY):   An F.

Another one of the boys, Jabari, expresses a further aspect of this fear of leaving childhood behind that is symbolized by entering the seventh grade and being inducted into a less secure environment. He is afraid of the violence so often reported in the newspaper and on television:

There's a lot of people today that are so afraid of going to seventh grade. I'm afraid to go to seventh grade. They bring guns to school. They're a lot of kids that bring guns to school. There's this boy named Joey. He got five days suspension for bringing Mace to school because he was scared. He can't fight. . . . There's this boy named Freddie in my class was fixing to beat up Joey and Joey was going to spray him with some Mace. So he gave it to Michael to hold for him so he wouldn't get in trouble. But Michael got caught and Joey got caught. Joey got five days suspension and Michael is in Juvenile Hall for a week.

Fear of having to fight and of guns and the urge for self-protection gets three friends into serious trouble.

There is no protection, no haven for childhood in this context of social terror. The boys observe that their parents when engaged in confrontations with school adults and public officials are a weak force face-to-face with institutional power. Children know that they have to learn how to take care of themselves, how to defend themselves. Friends become an essential line of defense and solidarity in navigating the hostile expanses of the public space.

The Importance of Friends

It is significant that *homies* has come to be a word that indicates friends and peers in contemporary black male youth culture.[7] *Homies,* or *homeboys,* constructs friends as home, a place of mythic and real security. Friends become as family, those who come from the same place of origin that you do, referencing shared conditions and experiences. At the same time, home becomes mobile, not a fixed space but multiply resident in those peers with whom you can "feel at home," "be at home."

The expansion of kin networks to incorporate friends into family

---

7. A brief history of the usage of *homie* and *homeboy* is provided in Frederic G. Cassidy, ed., *Dictionary of American Regional English* (Cambridge: Harvard University Press, 1991), 1065. *Homie* was used in the 1940s to designate a rural southern immigrant to the urban North, carrying with it the connotation of being a rustic or countrified person. In the late 1970s, "'home boy' refers either to someone from Harlem, Watts, or some other equally black community or to one's best friend." Its use has become part of popular parlance in hip-hop culture.

is not new to African Americans. Since enslavement, African Americans out of necessity and by choice have constructed family broadly with more flexible, inclusive boundaries than the traditional nuclear or even extended family.[8] Networks of kin, some related by blood, or marriage, some "fictive," were established to mobilize and maximize the limited material resources and social power of the individual members.[9]

But the term *homies* suggests a new, creative adaptation by youth to the already permeable boundaries of family under contemporary conditions. It speaks to their intensely felt need for networks that provide security and solidarity in the public arena as family itself seems increasingly unable to provide this support. Homies take on characteristics of community as well as of kin. In addition to the natural social urge of humans to be with peers, homies provide a show of group solidarity and strength in a deleterious context.

This imperative for friends among youth occurs in the face of the public perception of young black men in a group as threatening by their very presence and the concern of school and family that friends lead boys astray. The boys' need is to be out in a group. The group is seen as a threat.

Friendship is a fruitful relationship to explore in terms of the place it occupies in the trying out of alternative identities as passages to power and understanding. Homie is itself a sexed identity, connoting male bonds. Like the usage of the term *nigger*, it also references class location: the home referred to, the place of mutual origins, and the source of identities is the ghetto, the "bad" neighborhood, the black community.

I asked the boys who their friends were and what they looked for in a friend. One of the most frequently cited qualities was that friends were like yourself. So for starters, they are all male and, with one exception, African American. Friends also have qualities that you pride in having yourself. Kenny, a fifth-grader, told me, "All my good friends play football, just as I do."

Friendship is one of the key sites for trying out selves. Identities are performed and tested, reputations are constituted in a continuing cycle

---

8. Sudarkasa, "African-American Families"; Andrew Billingsley, *Climbing Jacob's Ladder: The Enduring Legacy of African-American Families* (New York: Simon and Schuster, 1992).

9. Stack, *All Our Kin.*

of presentation and response, testing for evidence of caring and trust, how far you can depend on someone else. At this age, the friends that the boys talked about were all males. The group, because it inspires feelings of power and self, encourages testing and grading each other.

> Friends fight. They fight when they think they're better than somebody else, when they think they're better than each other. Every friend usually competes. Like girls compete by how many boys they get or how good they look or stuff like that. And boys say how tough they are and, you know, stuff like that.

Friendship establishes boundaries that mark the group as being essentially masculine, and within the group there are pressures to conform to expectations of appropriate masculine behavior. Kenny explained that he did not want a friend who was "too much of a crybaby," but he went on to describe the friend who was like that, but who is changing in response to teasing from his peers:

> Any teeny-weeny little thing would happen, he would cry, and then he would go and tell his mommy and get her on the case. Sometimes me and him would get in arguments and stuff and then we would start to tangle a little bit and then he would start to cry and stuff, and then he would call his mom and then put all the blame on me. But he's changed. Yeah, he's changed a little bit. He doesn't cry as much. He doesn't go home and tell mommy anymore. I think people tell him that he was a nerd too much.

Friendship is a relationship that rarely cuts across race difference outside of school. Though Lamar has white friends at school, the friendship is not carried over into the world outside. He described one friend in particular who he played football with at recess. Because Tom is white, Lamar makes allowances for him and teaches him how to "act black" so that he will fit in and not get into trouble out of ignorance. He teaches him the fine points of "capping":

> I never did think he knew how to cap right because we, like, cap on people. We like to joke around a lot. When we in our class or when we outside and then if he say something, it don't hurt me because it's funny, I just laugh. Nobody get offended by him. . . . When I'm

around Tom I tell him don't be scared to cap because nothing bad going happen to you. We just joking around. . . . I tell him, we don't say things about your mother. Like before we even start we say, don't talk about mothers or grandparents 'cause I don't like nobody talking about that. And we say, okay. And we don't talk about anybody's mother.

Lamar feels it necessary to explain to Tom not to be afraid to hang out with black kids and to participate in their making fun. But this friendship does not spill over into a neighborhood association. "Nah, we just do things during school. I don't have his phone number so I don't call him."

Friends lose the aspect of just being individuals as they begin to forge bonds. Friends provide the sociality, the group camaraderie that the boys yearn for. They are the people you do things with after school: play football or video games at the arcade, go to the movies, just play, do homework. Claude and his friends go to school together either on the bus or riding bikes. They also provide the impetus and moral support for cutting classes:

We talk about what we want to do. Everybody say what they want to do. Lots of things you can do instead of go to school. Like somebody say they want to go on the subway. If they say no, we get on the bus—if they don't want to get on the bus, we walk. One of my friends he goin'ta get a car, then we can drive.

Friendship is learning lessons about sociality and establishing and maintaining networks of care and affection, erecting boundaries that enclose the group in some modicum of the security of "we-ness." These networks become increasingly important to the boys as families and blood relatives and community organizations are less and less able to be present to provide the context of play, protection, and guidance.

Horace articulated a quality that most of the boys singled out as most important: loyalty. The notion of loyalty, of trust, and of reciprocity were themes in their description of friendship. "Like people who don't like to talk about you. They don't pretend they're your friend and the next minute you hear them talking about you like this and that."

Friends are there as a support system, they back you up, you can count on them to back you up. Donte has had a friend since second grade. He lives right next door. "I expect him to be loyal, I can trust him." Claude described how friends act in a fight: "Like if when I get into a fight and somebody is going to jump them—I goin'ta help them. And if I get into a fight, somebody's going to jump me, they goin'ta help me." Security is found in a network of caring relations. As Dion put it, "If you get hurt, they'll care about you. Sometimes they get in fights and I try to break them up. They break me up. They definitely break me up."

This group support allows you to be yourself in ways that you might not be able to do alone. Friends help Dion, a boy who really doesn't want to fight, in his performance of masculinity as hot-tempered and bold but ready to get into the fray if he were not "restrained" by his friends. "I tell my friends—'man just hold me back, I don't want to fight. Somebody else just hold me back.' Because my friends know." On his own, Dion may be forced to prove himself by actually fighting.

Out in Public

Friendship groups become the solidarity support for negotiating the public space. Both Troublemakers and Schoolboys know that as young black males, even though they are still physically quite small, they become objects of fear and suspicion in public. Their presence in the group on the street, in shopping malls, commuter trains and buses makes adults uneasy. This "threatening" presence of adolescent black males on the street has been documented in other ethnographic work.[10]

The boys confront widespread hostility to their presence in public spaces. Shops have signs making clear that they expect youth—especially black males—to be thieves by advertising a limit on the number of children who can be in the shop at a certain time. Many of the boys described the experience of being followed around in stores by clerks who presumed they were there to steal something. More hurtful is that even when they enter businesses as customers their presence is stigmatized to such an extent that shopkeepers have strategies to get them off their premises as quickly as possible. Merchants maintain that the very presence of youth will drive away more desirable customers. As Horace

10. See, for example, Elijah Anderson, *Streetwise* (Chicago: University of Chicago Press, 1990); Majors and Billson, *Cool Pose.*

put it: "They don't want us around, they just want to take our money."

A newspaper item describes this relationship. The article describes patrons at a local mall as "jumpy," "anxious," "uneasy," because of the presence of what the article describes as "primarily black teenagers" gathering at a bus stop near the entrance. The mall manager has gone to the city council to ask that the bus stop be moved away from the mall. The manager agrees that the kids "have done little to justify their fearsome reputation." But he points out, "You have to provide an atmosphere [for shoppers] that is not only safe, but is *perceived* as safe." The article quotes the executive director of a youth services bureau as saying that "when they [black youth] get on an elevator, they're used to people grabbing their purses or getting off at the next floor. They've developed coping mechanisms for being discriminated against because of their age and ethnicity."[11]

These coping mechanisms involve processes of identification, the formation of self at the conjuncture of how one is seen and how one sees oneself. On one level, the boys treat the surveillance and fear as a joke, as flattering, a sign of their power to attract attention, be noticed. They heighten their effect by brazenly asserting their presence. They fill up sidewalks, occupy street corners, and invade "private" adult spaces. They act a part whose bodily styles and cool demeanor they learn from older youth, from popular films, from TV, and from music videos. This act can be momentarily rewarding, an emotional as well as a physical swagger. They threaten, misbehave, reciprocate in kind, displaying a power that reproduces the very stereotype of dangerous youth.

At another level, identities are constituted in relationship to the perceptions and expectations of other people. To be seen as a "beast" with a "fearsome reputation" incites one not just to play the role but to see oneself that way. To be recognized this way is to be, as Fanon put it, "Sealed into that crushing objecthood."[12] The danger is that in the desire for recognition, the subject of one's identification becomes the fantasmatic threatening figure of black masculinity. The act becomes the reality.

Yet another form of response is active critique and a challenge to— rather than a confirmation of—prevailing stereotypes and existing relations of power. Horace described one such action to me one day when I suggested we get an ice cream as we were passing a store selling frozen

11. *Express,* December 10, 1993.
12. Fanon, *Black Skins, White Masks,* 109.

yogurt. He explained that yes he wanted a cone, but we would have to go somewhere else because he was boycotting that store. Some weeks before, he and two friends had bought cones and were told by the person serving them that if they were going to eat at one of the tables in the store they would have to pay extra. So the boys said they weren't going to eat there, paid for the cones, then instead of leaving sat down at a table because, according to Horace, they knew that they were being charged extra because they were kids and she wanted to get rid of them. When the counter person ordered them to get out of the store, they replied that she didn't have the right to charge them extra because no sign was posted to that effect. The police were called and, as Horace put it, "acted big but know we ain't doing nothing wrong," so they left them there. With a grin of satisfaction, Horace recalled for me that they dawdled for over an hour over their cone. The owner who remained in the store watching them asked, "Do you always take this long?" They said, "No, only when we're dogged."

Horace learns in public, with family and with friends, the necessity of talking back to authority, to challenge power. His experience is that rules are contingent, that the kind of power you can muster to throw in the face of these rules is crucial. The performance of a tough masculinity is a fundamental part of this expression since the boys have little other power to muster.

Horace's ability and readiness to fight both verbally and physically has garnered a position of authority and respect for him among his peers. He explains to me one day that people look up to him. Horace means other kids in the school when he refers to "people," since he gets scant respect from school adults.

> Some people come running to me instead of Mr. Russell [the vice principal]. Sometimes, they'll go tell me there's a fight going on, right. If I think this fight's right I'm not going to stop it 'cause if this boy do something to this other boy—then he got to face it. I let it alone.

The fact that other "people" come to Horace for help to sort out difficult situations on the playground is not a signal to the school that he has leadership qualities that can be fostered and channeled. It indicates just the opposite. Horace becomes an individual to be watched as he gets involved in an alternative authority structure. His charismatic presence is seen as disruptive to the school's hierarchical order. The top-down system of administering power demands that children "tell an adult" who is invested with authority to judge and punish. This direct link between children unsettles the hierarchical reporting system that the school demands.

Another response involves having fun and challenging rules of social exclusion. Friends carry out "invasions" together. Claude explains what this means. "You know, like on TV when the army take over a place." Invasions are entering and making yourself known in a place that is strictly off-limits to kids. "You know, where they don't want you there. They keep you out. Like with guards." Moving into these spaces, occupying them for as long as you can with reasonable requests, is a way of making yourself visible, being seen, being noticed.

Claude described the invasion of the large recreation facility operated by the university across town. One evening he and a group of friends found an unsecured entrance to the building and got in. They cautiously made their way through the building doing their best not to attract the attention of the "guards." This dodging and making oneself as invisible as possible lasted for awhile, but that was not their intention. Finally, they found their way to the spot where they would make themselves visible, known. This was a small weight room on the second floor full of weights and exercise machines. They walked into the room and as two boys stopped to talk to the attendant at the door, the other three headed over and began examining and picking up weights. They scampered around, using the space and staying as long as possible without getting the police called. The goal is to be legitimately in the space even if only for a short while.

This form can be understood as a transgressive and delinquent act of trespassing on private property. It confirms the perception of gangs of kids roaming unsupervised, having fun without any regard for rules and authority. Yet if the wider social context within which this transgression occurs is introduced, the boys' act can be seen as redressing a fundamental social lack. The recreational facility that the boys entered has exactly the sort of equipment and services that does not exist in their own neighborhood that they could benefit from: a swimming pool, racquetball courts, weight rooms, fruit juice for snacks, adult professional supervisors. The boys in their own way are contesting their right to have access to the recreation that in our society today is available to only those who can pay.

Social Isolation: The Dangers of Friends

Parents find out what the boys have been up to with their friends when their forays result in the police being called. Because the group inspires feelings of commonality and strength, the boys are more likely to get in trouble in concert with others than when they are alone in public or isolated at home. So friendship is a field in which the work of family to shape and prepare kids for the future is visible. Adults consider the power and authority of friends as enormous and seek to control their kids through monitoring and regulating whom the boys socialize with. This is true for the parents of the Schoolboys as well as the Trouble-makers. They believe that who the boys are hanging out with determines how they are seen, how they see themselves. Friends reinforce or undermine strategies for class mobility.

Families as well as school have developed strategies for sealing the boys off from bad influences. To different degrees, all the boys I interviewed were isolated, separated for their own protection from infection by the "criminal element" in the community. Isolation is a typical approach, especially in the case of single working mothers whose children have no adults in their life for the hours before and after school. The description of children considered "bad" influences are first and foremost descriptive of kids perceived as from the same or a lower social class. As with school, the use of black vernacular is one of the defining features of this undesirability. The imposition of quarantine attempted to cut the boys off from the "bad" influences of black popular culture.

Chris's mother described herself as extremely vigilant about the outside influences that came into his life. She makes sure that he is always busy with organized activities:

> What can I say, I run a tight ship. He doesn't know much of this rock 'n' roll, rap music, in our house. Maybe he picks up some of it at school but we don't have that music in our house. Sundays we're playing church music before we go to service.
>
> ANN: What about after school?
>
> CHRIS'S MOTHER (SNORTS): He doesn't have time for anything like that after school. He has one free afternoon—Monday. Otherwise, he's playing baseball, soccer, he goes to tutoring. When he comes home he has homework, then the chores he has to do.

Thursday evening he's singing in the church choir. He doesn't have any time left over for all this bebop stuff and just hanging out with friends.

Families describe the characteristics of those children from whom they want to quarantine their own. These sound like the typical parental concerns about the other kids who lead their own children astray. Marilyn, Colin's mother, points out that

> for some reason my children both love, I call it the wrong type of kid. But it's not really the wrong type of kid, 'cause if they're their age they're just kids. But kids that have more freedom than I let my kids have. And then because of that, then my kids also want to hang out and they want to come home at seven, eight, nine at night and that kind of stuff. And I don't like that because it's just too easy for something to happen. Even if they're on their normal path, regular time, they could get in trouble. I don't like that part.

However, the consequences that Marilyn fears are that Colin might get entangled in the juvenile justice system. Being with the wrong type of kid even if they have the same parental supervision can get you in trouble. Marilyn is a single parent who has a full-time job with the city. They live in a small, comfortable apartment. She worries about the fact that there is no adult around to supervise Colin, one of the Schoolboys, and his older brother when they come home after school on the days that they do not go to after-school tutoring that she must pay for. She is especially concerned about their association with neighborhood kids:

> My rules are when you come home you can't open the door for anyone, of course. Nobody can visit. With kids you always have to say the whole thing because they always get you on things if you're not clear. They're always like, "Well, you said that they couldn't come in but you didn't say that I couldn't talk to them through the door or I couldn't talk to them out the window." Because my older son gave it to me all the time, so I learned how to be more specific and clear, so: "No, you can't open the door. No, you can't talk through the door. No one can stand on the porch when I'm not

here. Make sure all the doors are locked. All of them. Not just one lock."

Arlene also isolates Terrence as much as possible from associating with the other kids in the neighborhood.

He is not a visitor! He pretty much stays in. There are kids right here in this neighborhood who he plays with but not with a great deal of frequency where he's in and out of other people's houses. I mean, I just don't allow it. He isn't allowed to visit anybody he wants whenever he wants.

She identified the wrong kind of friend when she described one of the neighborhood kids whom she discouraged Terrence from playing with:

There's this little kid. I think he's cute. The kid's cute. He reminds me of what I saw when I was growing up. He's that element of black urban life who's been influenced by uncles, father whatever, but he's picked up all the slang. You hear this boy talk—you have to take a second look y'know to make sure you're not looking at a twenty-two-year-old kid 'cause he's speaking like he's been out on the streets a long time because he's streetwise. But the kid is a poor student, academically he is not a good student. I don't know what goes on in his home life because I do not have that kind of contact with his mom. But he's a very cute kid and I like to hear him do his thing. But I don't want my son to hang out with him. He's a nice kid. He just hasn't had the proper training or something.

The "right" kind of kid is apparently one who speaks Standard English, is a good student, has a supportive involved family. However, this "right" kind of kid as a friend can also produce dilemmas, especially if the friend is white. Helene's discussion of Horace's friendships is an interesting example of the complex ways in which the positive effects of friends from an upper-middle-class family living in a "good" neighborhood can be offset by class and racial privilege. Just as the effect of the rules is different for kids coming from different class backgrounds, assumptions about the real world are different in a racialized context. One context allows for the encouragement of social and cultural experimentation and acquiring a diverse group of friends, the other demands "repressive" measures, a kind of house arrest.

Helene has worked hard to regulate and oversee the friendships of Horace. She has discouraged his friendship with Roy in spite of the fact that she recognizes that Roy's own need for a family setting draws him to her house each evening and keeps him there in the relatively secure and stable setting of her small apartment.

> He has six children in his home, his father is on disability because of an injury, and his mother is on AFDC. He is like magnetized toward me because he'll come home after school every day with Horace and they'll do their homework, and then about six-thirty or seven when I expect him to go on home, he'll wanta stay later and later and later. And then I realize he doesn't have the parents at home. I'll say, "Don't you need to call your parent, let your parent know where you are?" and he says, "Well, I don't need to be home until eight-thirty." I say, "In my home I have a rule that you can't come every day after school. Once in a while, if there is a certain project you may," I said, "but my son has to be in the home between five-thirty and six everyday. If he has a game that's an exception." And I said, "So you're just going to have to leave."

She is worried about his association with Horace. What kind of family does Roy come from if he can stay out after dark without calling home? Her judgment is that she's sorry for him but she doesn't want to encourage his friendship with Horace who she already has enough of a hard time making sure gets home.

Yet Helene has encouraged Horace's friendship with Aron, who is a white boy from a well-off, professional family in the city. Aron is bused to the school. He lives in an area of beautiful, well-maintained older homes. Though Aron also lives in a mother-headed household, his lifestyle is very different because his mother is a well-known lawyer and his father is a professor.

Aron's mother, Barbara, has an extremely busy and demanding schedule that involves her professional life as well as the many community and social action projects to which she is committed. Because she is a liberal, she is delighted that Aron, her only son, has made friends with Horace, who is black and comes from a poor family. She believes this is an important part of Aron's learning to get along with a wide variety of people. She also interprets his fondness for Horace as revealing admirable character traits in her son. He is not a snob. Barbara does not see his friendship with Horace as a negative influence. He has too many influences in his life. Her feeling is that the more diverse the experiences he is exposed to, the better for him. For Barbara, Aron's proper growth and development is nourished by his participation with a broad range of friends, and experimentation is basic to learning.

Barbara's encouragement of Aron's experimenting with lifestyles, with experiences, on the other hand, is one of the reasons that Horace thoroughly enjoys spending time with Aron. Staying overnight at Aron's house is always a treat. He has told me that Aron has his own large room with a big sign on the door, "Do not enter without permission." Furthermore, Barbara respects this sign and always knocks on the door that is kept closed. Moreover, she is usually not at home on weekend nights, or when she is she heads into her room with a book. The boys are on their own.

Through the careful surveillance that Helene never relaxes over Horace and what Barbara tells her proudly in conversations, she has deduced that the boys had smoked marijuana that Aron has gotten hold of; that they sneak out after Barbara is asleep. Aron is also invited to evening parties and Horace wants to go along. Barbara wants to encourage Aron to have girlfriends, the pressure here being for Aron to display the fact that he's becoming a man through his interest in girls. Helene on the other hand is anxious to put off any relationship that Horace might have with girls for as long as possible. Her two older sons left the house soon after they became sexually involved with girls. She associates sexuality with loss of interest in school. She is terrified of drugs. She explained to me:

> It's one thing for Barbara to say she wants Aron to have as many girlfriends as he wants and to have fun. He's white, so it's different for him. She's a lawyer. If Aron gets into trouble, then she'll work it out. If Horace gets into trouble, then it's the police and I know where it will end.

Barbara is eager for Aron to go out and explore the world and learn about himself and others in the process. Helene is anxiously trying to isolate and control Horace's experiences for as long as she can.

The constitution of social identity through popular, local knowledge is a complex and many-faceted process. The popular knowledge is developed through experience, observation, practice within a specific material and social milieu. This learning, because it is used and elaborated in concrete situations, seems more relevant to the Troublemakers than school knowledge. A significant component is the importance of challenging authority figures and handling situations without relying on an adult. Practices develop leadership skills as well as a certain respect for peer teamwork and group struggle. A milieu of terror and material deprivation structures the emotions and the experiences that Troublemakers bring to the school day. This knowledge and the structures in which it is embedded are the interpretive frames through which the kids make sense of encounters, practices, school rituals, curriculum, authority. It is the ground from which a reverse discourse about race and a sense of "groupness" springs.

The theories, the stance, the style of communication that the boys bring to school are strategies, tools, that are forged in the contexts of family and public. All the families prepare their sons to inhabit a world in which they are in danger—an "endangered species"—and inculcate them with forms of defense and survival. However, the quality and quantity of resources that families can count on influence the type of strategies and tools that are promoted. The Troublemakers are more likely to come from households with little to cushion their experiences. Based on their observations and personal experiences, they expect to be engaged in confrontations with authority, to be able to stand up for themselves, to talk back, to defend themselves physically.

Talking back, disruption, and disorder are too often the only style for getting heard. Horace, for example, learned from his mother, from his own experience, that to accept authority categorically, to give in without a struggle, is to lose fundamental necessities such as one's money, one's shelter, one's self-respect. He learns these lessons in the ordinary setting of a yogurt store or a rent board hearing. The Schoolboys, in contrast, are more likely to come from families endowed with the financial and cultural means to provide protection. They can attempt to isolate and guard the youth from getting entangled in the system. Young boys are instructed in strategies of avoidance and enactments of submission. An approximation to a normative ideal figure is cultivated through modes of response to authority, forms of address and bodily styles. At the same time the differentiation from a black vernacular style is enforced as a strategy for producing boys who are "individually" different.

Donte lives with his mother, Mariana, and his brother in an apartment over a local fast-food restaurant on a busy street not far from a major intersection. The stairway up to the apartment is dark as night and gets darker the closer I get to the top of the stairs. There are two apartments on either side of the narrow landing; the doorways are about six feet apart. I have no idea which is Donte's apartment because it is so dark that I cannot even see the number on the door, so I knock on one door and wait. No one comes to the door, so I knock on the other door and this time Mariana appears. She invites me to come inside.

All the lights are on in the small room that I enter, but the room is still dim and depressing. I sit next to her on a couch that has a huge gaping hole in the middle. We sit on either side of the hole. In one corner of the room is a kitchen table and two chairs. To the right of the couch is a large TV with some framed photographs on top. Framed colored photographs also line the wall behind our heads on the couch. Family members have been captured in moments of success, triumph, passages into new life stages. I found these family photographs clustered on walls, TV sets, mantelpieces in almost every house that I visited as family members sat in graduation regalia, confirmation dresses, family portraits. Happiness shows on every face, hair perfectly combed, expressions purposeful, clothes neat and conventional. No clowning, candid, or spontaneous snapshots here. These portraits mark off the passage of the time and landmarks attained.

There is a photograph of Donte with his mother, smiling and poised. Several of the photographs are of Donte's sister, who is now going to a university in the South on a scholarship. Donte's mother is extremely proud of her daughter's accomplishments. They have been like two sisters, she tells me. There are pictures of the girl in her high school graduation cap and gown. There is one of Mariana wearing graduation cap and gown, her two sons and daughter on either side of her. She has worked hard to get her GED.

She begins to tell her story. I turn the tape recorder on. The following is a partial transcription of my interview with Mariana, who almost immediately after we begin starts telling me about the time she was arrested by the Arcadia police for beating Donte, or Tay as she calls him, with his belt one evening after the boy had been gone from home for several hours on his bicycle without telling his sister, who was babysitting, where he was going. Mariana had found him in another part of town and right there on the street had pulled off his belt and begun whipping him. Someone had called the police.

(This was spoken to me. You must read what Mariana had to say aloud. You cannot understand it unless you hear the words.)

I. THIS IS MY CHILD

They pulled the guns out
what did I do?
This is my child!
Don't tell me how to raise my child.

I was so upset at that time. The lady cop
she was checking his elbows and his knees.
He was scratched up

but I didn't do that.

[Her voice is thick with tears.]

And they write down
he has a hairline scratch on his back
so many inches long.
I was like,
I didn't do that
his sister did that
they was fighting one day
and she did that.

They read me my rights,
put my hands behind my back,
put handcuffs on me.
and I was like—
Why?
What did I do?

I cried
I actually cried

they told my boyfriend to leave
he said,
she didn't do anything
that's her baby son.
who slipped off from home.
She was worried.

And they told him
they said
        leave.
So he drove off
And he was looking back at me
as he drove off.
I mean I was hysterical
I had never been in trouble with the law
never been to jail
Never even dream of going to jail.

How could they tell me how to raise him?
This is my child.
These people have so much power over us.
This is my child.

I'm a black woman,
single black woman.
He's my little black kid.
If they tell us how to raise our children
what else will they do?

        [Mariana laughs bitterly.]

II.   A NIGHT IN HELL

I didn't know what to do. They took me down, they booked me, took my fingerprints and pictures. It was humiliating, it was a dream. It was a night I spent in hell.

III.   I LOVE MY MOMMA

So then they come back to jail
tell me that my son
was in very good health
that his blood count
his iron count
his potassium
is all in place.
Is this what you lock me up for
to tell me that my son eats well?

And I ask them again,
        why did you bring me to jail,
        if this is what you was going to come back and tell me?
They said
        he is a very smart little boy
        and he is very strong.
He showed me this book
I still have that book in the room
showed me this book
that they gave him
at the hospital.
They had him to draw these faces
and said
how do you feel now?
are you happy or sad?
And he drew a happy face
with a happy smile on it.
And they said
draw your family,
and he drew his brother,
his sister,
his mommy,
his cat.
And everybody had happy faces on it.

And they asked him
how do you feel about your mommy
and he wrote
I love my momma.

And I said
    Tay
    did they tell you to do this?
And he say,
    yeah.
He say
    I drew it.

And they asked him
What's your favorite food
what do your mom cook at home?
And he drew a hamburger,
his french fries
and a whole lot of
ketchup.

They asked you a lot of questions about me
didn't they?

He say,
    yeah
    they ask me a lot of questions
    and I told them,
        mom is good.
            She gets mad,
                I get in trouble,
                she whip me.

For them to do this has caused a lot of mental anguish. I'm still angry about it. It forced me. I haven't whipped Tay since that day.

[Mariana gives a dry laugh, a bitter laugh.]

IV.   I DON'T BELIEVE IT

Since I went to jail
I punish him,
I take away his Nintendo game,
I take away the TV,
I do a lot of screaming again.

I had stopped that.

It's not the same.
It hasn't been the same
with me and my family
since that night I went to jail
because they had labeled me
as a child abuser.

they said
 right now,
  you are charged with abusing your son
  and mental cruelty to his mind,

you guys
could actually fucking
charge the momma,
charge the momma of this child
with all of this shit
because you say
this is what I did to my son
when I know better what happen to my son.

you got the right to tell me I did all of these things
when he told you
that he fell offa the bike
and he scarred up his arm but—

you got the right to tell me I did this,

and you got the right to fill out a report
saying Mariana Tompkins
as of this day
1987
that I did this to my child.

I said
 all of this
  in this police report
  is a lie
I said,
 I would never let you
 charge me with that.

And the police officer said
    you already charged with it.

Everything in there was a lie. I still have that report in there now
[pointing to the bedroom] right now. It tells all these lies. And I let
my friend read it, the one I was telling you about, and he said, I don't
believe it.

V.   TIME

They put me in jail. I was there twelve hours
(I cried)
twelve hours.
and the sound of those doors
slamming behind me
it was like I was never going to come out of there.

Never been in jail
never been in any trouble
That was my first time
I thought it was going to be my last time
seeing the outside world
My freedom had been ripped away from me
for twelve hours.
With four other women
with a bunk bed
(the mattress was maybe a inch
as thick as that table
with a wool blanket that wouldn't even cover my feet)
on a steel bunk
the windows all the way up to the ceiling
you couldn't
see outside
and it was hella cold in that cell.
I was on my period.
I kept calling them
ask them,
    could you please
    please bring my sanitary napkins

they did not respond
they treat you like a animal right
the next morning about ten o'clock
that's when she came with the sanitary napkin
she told us
she said
you're supposed to be seeing the judge for nine o'clock

I did not see the judge till five-thirty
that Monday evening.

(They were so many people in that jail)

they handcuffed us
had our feet in chains
chained to another person's ankle
they had our hands
both our hands
chained to the other person's
they had us in a row of two
and they took us down this little long alleyway
around the corner
up the steps
into the courthouse
and they put us in a little room
maybe eight by six
it was small
it had a toilet
it had a little bench on each side
it was eight women in this little room
we was almost stacked
on top of each other
waiting to see the judge.

they called six women
before they called me out
all of those got sentenced to time in prison
They was in there for possession of drugs
beating up on other women
and stuff

they was charged with different things.
But I was the only one that was a child abuser.

VI.   THE LABEL

A woman there in the cell with me had told me
she said
they treat women that abuse children
dirty, real real bad
if you go to prison
they're going to dog you
the other inmates are going to kill you
because they got you labeled as child abuser

I'm not a child abuser
this is my child
if I don't chastise my child
teach him what is right from wrong
who will?

the white man don't care
hey
they don't care if this little boy
woulda got killed that night
they don't care
all they was in for
was arrest another black citizen
get one off the streets
put her in jail
they didn't care.

VII.   THE STORY

And I went to court
the judge she looked at me
she said
what did you do Miss Tompkins?
I said
well you have the papers in front of you.
She said

I want to hear your words

I said,
thank you
I told her my side of the story
    my son slipped off from home
    I work during the day
    sometimes from twelve o'clock to eight o'clock at night
    I work
    my daughter
    she's sixteen
    she was there
    she was babysitting
    and he slipped off
    on his bike
    did not let her know where he was
    I came home
    he wasn't there
    I was furious
    I was scared out of my mind
    thinking that my son
    was dead somewhere

She said
    and you whipped him?

I said
    I whipped him
    with his belt

they brought out the belt. She felt it. She waved it around.

she said
    who arrested you?

I said
    the lady officer sitting right there

she said
    this is a case
    that shoulda never came in front of me

I asked her

what would you have done
if that would have been your
little
seven year old
son

and she said
I would have did the same

and she said
don't let this happen again
Above all you have to do probation.

VIII.   PUNISHMENT

They punished me

She told the lady officer
she said
don't bring another case in front of me like this again

and she shook her head
but she still punished me
she gave me two years probation
with the mental health counselor
and I had to go to court
twice a month.

[Mariana is sobbing deeply. We stop for a long time.]

I went to court
they'd call me
Mariana Tompkins
and I'd get up
they'd lead me up to the little altar
right there where she was sitting
she was like
uummmm, your progress report is very clean
and
I see that you been doing all of your mental health time
and

you haven't been getting in any trouble
and
you keeping yourself up
come back again
may twelfth
nine-thirty in the morning

they'd write me a little slip
give me my little court sheet
and I'd leave
I didn't have to say anything

I did this for two years
Two years.
I was working during that time!
I was going to school in the morning
had to be in school for eight o'clock till twelve
had to leave school
be at my job for one o'clock.
I was a bartender
I was under a lot of pressure
I was a busy little momma
when I leave work sometimes
I would just go to Safeway
come home
if the kids want something to eat
fine
if they didn't want to eat
that was okay too
most of the time
they would cook something
and they eat because they would be big enough to.

The way the system treats you
with your children
these days
is wrong
they have a law
where you can't whip your children
If you do

you gotta do it in the privacy
of your own home
you cannot yell at your child
in a public place
or you go to jail
if you talk to them too roughly
you're going to jail
for that
but where do the parents have rights?
as for the child talking doggish
to the momma and the daddy
and not doing
what they are told to do
not coming home on time
that's why these kids is running around here
they out there on the corner
selling drugs
they're killing each other
that's exactly why
because the law is not on the parents' side

my son when he came home
two days later he told me
you can't whup me
that's child abuse

I said
        oh really
I said
        we'll see about that!

he kept throwing these little hints at me
My son
        Donte
he kept saying
        if you hit me
        I'll call the police
for the longest period
he threatened me
with that

IX.   MY LIFE SHATTERED

I was going to adult school then

It had gotten so bad
mentally I couldn't take it

things started falling apart around me
I mean my life shattered
it went down

I was meaner than ever
I didn't want to be around friends
I didn't want to talk to anyone on the phone
I even took a deferral from school

I stayed right here in my apartment
mentally in the dark
I didn't want to be bothered

it was like people
other people
was ruling
they had control of me
they told me where I go
twice a week
from nine-thirty to ten-thirty in the morning
they had control of my life
and for some strange reason
I kept thinking
that the police would pull up
in front of my apartment building
just to sit there
and see
what was going on
in my house.

X.   A WHITE WOMAN

The bad part about it
a social worker
would come to my house

twice a month
to check on little Donte
would get to my house
at three fifteen every evening
and stay till about six o'clock
twice a month
watch the kids
their behavior
talk to my son
ask him questions

[Mariana begins imitating the social worker by talking in a sugary
sweet voice.]

How is Donte doing in school?
and how is he?

when he come through the door
would give him a big hug
and a book
would sit there with my son
would talk

sometime
she would go in the kitchen

if we was eating dinner
I would offer her dinner
or coffee

she was here so long.

my daughter had nothing to do with her
she would not give this lady the time of day
she said
    you're out now momma
    but they're sending this lady
    this white woman
    in our house
    twice a month
    to put us under surveillance

[Pauses for a long time thinking. Then a long sigh.]

She became to be nice to me
at first I didn't agree with it
I was under surveillance
It was like they got my life in their hands
I wasn't free for two years
you know I was skeptical of this lady
this white lady
coming into this black house
she's not going to be comfortable here
I had to watch what I said
around her
the way I carried myself
around her
she would never let you know
     when she was coming
all I knew
it was twice a month
it was like sneak up visits
and each and every time
she came into my house
it was clean
I had dinner on the stove
I was dressed
my hair was combed
the kids were intact
they were coming in from school

she was amazed
     because my daughter
would come right in from school
     go to the table with her books
she would put her headphones on
     do her homework

but she never spent time
with this white lady
she said
     she shouldn't be

in our house
she said
  Momma
  what did you do so bad?
  what you did with Tay
  any momma woulda did that.

[At this moment Mariana's other son, Ronnie, who is about sixteen comes into the room and tells her he is going out. After he leaves she begins to talk about him.]

XI. WHERE DID YOU GET THE MONEY FROM RONNIE?

Ronnie is very dysfunctional!
I'm so afraid he's going to get killed

That room he never cleans it up

he talks back once he drew back to hit me
that was a no no

he threatened me
  he said I'll put my posse on you

I said
  oh you will huh!
  what do you call a posse?
  I got female posses
  they not dope dealers and dope smokers either
  they are concerned mothers
  I'll put my posse on you too

He was
  yeah
  all females huh?

I said
  but they love their children
  just like I love my son

he drew back to hit me
and I downed him right here

and we fought

You see how big he is now? He was taller than me at thirteen.
and bigger! we go through world war twenty sometime. I mean
verbally
we be going at it.

Sunday
he came in
he threatened me
I found money in his shoe
a lot of money.

[She holds up her fingers to indicate a fat stack of bills.]

I said
     I'm not going to give you
     this money

     you going to give me my money.

     No I'm not going to give you this money
     Where did you get it from?

     you don't need to know
     where I got the money

     Where did you get the money from
     Ronnie?

     ain't your business
     that's my money
     you ain't taking nothing

he got real vicious
like a dog
he had changed
his whole attitude
just popped in front of my eyes
I said
     I will not have you talk to me that way.

[Her voice is thunderous now.]

I brought you in this world
you never bite the hand that feed you
that's one thing you don't do.
I'm the only person
will probably care about you
in this whole world
I had to stress the point that I love my sons
I love you Ronnie!

I'm not a very cuddly huggable person
but I wanted to hug him   but I knew he woulda pushed me
away
so I didn't even try
I sit on the table in his room
he was in the bed
all curled up between the blankets

why don't you leave me alone
put my money back in the shoe.

I'm not going to give you the money back
I'm not putting the money back in the shoe
Ronnie.

XII. YOUR SON IS A MONSTER: LOCK HIM UP

When Tay was in third grade, he had this teacher
wear African clothing
she's into the cultures
she used to come up to my house all the time

I used to say
    Omigod
    here she come again
    it was always something
    about Donte

she told me
    lock your son up
    put him in a boys home
    lock him up

he's a monster

He was getting in a lotta trouble
he was lying
saying he was going to school
but he wasn't going to school
I said what are you doing Tay?

he be's with this little boy
Richard
his grandmother have custody of Richard
I met Richard
the courts took Richard away
from the mommy and daddy
the grandmother's old
she can't tame him

Teacher say
Richard is selling drugs for his uncle.
They found cocaine rocks on him
Richard didn't come to school today
Donte didn't come
and one other little boy
She say,
    they bad!
    the uncle is paying these boys to sell drugs
    at the subway station.

When I found this out
I start calling the police
to find my son
because after six o'clock
it's dark

Where's my son?
he's not here, y'know
I thought
something had happened
but I refused to go looking for him
I had been arrested once
I told him

I'm not going back to jail for you

The police
they used to tickle me
they used to come in the door
laughing at me
they said Miz Tompkins
you get paranoid now
I said
you damn right I do
I said
I'm not going to let you guys
lock me back up
because
if I find that little boy
I might just do him like that
and it's going to be over between him and me
I won't be his momma no more
I'll let you guys run the show
since you got my life in your hands
you run this show
I will let the police go look for this little runaway boy
let them get paid
the taxpayers are paying them money
for them to do a job
let them work it out

Every ten days
I was calling the police
    I'm Mariana Tompkins
    I'm looking for my son

They say
    oh here she come again.

Somedays Tay would not go to school
he would leave here
with his bookbag
throw his bookbag in the bushes
he would be missing from school

they would call me
I was going to job training
they call me as soon as I walk in that door
at 9 o'clock
Mariana, Donte teacher call

I say
oh my god
what is it now!
And I'd just start boo hooing
I cried all the time
I was so little
I had lost so much weight
I said
what is it now?
Teacher say, call the school
and I say
I don't want to know
I don't want to know
I don't want to know

I wouldn't call
I would sit there
and get my books
my books
would be soaking wet
from tears
teacher she say
call the school
I don't want to know
I ask Petra
that's one of the teachers there
I say
Petra would you call the school for me?
She say
I think you should
that made me think
something bad
had happened to my child

XIII.   THE SEARCH

the school they said
Donte didn't show up
for school
this morning

I left school
come home
put my tennis shoes on
my sweat pants
my sweatshirt
get on my feet

I walked fifty to sixty blocks
looking for my son

I asked the little kids in school
which direction did my son go?

I would go down these streets
hoping to find him

No luck

I gave up
I came home
called the police

they found him
they found him on the playground

it was raining that day
He was soaking wet
said he had been on the playground
all day
I found that very hard to believe
I asked him
       why would you sit on the playground?
       Who were you selling drugs for?

Nobody!!!

He was so offensive
when I said
    who were you selling drugs for
Nobody!!!

    But Tay
    don't you know
    somebody will kill you

I said
    I went to jail once for you
I said
    I won't do it again
I said
    somebody's going to kill you

no it's not,
I know what I'm doing

I said
    No you don't know
    what you doing.
    you're only ten years old
    how can you possibly know what you're doing?

XIV.   I WENT TO JAIL FOR YOU, ONCE

Then one day
he didn't come home
after school
the police brought him home
I told them
I said
    get him out of my house I don't want him here anymore
I said
    Donte
    you have disobeyed me
    you went against my punishment
    you didn't come home
    you're trying me
    I won't have that

I said
     I went to jail for you
once
I kept stressing that jail point
because that had mentally scarred me up here
I told him
     I don't have to whup you to get you outa my house
     Police are going to take you out

the two police officers
they didn't want to take him

I cried a little bit
and I wiped the tears away
I wouldn't let him see me cry
no more.

I told him
     go get your change of clothes
     and he wrote his little sister a note
     left it under her pillow

I went in there that evening and found the note:

     Nita, I am at Granville Place
     momma put me out
     I love you Nita
     and I'm going to miss you Nita

I cried a little bit over that.
The police took him away from here
put him in the back of the police car
took him to Granville Place
for a whole evening.
Nita said
     momma
     did you have to send him to Granville's like that?
I said
     we gotta teach him a lesson
she said

I know
because he's going to be just like Ronnie.
I said
Ronnie is like a footprint
a big giant footprint
Tay little feet steps in these big giant footprints
he wants to follow his big brother
that's the key to it all!

at that time I didn't realize it.

XV.   BECAUSE I AM AN ABUSER

The next day I had a GED test
I didn't pass
That made me angry.
Then this lady from child welfare called
she told me to come pick my child up
or
"I'll put your child out on the sidewalk in front of your house."
I said
if you do I'll sue the Arcadia Police Department
I said
I'll sue the whole damn county
She said
well its your responsibility to come and pick him up
I told her
remember when you locked me up
you guys put me in jail
for whupping him
I said
if you can raise my son better than I can
dammit you do it!

I hung up in her face.

The chief of police called me and said
the child welfare agency had dropped my son off
at the police department

and said the mother said she wasn't going to be responsible
'Cause I knew then that they was responsible for him.
They sent two officers out here
with my son and his bag
They said
        Miss Tompkins what you want us to do with him.
I said
I don't care what you do with him
take him to a foster home
I don't care
I said
you locked me up!
Fine!
Find a home for him.
Them foster people
oughta take care of him better than his mother

I said
        I won't have my child telling me I can't whip him
        I'll go to jail
        I will whip his ass
        and I'll whip him right in front of you.
The officers they just looked at me

I said
        I'm mad, I'm mad, I'm really mad right now
        It's not a good place for him to be right now
        because I am an ABUSER
        remember.

XVI.   THIS SYSTEM STINKS

So they say
        I don't think you an abuser
        If that was my son I woulda did the same thing.
I said
no
they told me I couldn't whip him

But when they take him away
they say I gotta have him back in my house
What is this!
What's going on with this system!

I told the police
I'm sick of this system
This system stinks.

chapter six
getting in trouble

Well you asked me
what my definition
of a homie is
a friend till the end
which starts off
when you kids
little "gargechos" that are always into something
doing something bad
acting like they did nothing

Well here's a little story
bout a homie named Frankie
had another little homie
that was down for hankie pankie
sorta like Spankie and Alfalfa
little rascals
doing what they do and getting away without a hassle
like going to the schoolyard
forging late pass to their class
cutting in lunchlines
leaving other students last
or strolling to the movies
to see a Rated R
when moms dropped them off
thought ET would be the star
still there was an issue
that just could not be ignored
taking tapes and forty-fives
from the local record stores
being good kids
to them was nothing but baloney
cos this is what you do when its you and your homies.

—LIGHTER SHADE OF BROWN, "HOMIES"

Horace has that drained look in his eyes that is always there when he first emerges from the classroom at the end of the day. He moves as if there is just enough energy left to get him through the door and out of school. I see the identical look of stunned exhaustion on the faces of teachers, but I am not surprised to find the aftermath of a hard work-day on adult faces. It is unexpected, unsettling to recognize that same slow, defeated posture on a twelve-year-old boy.

Outside the classroom, Horace catches sight of the crowded hall-way and his expression lightens. The corridor is choked with kids and adults moving eagerly toward the exits. Everyone, young and old, is in a rush to be outside, to get on with life. He breaks into a run, tossing his backpack playfully in the direction of another kid. I see his body shake loose as he bolts into the toilets in chase of another boy. Now there are shrieks, yells, roars coming from that room into which I, a female adult, cannot follow.

I tutor Horace in an after-school program once a week. He is one of the boys identified as a "troublemaker" by the school. His name had appeared on every list of the school adults whom I had asked to iden-tify boys "getting in trouble" for me to interview. This is the boy described by one of the teachers as "on the fast track to the peniten-tiary," whose name had become the norm among school adults against which other children could be ranked in terms of their tractability.

Horace shakes off a day in which there have been few rewards, intense surveillance, and the virtual eradication of all that he brings to school. He has been marginalized to ranks and spaces that are full of disgrace. What lessons does Horace learn about self and school as he journeys from classroom to Punishing Room to Jailhouse? How does he fashion selfhood within this context? What is the connection between this self-fashioning and getting in trouble?

In this chapter, we examine masculinity as a nexus of identification and self-fashioning during the school day, a ritualized source of articu-lating power, of making a name for oneself, of getting respect under conditions where the officially sanctioned paths to success are recog-nized as blocked. Masculinity, however, exists in a dynamic and struc-turing relationship with other coordinates of social identity: race and class. Therefore, in the discussion that follows I will elaborate on how gender acts are always and already modulated through race at the con-stitutive embodied level as well as that of the imaginary and representa-tional.

Schoolwork

School is a workplace. This seems obvious for the adults who work there, from custodians and cafeteria workers to teachers and administrators. But school is also a workplace for children. Certainly what children do in school is characterized as "work" by both adults and kids.

I found many examples in the discipline records of the relationship between "work" and "trouble." Children are described as "working hard" or as "refusing to work."[1] One teacher had scribbled on the referral form, "He has refused to do any work today," as the reason a boy was sent to the Punishing Room. In another case, the charge was that "he won't do the work, won't read, won't write, sits and refuses." Some children are characterized as "good workers," while others defy the conditions of work, go on strike openly or use slowdown tactics through procrastination and escape avoidance. The work of school is compulsory labor: children must, by law, attend school. They have no control over the materials they work with, what they produce, the nature of the rewards for their exertions and performance.

I was interested in how the boys that I interviewed felt about schoolwork so I asked them to describe the school day. Both Schoolboys and Troublemakers characterized it as boring, uneventful, dull, a stretch of time in which you did nothing interesting. The following comment was a fairly typical answer: "Nothing happens—you go to classes and do your work."

When I asked Eddie what was his least favorite part of the day, his answer was, "My teachers. Homework. And classwork, yeah, class. When you have to sit there and write and do nothing but listen." Even Ricky, described as an "ideal" student by the teacher, was lukewarm, indifferent about schoolwork. Math was "the worst" and P.E. was his favorite part of the day because it was "fun." Claude, one of a group of boys most marginalized by the school who was described by the principal as a "thug," seemed most alienated from schoolwork. He flatly told

---

1. I was surprised to find that getting in trouble happened more frequently during work time or transitions back to work than during play and recreation periods of the school day. Interestingly enough, studies of juveniles have found that delinquent acts decline significantly when public schools are not in session, and that youth who leave school during the academic year are involved in fewer crimes than those who are currently enrolled. For example, see James W. Messerschmidt, *Masculinities and Crime: Critique and Reconceptualization of Theory* (Lanham, Md.: Rowman and Littlefield, 1993), 87.

me, "School, I don't like school. Really, it's boring. No way. There isn't a single thing about school for me."

In their descriptions, both Troublemakers and Schoolboys presented a timetable of their movement from one set of tasks to another, from one space in school to another. They recalled the mechanics of work: getting books out, writing, listening to the teacher, reading aloud. But they generally found it difficult to come up with the substance of what they actually learned in classrooms, what or who they read or wrote about, for example. This is not surprising since the routine is indeed what the school emphasizes through sheer repetition as the most noteworthy aspect of the school day. Being in the right place at the right time and the physical acts of going about the tasks called for when you are there is the fundamental knowledge about work impressed on the children. The kids recognize this. They have registered that the timetable, the form, not the content of the curriculum, is the significant element in their education. In a context of extremely scarce rewards, this physical conformity is positively acknowledged by teachers with verbal recognition such as, "Everyone have their books out and open at page 6? Good." There is also a personal, sensuous reason for recollecting the daily agenda: the compartmentalization of activity into time and space and the motion from one to another gives a rhythm to the day, the change that breaks up the monotony of the routine.

My own experience as a participant observer in a classroom corroborated the description of the school day as one that was tedious, interminable, and deadening of any imaginative impulse or insight. My field notes, soon after I began observing in the sixth-grade room, record one afternoon when I found myself caught up in a collective effort to break out of the passive mold and do something active to keep myself awake. This spontaneous activity made clear to me that even the children who were most successful in the class had their own methods for helping to pass the time.

> I catch the eye of Chris who I notice has made a clever paper gizmo that opens and closes in his hand displaying a little message which he flashes at me. I smile in acknowledgement of receipt. Chris is a white boy who is bussed in to the school. He is a good student, quiet and cooperative who tackles his work with the dedicated fortitude of someone who wants to get it done as quickly as possible

so that he can get on with something else. This something else is often a book from the class library which he escapes into. The gizmo, which I learn later is called a "cootie catcher," looks simple enough so I begin to construct one with paper from my notebook as silently and surreptitiously as possible. I have to tear out a sheet of paper without making a loud crackling noise and call attention to myself. Carefully. Chris watches me encouragingly shaking his head as I make a wrong move and guiding me by partly undoing his own creation. As I signal back to him, my work completed, I notice that a few other kids in the room also have cootie catchers. They know what I am doing. We signal back and forth. It is a moment of thrilling complicity. I remember that we are supposed to be sitting listening to other children reading aloud about the Egyptians from the social science textbook. I have not registered a word in the last few minutes. Others are passing time differently. One girl is braiding the hair of one of the girls at her table; some children are openly daydreaming. Surely the teacher is aware of all these activities which she would certainly have stopped instantly earlier in the day. It seems that everybody knows that we are just passing time, waiting for the bell to ring. We are all tired, drowsy, bored, and ready to go home.

When the teacher signals that it is okay to pass time this way, that she will turn a blind eye, even conforming kids fool around. This play at work does not disrupt the routine; rather, it helps to make it more tolerable.

Note passing also helps to make the minutes go faster. It is about the need to communicate with others across a space in which communication is technically only allowed through the adult. Some children pass notes surreptitiously, discreetly. Occasionally a child decides to make the note passing public in order to make things happen by engineering the discovery of a note that will cause adult consternation and "finger" another kid. So Lonnie was banished to the Jailhouse for an entire day when he passed a scrap of paper with a penis drawn on it to a friend who looked at the contents and reacted in a way to draw attention to the communication.

Nothing, however, is as finely practiced an art as getting out of work at the same time as appearing to do it. This usually involves slowing down the pace of task completion to one that would make a snail seem a speedster. Horace's teacher would often complain about his inability to follow instructions promptly; pointing out to me how long it took him to move from one task to another. Long after he has been told to get his book out and turn to a particular page, his head is still in his desk as he ostensibly searches for the book. Once it is out, he stares fixedly into space while the teacher asks him to turn to the page: "Everybody else already has it open in front of them. We're waiting."

One of the few periods of the day that the boys say they look forward to is recess. In contrast to class time, this is the interlude when kids have some control, though still limited and highly surveilled, over what they do and with whom. This is a moment when you can play games, socialize with friends, run around, shout, laugh, eat.[2]

Frequently, I noticed that Troublemakers engineered subversion as a way of exercising some command over the pattern of work and play during the day. Sometimes this involved prolonging recess through a trip to the Punishing Room. I saw this played out several times in a scenario where Boy Number One would be sent by the teacher to the Punishing Room, where he would tell a story that implicated Boy Number Two, and possibly Three and Four, in an action that happened during recess. So Boy Number One would be sent back to the classroom to bring the others in to tell their story. Trips up and down the hallway, peeking into rooms, making faces in passing, extended the length of time away from class. This was a con-game that worked from time to time.

A variation on this theme was using misbehavior to prolong an outing. So Horace and Lamond, who had behaved like model students on the field trip, on the way home ran ahead of the group in the last few blocks, scaled the school fence rather than going through the gate, and got sent to the office.

While schoolwork was described as boring and hard, getting in trouble was described as "easy" by the Troublemakers. Claude explained to me that it was "easier than staying good" for him. Within the field of power of school, trouble is the condition of being a child, while conformity takes work: "Somebody gets spotted and they just pick out that

2. McNeil reports that teachers who also labor under alienating work conditions and whose work has become increasingly routinized with the adoption of scientific management techniques of controlling children also look forward to recess. This is time when teachers have some modicum of free activity themselves. Linda M. McNeil, *Contradictions of Control: School Structure and School Knowledge* (New York: Routledge and Kegan Paul, 1986).

person," was how he described it to me with a shrug. Like the other Troublemakers, he grounded his conclusion in his observation that troublesome behavior was not all that unusual an occurrence for a kid in school. Another of the boys told me,

> Everybody gets in trouble sometimes. Laura [a white girl in the class who is a very good worker], even she gets in trouble sometimes. Everybody does. [Pauses to reflect for a moment.] Maybe Marsha and Simone [two other white girls], they barely get in trouble.

Under tedious, routinized conditions of work and learning, activities that risk trouble, even trouble itself, function to spice up the workday and make time go faster through creative attempts to make things happen and disrupt the routine. This is one of the more obvious functions of trouble for, as I have pointed out, even the most conforming kids.

However, for African American children the conditions of schooling are not simply tedious; they are also replete with symbolical forms of violence. Troublemakers are conscious of the fact that school adults have labeled them as problems, social and educational misfits; that what they bring from home and neighborhood—family structure and history, forms of verbal and nonverbal expression, neighborhood lore and experiences—has little or even deficit value. The convergence of the routine with the harsh, exclusionary ambience of school calls forth a more intensive mode of identity work. My concern now is to home in on this work through an examination of the relationship between trouble and masculinity; of the specific circular relationship between risky, rule-breaking behavior, getting in trouble, and the experience of being and becoming male. Making a name for yourself through identity work and self-performance, even if the consequence is punishment, becomes a highly charged necessity given the conditions of school for the Troublemakers.

Making a Name for Yourself: Transgressive Acts and Gender Performance

Though girls as well as boys infringe the rules, the overwhelming majority of violations in every single category, from misbehavior to obscenity, are by males. In a disturbing tautology, transgressive behavior is that which constitutes masculinity. Consequently, African American males in the very act of identification, of signifying masculinity, are likely to be breaking rules.

I use the concept of sex/gender not to denote the existence of a stable, unitary category that reflects the presence of fundamental, natural biological difference, but as a socially constructed category whose form and meaning varies culturally and historically. We come to know ourselves and to recognize others as of a different sex through an overdetermined complex process inherent in every sphere of social life at the ideological and discursive level, through social structures and institutional arrangements, as well as through the micropolitics of social interactions.[3] We take sex difference for granted, as a natural form of difference as we look for it, recognize it, celebrate it; this very repetition of the "fact" of difference produces and confirms its existence. Indeed, assuming sex/gender difference and identifying as one or the other gender is a precursor of being culturally recognizable as "human."

While all these modes of constituting gender as difference were palpable in the kids' world, in the following analysis of sex/gender as a heightened and highly charged resource for self-fashioning and making a name for oneself, the phenomenological approach developed by ethnomethodologists and by poststructuralist feminist Judith Butler is the most productive one to build on. Here gender is conceptualized as something we do in a performance that is both individually and socially meaningful. We signal our gender identification through an ongoing performance of normative acts that are ritually specific, drawing on

---

3. Here are a very few examples of the enormous body of work concerned with the production of gender differences in the last two decades. At the ideological and discursive level see Mullings, "Images, Ideology"; Teresa de Lauretis, *Technologies of Gender: Essays on Theory, Film, and Fiction* (Bloomington: Indiana University Press, 1987); and Michele Barrett, *Women's Oppression Today: Problems in Marxist Feminist Analysis* (London: New Left Books, 1980). For processes of social structure and institutional arrangements see R. W. Connell et al., *Making the Difference: Schools, Families, and Social Division* (London: George Allen and Unwin, 1982); Mariarosa Dalla Costa, "Women and the Subversion of the Community," in *The Power of Women and the Subversion of Community,* ed. Mariarosa Dalla Costa and Selma James (Bristol, England: Falling Wall Press, 1973); Catharine A. MacKinnon, *Feminism Unmodified: Discourses on Life and Law* (Cambridge: Harvard University Press, 1987). For micropolitics see Arlie Russell Hochschild, *The Second Shift: Working Parents and the Revolution at Home* (New York: Viking, 1989); Donna Eder, Catherine Colleen Evans, and Stephen Parker, *School Talk: Gender and Adolescent Culture* (New Brunswick, N.J.: Rutgers University Press, 1995); and Candace West and Don H. Zimmerman, "Doing Gender," *Gender and Society* 1, no. 2 (1987).

well-worked-over, sociohistorical scripts and easily recognizable scenarios.[4]

Butler's emphasis on the coerced and coercive nature of these performances is especially useful. Her work points out that the enactment
of sex difference is neither voluntary nor arbitrary in form but is a compulsory requirement of social life. Gender acts follow sociohistorical
scripts that are policed through the exercise of repression and taboo.
The consequences of an inadequate or bad performance are significant,
ranging from ostracism and stigmatization to imprisonment and death.
What I want to emphasize in the discussion that follows are the rewards
that attach to this playing out of roles; for males, the enactment of masculinity is also a thoroughly embodied display of physical and social
power.

Identification as masculine through gender acts, within this framework, is not simply a matter of imitation or modeling, but is better
understood as a highly strategic attachment to a social category that has
political effects. This attachment involves narratives of the self and of
Other, constructed within and through fantasy and imagination, as
well as through repetitious, referential acts. The performance signals
the individual as socially connected, embedded in a collective membership that always references relations of power.

African American boys at Rosa Parks School use three key constitutive strategies of masculinity in the embrace of the masculine "we" as
a mode of self-expression. These strategies speak to and about power.
The first is that of heterosexual power, always marked as male. Alain's
graffiti become the centerpiece of this discussion. The second involves
classroom performances that engage and disrupt the normal direction
of the flow of power. The third strategy involves practices of "fighting."
All three invoke a "process of iterability, a regularized and constrained
repetition of norms," in doing gender; constitute masculinity as a natural, essential corporeal style; and involve imaginary, fantasmatic
identifications.[5]

These three strategies often lead to trouble, but by engaging
them a boy can also make a name for himself as a real boy, the Good
Bad Boy of a national fantasy. All three illustrate and underline the

4. Judith Butler. "Performative Acts and Gender Constitution: An Essay in Phenomenology and Feminist Theory," *Theatre Journal* 40, no. 4 (1988).
5. Judith Butler, *Bodies That Matter: On the Discursive Limits of "Sex"* (New York:
Routledge, 1993), 95.

way that normative male practices take on a different, more sinister inflection when carried out by African American boys. Race makes a significant difference both in the form of the performance as well as its meaning for the audience of adult authority figures and children for whom it is played.

Heterosexual Power: Alain's Graffiti

One group of transgressions specifically involves behavior that expresses sexual curiosity and attraction. These offenses are designated as "personal violations" and given more serious punishment. Inscribed in these interactions are social meanings about relations of power between the sexes as well as assumptions about male and female difference at the level of the physical and biological as well as the representational. It is assumed that females are sexually passive, unlikely to be initiators of sexual passes, while males are naturally active sexual actors with strong sexual drives. Another assumption is that the feminine is a contaminated, stigmatizing category in the sex/gender hierarchy.

Typically, personal violations involved physical touching of a heterosexual nature where males were the "perpetrators" and females the "victims." A few examples from the school files remind us of some of the "normal" displays of sexual interest at this age.

- Boy was cited with "chasing a girl down the hall" [punishment: two days in the Jailhouse].
- Boy pulled a female classmate's pants down during recess [punishment: one and a half days in the Jailhouse].
- Boy got in trouble for, "touching girl on private parts. She did not like" [punishment: a day in the Jailhouse].
- Boy was cited for "forcing girl's hand between his legs" [punishment: two and a half days in the Jailhouse].

In one highly revealing case, a male was cast as the "victim" when he was verbally assaulted by another boy who called him a girl. The teacher described the "insult" and her response to it on the referral form in these words:

During the lesson, Jonas called Ahmed a girl and said he wasn't staying after school for detention because "S" [another boy] had done the same thing. Since that didn't make it ok for anyone to speak this way I am requesting an hour of detention for Jonas. I have no knowledge of "S" saying so in my presence.

This form of insult is not unusual. When boys want to show supreme contempt for another boy they call him a girl or liken his behavior to female behavior. What is more troubling is that adults capitulate in this stigmatization. The female teacher takes for granted that a comment in which a boy is called a girl is a symbolic attack, sufficiently derogatory to merit punishment. All the participants in the classroom exchange witness the uncritical acknowledgment of adult authority to a gender order of female debasement.

Of course, this is not news to them. Boys and girls understand the meaning of being male and being female in the field of power; the binary opposition of male/female is always one that expresses a norm, maleness, and its constitutive outside, femaleness. In a conversation with a group of boys, one of them asserted and then was supported by others that "a boy can be a girl, but a girl can never be a boy." Boys can be teased, controlled, punished by being accused of being "a girl." A boy faces the degradation of "being sissified," being unmanned, transferred to the degraded category of female. Girls can be teased about being a tomboy. But this is not the same. To take on qualities of being male is the access to and performance of power. So females must now fashion themselves in terms of male qualities to partake of that power. Enactments of masculinity signal value, superiority, power.

Let us return to Alain, the eleven-year-old boy who while cooling off and writing lines as a punishment in the antechamber of the Punishing Room, writes on the table in front of him: "Write 20 times. I will stop fucking 10 cent teachers and this five cent class. Fuck you. Ho! Ho! Yes Baby." Alain's message can be read in a number of ways. The most obvious way is the one of the school. A child has broken several rules in one fell swoop and must be punished: he has written on school property (punishable); he has used an obscenity (punishable); he has committed an especially defiant and disrespectful act because he is already in the Punishing Room and therefore knows his message is likely to be read (punishable). Alain is sent home both as a signal to him and to the other witnesses as well as to the students and adults who will hear it through the school grapevine that he cannot get away with such flagrant misbehavior.

An alternative reading looks at the content of the message itself and the form that Alain's anger takes at being sent to the Punishing Room. Alain's anger is being vented against his teacher and the school itself, expressing his rejection, his disidentification with school that he devalues as monetarily virtually worthless. His message expresses his anger through an assertion of sexual power—to fuck or not to fuck—one sure way that a male can conjure up the fantasmatic as well as the physical specter of domination over a female of any age. His assertion of this power mocks the authority of the teacher to give him orders to write lines. His use of "baby" reverses the relations of power, teacher to pupil, adult to child; Alain allies himself through and with power as the school/teacher becomes "female," positioned as a sex object, as powerless, passive, infantilized. He positions himself as powerful through identification with and as the embodiment of male power as he disidentifies with school. At this moment, Alain is not just a child, a young boy, but taking the position of "male" as a strategic resource for enacting power, for being powerful. At the same time, this positioning draws the admiring, titillated attention of his peers.

These moments of sex trouble exemplify some of the aspects of the performance of sex/gender difference that is naturalized through what is deemed punishable as well as punishment practices. Judging from the discipline records, girls do not commit sexual violations. It is as if by their very nature they are incapable. To be female is to be powerless, victimizable, chased down the hallway, an object to be acted upon with force, whose hand can be seized and placed between male legs. To be female is also to be sexually passive, coy, the "chaste" rather than the chaser, in relation to male sexual aggressiveness. In reality, I observed girls who chased boys and who interacted with them physically. Girls, in fact, did "pants" boys, but these acts went unreported by the boys. For them to report and therefore risk appearing to be victimized by a girl publicly would be a humiliating outcome that would only undermine their masculinity. In the production of natural difference, boys' performances work as they confirm that they are active pursuers, highly sexualized actors who must be punished to learn to keep their burgeoning sexuality under control. There is a reward for the behavior even if it may be punished as a violation. In the case of African American boys, sex trouble is treated as egregious conduct.

African American males have historically been constructed as hypersexualized within the national imagination. Compounding this is the process of the adultification of their behavior. Intimations of sexuality on their part, especially when directed toward girls who are bused in—white girls from middle-class families—are dealt with as grave transgressions with serious consequences.

Power Reversals: Class Acts

Performance is a routine part of classroom work. Students are called upon to perform in classes by teachers to show off their prowess or demonstrate their ineptitude or lack of preparation. They are required to read passages aloud, for example, before a highly critical audience of their peers. This display is teacher initiated and reflects the official curricula; they are command performances with well-scripted roles, predictable in the outcome of who has and gets respect, who is in control, who succeeds, who fails.

Another kind of performance is the spontaneous outbreaks initiated by the pupils generally defined under the category of "disruption" by the school. These encompass a variety of actions that punctuate and disrupt the order of the day. During the school year about two-thirds of these violations were initiated by boys and a third by girls. Here are some examples from the discipline files of girls being "disruptive":

- Disruptive in class—laughing, provoking others to join her. Purposely writing wrong answers, being very sassy, demanding everyone's attention.
- Constantly talking; interrupting; crumpling paper after paper; loud.

Some examples of boys' disruption:

- Constant noise, indian whoops, face hiccups, rapping.
- Chanting during quiet time—didn't clean up during art [punishment: detention].
- Joking, shouting out, uncooperative, disruptive during lesson.

From the perspective of kids, what the school characterizes as "disruption" on the referral slips is often a form of performance of the self: comedy, drama, melodrama become moments for self-expression and display. Disruption adds some lively spice to the school day; it injects laughter, drama, excitement, a delicious unpredictability to the classroom routine through spontaneous, improvisational outbursts that add flavor to the bland events.

In spite of its improvisational appearance, most performance is highly ritualized with its own script, timing, and roles. Teachers as well as students engage in the ritual and play their parts. Some kids are regular star performers. Other kids are audience. However, when a substitute is in charge of the class and the risk of being marked as a troublemaker is minimal, even the most timid kids "act up." These rituals circulate important extracurricular knowledge about relations of power.

These dramatic moments are sites for the presentation of a potent masculine presence in the classroom. The Good Bad Boy of our expectations engages power, takes risks, makes the class laugh, and the teacher smile. Performances mark boundaries of "essential difference"—risk taking, brinkmanship. The open and public defiance of the teacher in order to get a laugh, make things happen, take center stage, be admired, is a resource for doing masculinity.

These acts are especially meaningful for those children who have already been marginalized as outside of the community of "good," hardworking students. For the boys already labeled as troublemakers, taking control of the spotlight and turning it on oneself so that one can shine, highlights, for a change, one's strengths and talents. Already caught in the limelight, these kids put on a stirring performance.

Reggie, one of the Troublemakers, prides himself on being witty and sharp, a talented performer. He aspires to two careers: one is becoming a Supreme Court justice, the other an actor. He had recently played the role of Caliban in the school production of *The Tempest* that he described excitedly to me:

> I always try to get the main character in the story 'cause I might turn out to be an actor because I'm really good at acting and I've already did some acting. Shakespeare! See I got a good part. I was Caliban. I had to wear the black suit. Black pants and top. Caliban was a beast! In the little picture that we saw, he looks like the . . . the. . . [searching for image] the beast of Notre Dame. The one that rings the bells like *fing! fing! fing!*

Here is one official school activity where Reggie gets to show off something that he is "good at." He is also proud to point out that this is not just a role in any play, but one in a play by Shakespeare. Here his own reward, which is not just doing something that he is good at, but doing it publicly so that he can receive the attention and respect of adults and peers, coincides with the school's educational agenda of creating an interest in Shakespeare among children.

Reggie also plays for an audience in the classroom, where he gets in trouble for disruption. He describes one of the moments for me embellished with a comic imitation of the teacher's female voice and his own swaggering demeanor as he tells the story:

> The teacher says [he mimics a high-pitched fussy voice], "You not the teacher of this class." And then I say [adopts a sprightly cheeky tone], "Oh, yes I am." Then she say, "No, you're not, and if you got a problem, you can just leave." I say, "Okay" and leave.

This performance, like others I witnessed, are strategies for positioning oneself in the center of the room in a face-off with the teacher, the most powerful person up to that moment. Fundamental to the performance is engagement with power; authority is teased, challenged, even occasionally toppled from its secure heights for brief moments. Children-generated theatrics allow the teasing challenge of adult power that can expose its chinks and weaknesses. The staged moments heighten tension, test limits, vent emotions, perform acts of courage. For Reggie to have capitulated to the teacher's ultimatum would have been to lose what he perceives as the edge in the struggle. In addition, he has won his escape from the classroom.

Horace describes his challenge to the teacher's authority in a summer school math class:

> Just before the end of the period he wrote some of our names on the board and said, "Whoever taught these students when they were young must have been dumb." So I said, "Oh, I didn't remember that was you teaching me in the first grade." Everyone in the room cracked up. I was laughing so hard, I was on the floor. He sent me to the office.

Horace is engaging the teacher in a verbal exchange with a comeback to an insult rather than just passively taking it. In this riposte, Horace not only makes his peers laugh at the teacher, but he also defuses the insult through a quick reversal. The audience in the room, raised on TV sitcom repartee and canned laughter, is hard to impress, so the wisecrack, the rejoinder, must be swift and sharp. Not everyone can get a laugh at the teacher's expense, and to be topped by the teacher would be humiliating; success brings acknowledgment, confirmation, applause from one's peers. For Horace, this is a success story, a moment of gratification in a day that brings few his way.

The tone of the engagement with power and the identity of the actor is highly consequential in terms of whether a performance is overlooked by the teacher or becomes the object of punishment. In a study of a Texas high school, Foley documents similar speech performances.[6] He describes how both teacher and students collaborate to devise classroom rituals and "games" to help pass the time given the context of routinized, alienating classroom work. He observes that upper-middle-class male Anglo students derail boring lessons by manipulating teachers through subtle "making out" games without getting in trouble. In contrast, low-income male Hispanic students, who were more likely to challenge teachers openly in these games, were punished. Foley concluded that one of the important lessons learned by all participants in these ritual games was that the subtle manipulation of authority was a much more effective way of getting your way than openly confronting power.

Style becomes a decisive factor in who gets in trouble. I am reminded of comments made by one of the student specialists at Rosa Parks who explained the high rate of black kids getting in trouble by remarking on their different style of rule breaking: "The white kids are sneaky, black kids are more open."

So why are the black kids "more open" in their confrontations with power? Why not be really "smart" and adopt a style of masculinity that allows them to engage in these rituals that spice the school day and help pass time, but carry less risk of trouble because it is within certain mutually understood limits?

These rituals are not merely a way to pass time, but are also a site for constituting a gendered racial subjectivity. For African American boys, the performance of masculinity invokes cultural conventions of speech performance that draws on a black repertoire. Verbal performance is an important medium for black males to establish a reputa-

---

6. Douglas E. Foley, *Learning Capitalist Culture: Deep in the Heart of Tejas* (Philadelphia: University of Pennsylvania, 1990).

tion, make a name for yourself, and achieve status.[7] Smitherman points out that black talk in general is

> a functional dynamic that is simultaneously a mechanism for learning about life and the world and a vehicle for achieving group recognition. Even in what appears to be only casual conversation, whoever speaks is highly conscious of the fact that his personality is on exhibit and his status at stake.[8]

Oral performance has a special significance in black culture for the expression of masculinity. Harper points out that verbal performance functions as an identifying marker for masculinity only when it is delivered in the vernacular and that "a too-evident facility in white idiom can quickly identify one as a white-identified uncle Tom who must also be therefore weak, effeminate, and probably a fag."[9] Though the speech performances that I witnessed were not always delivered in the strict vernacular, the nonverbal, bodily component accompanying it was always delivered in a manner that was the flashy, boldly flamboyant popular style essential to a good performance. The body language and spoken idiom openly engage power in a provocative competitive way. To be indirect, "sly," would not be performing masculinity.

This nonstandard mode of self-representation epitomizes the very form the school seeks to exclude and eradicate. It is a masculine enactment of defiance played in a black key that is bound for punishment. Moreover, the process of adultification translates the encounter from a simple verbal clash with an impertinent child into one interpreted as an intimidating threat.

Though few white girls in the school were referred to the office for disruptive behavior, a significant number of African American girls staged performances, talked back to teachers, challenged authority, and were punished. But there was a difference with the cultural framing of their enactments and those of the boys. The bottom line of Horace's

---

7. Geneva Smitherman, *Talkin and Testifyin: Language of Black America* (Detroit: Wayne State University Press, 1977); Lawrence Levine, *Black Culture and Black Consciousness: Afro-American Folk Thought from Slavery to Freedom* (New York: Oxford University Press, 1977); Philip Brian Harper, *Are We Not Men? Masculine Anxiety and the Problem of African-American Identity* (New York: Oxford University Press, 1996); Keith Gilyard, *Voices of the Self: A Study of Language Competence* (Detroit: Wayne State University Press, 1991).

8. Smitherman, *Talkin and Testifyin,* 80.

9. Harper, *Are We Not Men?* 11.

story was that "everyone in the room cracked up." He engaged authority through a self-produced public spectacle with an eye for an audience that is at home with the cultural icon of the Good Bad Boy as well as the "real black man." Boys expect to get attention. Girls vie for attention too, but it is perceived as illegitimate behavior. As the teacher described it in the referral form, the girl is "demanding attention." The prevailing cultural framework denies her the rights for dramatic public display.

Male and female classroom performance is different in another respect. Girls are not rewarded with the same kind of applause or recognition by peers or by teachers. Their performance is sidelined; it is not given center stage. Teachers are more likely to "turn a blind eye" to such a display rather than call attention to it, for girls are seen as individuals who operate in cliques at most and are unlikely to foment insurrection in the room. Neither the moral nor the pragmatic principle prods teachers to take action. The behavior is not taken seriously; it is rated as "sassy" rather than symptomatic of a more dangerous disorder. In some classrooms, in fact, risk taking and "feistiness" on the part of girls is subtly encouraged given the prevailing belief that what they need is to become more visible, more assertive in the classroom. The notion is that signs of self-assertion on their part should be encouraged rather than squelched.

Disruptive acts have a complex, multifaceted set of meanings for the male Troublemakers themselves. Performance as an expression of black masculinity is a production of a powerful, subjectivity to be reckoned with, to be applauded; respect and ovation are in a context where none is forthcoming. The boys' anger and frustration as well as fear motivate the challenge to authority. Troublemakers act and speak out as stigmatized outsiders.

Ritual Performances of Masculinity: Fighting

Each year a substantial number of kids at Rosa Parks get into trouble for fighting. It is the most frequent offense for which they are referred to the Punishing Room. Significantly, the vast majority of the offenders are African American males.[10]

---

10. One-quarter of the 1,252 referrals to the Punishing Room were for fighting; four-fifths of the incidents involved boys, nine out of ten of whom were African Americans. All except three of the girls who were in fights were black.

The school has an official position on fighting: it is the wrong way to handle any situation, at any time, no matter what. Schools have good reasons for banning fights: kids can get hurt and when fights happen they sully the atmosphere of order, making the school seem like a place of danger, of violence.

The prescribed routine for schoolchildren to handle situations that might turn into a fight is to tell an adult who is then supposed to take care of the problem. This routine ignores the unofficial masculine code that if someone hits you, you should solve the problem yourself rather than showing weakness and calling an adult to intervene. However, it is expected that girls with a problem will seek out an adult for assistance. Girls are assumed to be physically weaker, less aggressive, more vulnerable, more needy of self-protection; they must attach themselves to adult (or male) power to survive. This normative gender distinction, in how to handle both problems of a sexual nature and physical aggression, operates as a "proof" of a physical and dispositional gender nature rather than behavior produced through discourses and practices that constitute sex difference.

Referrals of males to the Punishing Room, therefore, are cases where the unofficial masculine code for problem resolution has prevailed. Telling an adult is anathema to these youth. According to their own codes, the act of "telling" is dangerous for a number of reasons. The most practical of these sees it as a statement to the "whole world" that you are unable to deal with a situation on your own—to take care of yourself—an admission that can have disastrous ramifications when adult authority is absent. This is evident from the stance of a Troublemaker who questions the practical application of the official code by invoking knowledge of the proper male response when one is "attacked" that is shared with the male student specialist charged with enforcing the regulation: "I said, 'Mr. B., if somebody came up and hit you, what would you do?' 'Well,' he says, 'We're not talking about me right now, see.' That's the kind of attitude they have. It's all like on you."

Another reason mentioned by boys for not relying on a teacher to take care of a fight situation is that adults are not seen as having any real power to effectively change the relations among kids:

If someone keep messing with you, like if someone just keep on and you tell them to leave you alone, then you tell the teacher. The teacher can't do anything about it because, see, she can't hit you or nothing. Only thing she can do is tell them to stop. But then he keep on doing it. You have no choice but to hit 'em. You already told him once to stop.

This belief extends to a distrust of authority figures by these young offenders. The assumption that all the children see authority figures such as teachers, police, psychologists as acting on their behalf and trust they will act fairly may be true of middle- and upper-class children brought up to expect protection from authority figures in society. This is not the case with many of the children at the school. Their mistrust of authority is rooted in the historical and locally grounded knowledge of power relations that come from living in a largely black and impoverished neighborhood.

Fighting becomes, therefore, a powerful spectacle through which to explore trouble as a site for the construction of manhood. The practice takes place along a continuum that ranges from play—spontaneous outbreaks of pummeling and wrestling in fun, ritualistic play that shows off "cool" moves seen on video games, on TV, or in movies—to serious, angry socking, punching, fistfighting. A description of some of these activities and an analysis of what they mean provides the opportunity for us to delve under the surface of the ritualized, discrete acts that make up a socially recognizable fight event into the psychic, emotional, sensuous aspects of gender performativity. The circular, interactive flow between fantasmatic images, internal psychological processes, and physical acts suggest the dynamics of attachment of masculine identification.

Fighting is one of the social practices that add tension, drama, and spice to the routine of the school day. Pushing, grabbing, shoving, kicking, karate chopping, wrestling, fistfighting engage the body and the mind. Fighting is about play and games, about anger, and pain, about hurt feelings, about "messing around." To the spectator, a fight can look like serious combat, yet when the combatants are separated by an adult, they claim, "We were only playing." In fact, a single fight event can move along the continuum from play to serious blows in a matter of seconds. As one of the boys explained, "You get hurt and you lose your temper."

Fighting is typically treated as synonymous with "aggression" or "violence," terms that already encode the moral, definitional frame that obscures the contradictory ways that the practice, in all its manifestations, is used in our society. We, as good citizens, can distance ourselves from aggressive and violent behavior. "Violence" as discourse constructs "fighting" as pathological, symptomatic of asocial, dangerous tendencies, even though the practice of "fighting" and the discourses that constitute this practice as "normal," are in fact taken for granted as ritualized resources for "doing" masculinity in the contemporary United States.

The word *fighting* encompasses the "normal" as well as the pathological. It allows the range of meanings that the children, specifically the boys whom I interviewed and observed, as well as some of the girls, bring to the practice. One experience that it is open to is the sensuous, highly charged embodied experience before, during, and after fighting; the elating experience of "losing oneself" that I heard described in fight stories.

War Stories

I began thinking about fights soon after I started interviews with the Troublemakers and heard "fight stories." Unlike the impoverished and reluctantly told accounts of the school day, these stories were vivid, elaborate descriptions of bodies, mental states, and turbulent emotional feelings. They were stirring, memorable moments in the tedious school routine.

Horace described a fight with an older boy who had kept picking on him. He told me about the incident as he was explaining how he had broken a finger one day when we were trading "broken bones" stories.

> When I broke this finger right here it really hurt. I hit somebody in the face. It was Charles. I hit him in the face. You know the cafeteria and how you walk down to go to the cafeteria. Right there. That's where it happened. Charles picked me up and put me on the wall, slapped me on the wall, and dropped me. It hurt. It hurt bad. I got mad because he used to be messing with me for a long time so I just swung as hard as I could, closed my eyes, and just *pow,* hit him in the face. But I did like a roundhouse swing instead of doing it straight and it got the index finger of my right hand. So it was right there, started right here, and all around this part [he is

showing me the back of his hand] it hurt. It was swollen. Oooh! It was like this! But Charles, he got hurt too. The next day I came to school I had a cast on my finger and he had a bandage on his ear. It was kinda funny, we just looked at each other and smiled.

The thing that most surprised and intrigued me about Horace's story was that he specifically recalled seeing Charles the next day and that they had looked at each other and smiled. Was this a glance of recognition, of humor, of recollection of something pleasing, of all those things? The memory of the exchanged smile derailed my initial assumption that fighting was purely instrumental. This original formulation said that boys fight because they have to fight in order to protect themselves from getting beaten up on the playground. Fighting from this instrumental perspective is a purely survival practice. Boys do fight to stave off the need to fight in the future; to stop the harassment from other boys on the playground and in the streets. However, this explains only a small group of boys who live in certain environments; it relegates fighting to the realm of the poor, the deviant, the delinquent, the pathological. This position fails to address these physical clashes as the central normative practice in the preparation of bodies, of mental stances, of self-reference for manhood and as the most effective form of conflict resolution in the realm of popular culture and international relations.

I listened closely to the stories to try to make sense of behavior that was so outside of my own experience, yet so familiar a part of the landscape of physical fear and vulnerability that I as a female walked around with every day. I asked school adults about their own memories of school and fighting. I was not surprised to find that few women seemed to recall physical fights at school, though they had many stories of boys who teased them or girlfriends whom they were always "fighting" with. This resonated with my own experience. I was struck, however, by the fact that all of the men whom I talked to had had to position themselves in some way with regard to fighting. I was also struck that several of these men framed the memory of fighting in their past as a significant learning experience.

Male adults in school recall fighting themselves, but in the context both of school rules and of hindsight argue that they now know better. One of the student specialists admitted that he used to fight a lot. I found it significant that he saw "fighting" as the way he "learned":

I used to fight a lot. [Pause.] I used to fight a lot and I used to be real stubborn and silent. I wouldn't say anything to anybody. It would cause me a lot of problems, but that's just the way I learned.

The after-school martial arts instructor also admitted to fighting a lot when he was younger:

There were so many that I had as a kid that it's hard to remember all of them and how they worked out. But yes, I did have a lot of arguments and fights. A lot of times I would lose my temper, which is what kids normally do, they lose their temper, and before they have a chance to work things out they begin punching and kicking each other. Right? Well I did a lot of those things so I know from experience those are not the best thing to do.

As I explored the meaning of fighting I began to wonder how I, as female, had come to be shaped so fighting was not a part of my own corporeal or mental repertoire. A conversation with my brother reminded me of a long forgotten self that could fight, physically, ruthlessly, inflict hurt, cause tears. "We were always fighting," he recalled. "You used to beat me up." Memories of these encounters came back. I am standing with a tuft of my brother's hair in my hand, furious tears in my eyes. Full of hate for him. Kicking, scratching, socking, feeling no pain. Where had this physical power gone? I became "ladylike" repressing my anger, limiting my physical contact to shows of affection, fearful. I wondered about the meaning of being female in a society in which to be female is to be always conscious of men's physical power and to consciously chart one's everyday routines to avoid becoming a victim of this power, but to never learn the bodily and mental pleasure of fighting back.

Bodily Preparations: Pain and Pleasure

Fighting is first and foremost a bodily practice. I think about fighting and physical closeness as I stand observing the playground at recess noticing a group of three boys, bodies entangled, arms and legs flailing. In another area, two boys are standing locked closely in a wrestling embrace. Children seem to gravitate toward physical contact with each other. For boys, a close, enraptured body contact is only legitimate when they are positioned as in a fight. It is shocking that this bodily closeness between boys would be frowned on, discouraged if it were read as affection. Even boys who never get in trouble for "fighting" can be seen engaging each other through the posturing and miming, the grappling of playfight encounters.

This play can lead to "real" fights. The thin line between play and anger is crossed as bodies become vulnerable, hurt, and tempers are lost. One of the white boys in the school who was in trouble for fighting describes the progression this way:

> Well we were messing with each other and when it went too far, he started hitting me and then I hit him back and then it just got into a fight. It was sorta like a game between me, him and Thomas. How I would get on Thomas's back an—he's a big guy—and Stephen would try to hit me and I would wanta hit him back. So when Thomas left it sorta continued and I forgot which one of us wanted to stop—but one of us wanted to stop and the other one wouldn't.

Fighting is about testing and proving your bodily power over another person, both to yourself and to others through the ability to "hurt" someone as well as to experience "hurt."

> HORACE: You know Claude. He's a bad boy in the school. When I was in the fifth grade, he was in the fifth grade. I intercepted his pass and he threw the ball at my head and then I said, "You're mad," and I twisted the ball on the floor. I said, "Watch this," and y'know spiraled it on the floor, and he kicked it and it hit my leg, and I said, "Claude, if you hit me one more time with the ball or anything I'm going to hurt you." He said, "What if you do?" I said, "Okay, you expect me not to do anything, right?" He said, "Nope." Then I just *pow, pow, pow,* and I got him on the floor and then I got him on his back. I wanted to hurt him badly but I couldn't.
>
> ANN: Why couldn't you?
>
> HORACE: I didn't want to get in trouble. And if I did really hurt him it wouldn't prove anything anyway. But it did. It proved that I could hurt him and he didn't mess with me anymore.

Pain is an integral part of fighting. Sometimes it is the reason for lashing out in anger. This description by Wendell also captures the loss of self-control experienced at the moment of the fight:

> Sometimes it starts by capping or by somebody slams you down or somebody throws a bullet at you. You know what a bullet is, don't you? [He chuckles delightedly because I think of a bullet from a gun.] The bullet I am talking about is a football! You throw it with all your might and it hits somebody. It just very fast and they call it bullets. You off-guard and they throw it at your head, and bullets they throw with all their might so it hurts. Then that sorta gets you all pissed off. Then what happens is, you kinda like, "Why you threw it?" "'Cause I wanted to. Like, so?" "So you not going to do that to me." Then: "So you going to do something about it?" Real smart. "Yeah!" And then you tap the person on the shoulder and your mind goes black and then *shweeeee* [a noise and hand signal that demonstrates the evaporation of thought] you go at it. And you don't stop until the teacher comes and stops it.

Fighting is a mechanism for preparing masculinized bodies through the playful exercise of bodily moves and postures and the routinized rehearsal of sequences and chains of stances of readiness, attack, and defense. Here it is crucial to emphasize that while many boys in the school never ever engage in an actual physical fight with another boy or girl during school hours, the majority engage in some form of body enactments of fantasized "fight" scenarios. They have observed boys and men on TV, in the movies, in video games, on the street, in the playground adopting these stances.

These drills simultaneously prepare and cultivate the mental states in which corporeal styles are grounded. So for instance, boys are initiated into the protocol of enduring physical pain and mental anguish— "like a man"—through early and small infusions of the toxic substance itself in play fights. The practice of fighting is the site for a hot-wiring together of physical pain and pleasure, as components of masculinity as play and bodily hurt inevitably coincide.

Consequently, it also engages powerful emotions. Lindsey described the feelings he experienced prior to getting into a fight:

Sometimes it's play. And sometimes it's real. But that's only sometimes, because they can just suddenly make you angry and then,
it's like they take control of your mind. Like they manipulate your
mind if you angry. Little by little you just lose it and you get in a
temper.

One of the white boys in the school who had gotten in trouble for
fighting described his thoughts and feelings preceding a fight and the
moment of "just going black" in a loss of self:

My mind would probably be going through how I would do this.
If I would stop it now or if I would follow through with it. But
once the fight actually happens I sort of go black and just fight 'em.

Fighting is a practice, like sports, that is so symbolically "masculine" that expressions of emotion or behavior that might call one's manhood into question are allowed without danger of jeopardizing one's
manliness. Even crying is a permissible expression of "masculinity"
under these circumstances. One of the boys who told me he never
cried, corrected himself:

But if I be mad, I cry. Like if I get into a fight or something like
that, I cry because I lose my temper and get so mad. But sometimes, I play football and if I cry that mean I'm ready to tumble—
throw the ball to me because I'm going.

Fighting in school is a space in which boys can feel free to do emotional
work.[11] In a social practice that is so incontrovertibly coded as masculine, behaviors marked as feminine, such as crying, can be called upon
as powerful wellsprings for action.

One of the questions that I asked all the boys about fighting came
out of my own ignorance. My query was posed in terms of identity
work around the winning and losing of fights. Did you ever win a fight?
Did you ever lose a fight? How did you feel when you lost? How did
you feel when you won? I found the answers slippery, unexpected, con-

11. Arlie Russell Hochschild, *The Managed Heart: Commercialization of Human Feeling* (Berkeley and Los Angeles: University of California Press, 1983). Hochschild explores
the feeling rules that guide and govern our own emotional displays as well as how we interpret the emotional expression of others.

tradictory. I had anticipated that winning would be described in proud and boastful ways, as success stories. But there seemed to be a surprising reluctance to embellish victory. I learned that I was missing the point by posing the question the way I had in terms of winning and losing. Trey enlightened me when he explained that what was at stake was not winning or losing per se but in learning about the self:

> I won a lot of fights. You know you won when they start crying and stuff or when they stop and leave. I lost fights. Then you feel a little okay. At least you lost. I mean like you ain't goin' win every fight. At least you fought back instead of just standing there and letting them hit you.

Another boy expressed the function that fighting played in establishing yourself as being a particular kind of respectable person:

> It's probably like dumb, but if somebody wants to fight me, I mean, I don't care even if I know I can't beat 'em. I won't stop if they don't stop. I mean I'm not scared to fight anybody. I'm not a coward. I don't let anybody punk me around. If you let people punk you around, other peoples want to punk you around.

Proving yourself to others is like a game, a kind of competition:

> Me and Leslie used to fight because we used to be the biggest boys, but now we don't care anymore. We used to get friends and try and fight each other. I fought him at Baldwin school all the time. We stopped about the fifth grade [the previous year]. Just got tired, I guess.

Standing and proving yourself today can be insurance against future harassment in the yard as you make a name for yourself through readiness to fight: "Like if somebody put their hands on you, then you have to, you have to hit them back. Because otherwise you going be beat up on for the rest of your life."

Eddie, who has avoided fights because he does not want to get in trouble, is now seen as a target for anyone to beat up, according to one of his friends, who characterized Eddie's predicament this way: "He can't fight. *He can't fight.* Every girl, every boy in the whole school fixing to beat him up. Badly. They could beat him up badly."

Eddie explains his own perspective on how he has come to actually lose a reputation.

> Yeah, I won a fight in preschool. Like somebody this tall [his gesture indicates a very tall someone] I had to go like this [reaches up to demonstrate] so I could hit him. He was older than me. He was the preschool bully. Till I mess him up.

But Eddie's parents came down hard on him for getting in trouble for fighting in elementary school:

> Yeah, I lost fights. See when I got to Rosa Parks my parents told me not to fight unless I had to—so I lost my face. 'Cause I was so used to telling them to stop, don't fight, don't fight.

In constructing the self through fight stories, it is not admirable to represent oneself as the aggressor or initiator in a fight. All the boys whom I talked to about fighting presented themselves as responding to a physical attack that had to be answered in a decisive way. No one presented himself as a "bully," though I knew that Horace had that reputation. Yet he told me that "only fights I been in is if they hit me first."

There are, however, times when it is legitimate to be the initiator. When verbal provocation is sufficient. This is when "family" has been insulted. Talking about "your momma" is tantamount to throwing down the gauntlet:

> Mostly I get in fights if somebody talk about my grandfather because he's dead. And I loved my grandfather more than I love anybody and then he died. [Tears are in Jabari's eyes as we talk.] That's why I try to tell people before they get ready to say anything, I'm like, "Don't say anything about my grandfather, 'cause if you say something about him, I'm goin' hit you."

The boys talked about how they learned to fight. How one learns to fight and what one learns about the meaning of fighting—why fight, to fight or not to fight—involved both racial identity and class positioning. Ricky and Duane, two of the Schoolboys, have been enrolled by their parents in martial arts classes. Fighting remains a necessary accoutrement of masculinity that is "schooled," not a "natural" acquisition of doing. As such, it becomes a marker of higher class position. Fighting takes place in an institutionalized arena rather than spontaneously in just any setting. The mind seems to control the body here, rather than vice versa.

Horace, on the other hand, like the majority of boys with whom I talked, explained that he had learned to fight through observation and practice:

> I watched people. Like when I was younger, like I used to look up to people. I still do. I look up to people and they knew how to fight so I just watched them. I just like saw people fight on TV, you know. Boxing and stuff.

Another boy told me that he thought kids learned to fight "probably from theirselves. Like their mom probably say, if somebody hit you, hit them back." This advice about proper behavior is grounded in the socialization practices that are brought into school as ways of responding to confrontations.

Gender Practice and Identification

Fighting acts reproduce notions of essentially different gendered natures and the forms in which this "difference" is grounded. Though class makes some difference in when, how, and under what conditions it takes place, fighting is the hegemonic representation of masculinity. Inscribed in the male body—whether individual males fight or not, abjure fighting or not—is the potential for this unleashing of physical power. By the same token, fighting for girls is considered an aberration, something to be explained.

Girls do get in fights at school. Boys asserted that girls can fight, even that "sometimes they get in fights easier. Because they got more attitude." Indeed, girls do make a name for themselves this way. One of the girls at Rosa Parks was in trouble several times during the school year for fighting. Most of her scraps were with the boys who liked to tease her because she was very tall for her age. This, however, was not assumed to be reflective of her "femaleness" but of her individuality. Mr. Sobers, for example, when I asked him about her, made a point of this singularity rather than explaining her in terms of race, class, or gender: "Oh, Stephanie is just Stephanie."

Fighting is not a means of "doing gender" for girls. They do not use physical clashes as a way to relate to each other in play. Girls did not practice "cool" moves or engage in play fights with each other. They used other strategies for making the day go by, such as the chain of stories about other children, the "he said, she said," which can build up to a more physical confrontation.[12] More often it leads to injured feelings, the isolation and ostracism of individuals, and the regrouping of friendships. On the playground at Rosa Parks, girls were more likely to interact physically with boys than with other girls. They often initiated encounters with boys to play chase games by pushing, prodding, hitting, or bumping into them.

Through male fighting we can see how gender difference is grounded in a compulsory and violently enforced heterosexuality. The interaction involves the convergence of the desire for physical and emotional closeness with another, the anxiety over presenting a convincing performance of a declarative act of identification, and the risk of ostracism or punishment. Boys from an early age learn that affectionate public physical contact such as an embrace with those who are seen as most like oneself, other males, is taboo. For them, a physical embrace, the close intertwining of bodies is culturally permissible only in the act of the rituals of the fight.[13] Thus the fulfillment of desire for physical intimacy, for body contact, can most safely be accomplished publicly through the apparent or actual infliction and experience of bodily pain. A desire for closeness, for identification with a reflection of oneself, can be achieved through an act that beckons and embraces using apparently threatening and hostile gestures. In a revealing story of the constraining boundaries of male self-expression, Mac an Ghaill recounts how the public exchange of flowers between two males in a high school was regarded by personnel as more unnatural, reprehensible, and threatening than the physical violence of the fight that the gesture provoked.[14]

---

12. For a full discussion of this strategy see Marjorie Harness Goodwin, *He-Said–She-Said: Talk as a Social Organization among Black Children* (Bloomington: Indiana University Press, 1990).

13. In the U.S. context, we see passionate public embraces between males in certain high-contact team sports such as football, basketball, and soccer in moments of great emotion. It is less likely to be witnessed in sports such as tennis or golf where team camaraderie cannot develop or where the masculinity of the participants is not so indubitably demonstrated.

14. Mairtin Mac an Ghaill, *The Making of Men: Masculinities, Sexualities, and Schooling* (Buckingham, England: Open University Press, 1994), 1.

Most men don't have to actually fight; they can participate in the inscription of power on male bodies through watching. Fighting acts are a major form of entertainment in our society. From popular cultural figures on television, screen, in video games, boxing and wrestling matches, the use of fists and agile feet deeply encode the hegemonic representation of masculinity. Even as the pantheon of cultural super-heroes real and fantasy, such as Mike Tyson, Dennis Rodman, Schwarznegger's "Terminator" and Stallone's "Rambo," are supplemented by cultural representations of the "New Man" who is a more fitting partner for the stronger images of the liberated woman—Kevin Costner's Robin Hood or Keaton's Batman, for instance—these more "sensitive" heroes are also still skilled and courageous physical fighters. They become "real men" because they can, when inevitably called upon to do so, physically vanquish the villain and save the female "victim." The fight scene/shootout between hero and villain continues to be the most enduring convention of climax and resolution in film and television. Violence remains the most predictable way of males resolving conflict and problems in the popular culture as well as in world events.

The presence of spectators is a key element. The performance of fighting in settings such as the playground, the boxing ring, the movie theater, the sports arena is not only rousing entertainment for an audience, but a reinscription of an abstract masculine power. This performance is affirmed by ardent spectators, mostly men but some women, who consume the ritualistic enactment of raw, body power. Video games are an excellent example of how even males who avoid physical aggressive behavior in their own personal life symbolically perform a violent masculinity in order to play the game at all.[15]

Fighting is the emblematic ritual performance of male power. Participation in this ritual for boys and for men is not an expression of deviant, antisocial behavior but is profoundly normative, a thoroughly social performance. Though it is officially frowned on as a means of resolving personal problems, it is in fact culturally applauded as a way of settling differences among men. As boys mock fight through imitating martial arts movements with or without an audience, playfight with peers, play video games, they bodily and psychically inhabit male power through fantasy and imagination.

For Troublemakers, who are already sidelined as academic failures,

15. R. W. Connell, "Teaching the Boys: New Research on Masculinity and Gender Strategies for Schools," *Teachers College Record* 98, no. 2 (1996).

one route to making a name for yourself, for expressing "normalcy," competency, and humanity, is through this identification with physical power. Once again, a sense of anger and frustration born of marginalization in school intensifies the nature of these performances.

Race makes a difference in how physical power is constituted and perceived. African American boys draw on a specific repertoire of racial images as well as the lived experience and popular knowledge from the world outside the school. Most of the black boys live in an environment where being mentally and physically prepared to stand up for oneself through words and deeds is crucial. However, there is another reason specifically grounded in the history and evolution of race relations in the United States. Up to the 1960s, physical violence wielded by whites in the form of individuals, mobs, or the state was the instrument used to police the racial order; demonstrations of male privilege or assertions of rights on the part of black men was the cause for brutal retaliation. The prevailing wisdom in black communities was that in order to survive males had to be carefully taught to mask any show of power in confrontations with whites. With the emergence of Black Power as an ideology and a practice, the right of black men to stand up for their manhood and their racial pride through physical force was asserted. This was the right to have the physical privileges of white men. This "right" is inculcated into young black males in family and community, many of whom are taught, "Don't let anyone take advantage of you. If someone hits you, you hit them back." First blows are not always physical, but sometimes symbolic; racial epithets are violent attacks. A physical response is especially likely on the part of the Troublemakers, who have a heightened racial consciousness.

Simultaneously, this manifestation of physicality is the very material presence that the school seeks to exclude: black males are already seen as embodying the violence and aggression that will drive away "desirable" families and their children. Fighting on the part of black boys is more visible as a problem, so it is viewed with extreme concern and responded to more swiftly and harshly. Once again, the process of adultification of black male behavior frames the act as symptomatic of dangerous tendencies. The Troublemakers, who have already been labeled as bound for jail, have little to lose and everything to gain in using this form of rule breaking as a way of making a name for themselves, gaining recognition through performances of masculinity.

field note
ODD SYMPTOMS

My conviction that children's school behavior was becoming widely explained and understood as a matter of *individual* children's pathology extracted from any social context deepened when, in 1994, children's disobedience was officially classified as a mental illness by the American Psychiatric Association (APA). This classification, designated as Oppositional Defiant Disorder (ODD), appeared in the official diagnostic reference book of the American Psychiatric Association that contains classifications of all mental disorders recognized that year.[1] The following description of the symptoms of the disorder is excerpted from the APA's *Diagnostic and Statistical Manual of Mental Disorders:*

> Code 313.81. "Oppositional Defiant Disorder" (ODD). The essential feature of Oppositional Defiant Disorder is a recurrent pattern of negativistic, defiant, disobedient, and hostile behavior toward authority figures that persists for at least 6 months (Criterion A) and is characterized by the frequent occurrence of at least four of the following behaviors: losing temper (Criterion A1), arguing with adults (Criterion A2), actively defying or refusing to comply with the requests or rules of adults (Criterion A3), deliberately doing things that will annoy other people (Criterion A4), blaming others for his or her own mistakes or misbehavior (Criterion A5), being touchy or easily annoyed by others (Criterion A6), being angry and resentful (Criterion A7), or being spiteful or vindictive (Criterion A8). To qualify for Oppositional Defiant Disorder, the behaviors must occur more frequently than is typically observed in individuals of comparable age and developmental level and must lead to significant impairment in social, academic or occupational functioning (Criterion B). The diagnosis is not made if the disturbance in behavior occurs exclusively during the course of a Psychotic or Mood Disorder (Criterion C) or if

---

1. American Psychiatric Association, *Diagnostic and Statistical Manual of Mental Disorders,* 4th ed. (Washington, D.C.: American Psychiatric Association, 1994).

criteria are met for Conduct Disorder or Antisocial Personality Disorder (in an individual over 18 years).

Negativistic and defiant behaviors are expressed by persistent stubbornness, resistance to directions, and unwillingness to compromise, give in, or negotiate with adults or peers. Defiance may also include deliberate or persistent testing of limits, usually by ignoring orders, arguing, and failing to accept blame for misdeeds. Hostility can be directed at adults or peers and is shown by deliberately annoying others or by verbal aggression (usually without the more serious physical aggression seen in Conduct Disorder). Manifestations of the disorder are almost invariably present in the home setting, but may not be evident at school or in the community. Symptoms of the disorder are typically more evident in interactions with adults or peers whom the individual knows well, and thus may not be apparent during clinical examination. Usually individuals with this disorder do not regard themselves as oppositional or defiant, but justify their behavior as a response to unreasonable demands or circumstances.[2]

2. Ibid., 91–92.

chapter seven
unreasonable circumstances

To the real question, "How does it feel to be a problem?" I answer seldom a word. And yet, being a problem is a strange experience.

—W. E. B. DU BOIS, *Souls of Black Folk*

By what sends
the white kids
I ain't sent:
I know I can't
be President.
What don't bug
them white kids
sure bugs me:
We know everybody
ain't free.
Lies written down
for white folks
ain't for us a-tall:
"Liberty And Justice"—
Huh!—for All?

—LANGSTON HUGHES, "CHILDREN'S RHYMES"

Just a few days after the 1992 riots that followed the acquittal of the Los Angeles policemen who had beaten Rodney King, I overheard a conversation between a teacher and the PALS counselor in the hallway of Rosa Parks School. The teacher, a white woman, was deploring the behavior of an eleven year old African American boy, D'Andre, in her class. During a discussion of the riots, some of the children had said that it was Simi Valley that should have gone up in smoke not South Central Los Angeles.[1] At this, the white student teacher, Laura, told the children that she had an uncle who lived in Simi Valley, to which D'Andre had retorted, "I'd burn his house down too."

According to the hallway account, Laura was extremely upset by this response. Her feelings were hurt that a child she had worked with closely in the classroom for almost a whole year would have said something so hateful to her. D'Andre was sent off to the Punishing Room for his remark. "You must do something about that boy's attitude," the teacher told the counselor. "He's such a hostile kid. He says he doesn't like white people."

This anecdote about D'Andre is a dramatic illustration of the way that "race" enters the school and structures the interactions of the school day. The story of D'Andre and the student teacher gives a glimpse of how processes of racial identification and group membership conflict with the school's discourse about difference as individual and getting in trouble as a matter of personal choice or individual pathology. Race is a highly charged nexus for identification and for generating theories about school failure and trouble. Troublemakers contest the school's claim to use neutral, race-blind criteria for judgments by articulating a counterdiscourse about a collective condition that contends that it is children's race that determines how punishment is meted out by school adults. They bring to the events of the school day knowledge and feelings about the racialized relations of power in the wider social world in which the school is embedded. They formulate a critique of the institutional racism that they encounter in school. This critique is expressed in a myriad of ways: obliquely through the adoption of bodily attitudes, style, clothing, and language, as well as directly through political action using confrontational tactics.

We will examine the social costs and benefits of racial identification. Positioning oneself as "raced" or as "raceless" simultaneously involves the playing out and expression of present class location as well as the engagement with or disengagement from anticipatory social mobility strategies. Schoolboys especially are faced with dilemmas of

---

1. Simi Valley is the predominately white Los Angeles suburb to which the trial of the Los Angeles policemen had been moved and where, it was reputed, a number of policemen and families lived.

racial identification that bear serious implications for their gender practice as well as render pathways for class mobility problematic.

The hallway story also captures the emotional ingredients—fear, anger, resentment, hurt feelings—that lie just under the surface and seethe into the open when race as a feature of social division enters the discussion. Unlike masculinity, race is a highly contested, inflammatory, politically charged category. School adults interpret public assertions of race identification by kids as rude, disruptive, and illegitimate, as personal attacks on their own probity. Kids bring feelings of anger and frustration about racial inequality gleaned from personal experience, from family, neighborhood, television, movies, and popular music to decipher struggles with authority figures.

Competing Frameworks: (Un)Reasonable Circumstances

Is D'Andre a rude, aggressive kid with an emotional problem? Or is his disruptive behavior "reasonable" when we take the "circumstances" and events surrounding the behavior into account? Let us look more closely at two disparate frameworks inherent in the D'Andre anecdote for different readings of the outburst. From the school's perspective, D'Andre's response is indeed disturbingly aggressive and antisocial. It contravenes several basic precepts that are widely promulgated: the proper way to resolve conflict is through established channels and verbal negotiation not through violence and lawbreaking; laws should be observed, and breaking them constitutes criminal activity; private property should be respected so that the act of burning down someone's house or, by extension to the events in South Central Los Angeles, looting and burning neighborhood buildings, is reprehensible behavior that should not be condoned. D'Andre's espousal of such tactics and his identification as someone who doesn't like white people reveals the distorted values and emotions of a psychologically troubled youth. The boy is referred to the counselor, a psychotherapist, for an attitude adjustment.

This standpoint is one that extracts children from the larger social and political context in which they exist and that they bring to school, treating them as individual actors in isolation. Within this individualized framework for understanding troubling behavior, the remedy involves the diagnosis and treatment of an individual and his problem. D'Andre is characterized as emotionally disturbed. From this psychologized perspective, he is one of a growing number of children whose disruptive outbursts are explained as a personality disorder. He could very likely be diagnosed as suffering from "Oppositional Defiant Disorder" (ODD), the illness recently "discovered" by the American Psychiatric Association (APA) and described in the field note that precedes this chapter.[2] In fact, D'Andre displays the necessary four symptoms requisite for a diagnosis of this illness: "losing temper" (Criterion A1); "being touchy or easily annoyed by others" (Criterion A6); "being angry and resentful" (Criterion A7); and "being spiteful and vindictive" (Criterion A8).

The APA goes to pains to underscore the origins of the disorder as within the individual and not the result of external circumstances: "Usually individuals with this disorder do not regard themselves as oppositional or defiant, but justify their behavior as a response to unreasonable demands or circumstances."[3] So diagnosticians are instructed to discount the social environment and to reject any claims on the part of the individual that external forces have contributed to the problem. In fact, according to the wording the very making of this kind of claim is a clear symptom of the disorder.

Let us take the boy's standpoint for a change. Let us situate the behavior within a specific and highly relevant social context. We shall take into consideration a few of the "unreasonable demands or circumstances" by which D'Andre might justify his behavior. Otherwise we cannot begin to understand or address his undeniably disruptive and hostile outburst.

When the teacher tells her story, the fact that D'Andre is African American and the student teacher is white is never mentioned, nor is the fact that Simi Valley is a predominately white, middle-class suburb of Los Angeles, and that South Central Los Angeles is an urban area with a concentration of poor and low-income black and minority residents. She treats these social distinctions as irrelevant details to her story. The only person in her account it would seem for whom race seems to matter is D'Andre, whom she reports as saying "he doesn't like white people." He becomes the sole bearer of a disturbing bigotry that sees people in terms of race rather than as individuals. He is presented as injecting a way of seeing the world into the discourse of the community that is otherwise absent.

2. American Psychiatric Association, *Diagnostic and Statistical Manual,* 91–92.
3. Ibid., 92.

However, D'Andre's anger is both predictable and intelligible through a racial lens. He is bringing to school with him, along with schoolbag, textbooks, pencils, and paper, powerful feelings of anger, sadness, and fear after watching conflict and conflagration in Los Angeles on television for three days following the acquittal of the four white policemen whom he had watched on TV beating Rodney King, a black man, by an all-white jury in Simi Valley. The spectacle of King's savage beating had stirred up strong feelings of outrage in citizens across the nation. In D'Andre's neighborhood, where police harassment and beating of black men was not unusual but had just never been caught on videotape, feelings of anger were tinged by vindication and the unrealized hope of a national spectacle of justice and retribution at the climax of the trial of the police.

Undoubtedly, D'Andre and his family had spent hours watching television and talking about these events with mixed feelings of sadness, rage, and horror. Certainly in millions of households across the land, there was a feeling that as local neighborhoods were pillaged, vengeance was being wreaked against the wrong target. D'Andre identifies himself with the rioters, who not only look very much like his family and himself but who are facing similar social and economic problems. His explosion of feeling is based on his consciousness of the historic and social connection of black people in the United States, a connection recurringly forged through events such as the beating of King. A heightened racial identification is something that he and more than half of the children at Rosa Parks bring into school as an interpretive lens.

These kids come from a milieu in which race is a fundamental attribute of self not as an abstract circumstance but as a meaningful identity that must be taken into consideration at every step. The formation of black identity takes place within a mixed social and feeling context of pride, rage, shame. The sentiments that D'Andre expressed are not just representative of his personal feelings of disaffection but are grounded in a sense of group condition. It is this sensation of a groupness and a collective identity that some of the boys whom I got to know bring to school to counter the school's evaluation of them as antisocial individuals who are potential dangers to society.

The student teacher also takes sides by establishing her connection with the people of Simi Valley. This bond is both one of kinship and, what remains unstated, of race. She uses her classroom status as one of the "good guys" to personify the point that it is individuals like herself who would be attacked; but D'Andre refuses to accept the substitution of individual difference for group status in the exchange. The student teacher demonstrates the invisibility of whiteness, of race as a position of power and privilege. This elision of group privilege and its recasting as individual in character is a fundamental aspect of the discourse of individual choice.

Individual Choice: Acting White

The school's ubiquitous message is that success and failure is a matter of personal choice. This discourse is expressed in the school rules and in the verbal exhortations of adults to kids: "Success is up to you." This could be an encouraging, motivational message. However, the homily obscures both the material and social constraints that prevent African American children from succeeding. The way school is organized to promote dominant cultural values and expressive modes favors the middle-class white minority students at the expense of the African American majority. Race and class make a difference in children's chances for success at school.

In a racialized society such as the United States, the essential feature for maintaining white hegemony is the elevation of the physical and cultural attributes of whiteness: the dominant group becomes the standard against which "individuals" are measured. Children are individuated in relation to an idealized figure who is both white and middle class. To invest the dominant group's way of life with the stamp of "ideal" or "norm" means that the subordinate group's family patterns, language, relational styles are constituted as deviant, pathological, deficient, inferior. Blackness, as the Other, the outside category, becomes the racially marked presence that constitutes the norm, the seemingly raceless individual, by its very representation as undifferentiated. This apparent absence of race in whites, this presence as raceless, permits their cultural forms to be known as, even experienced as, individuality. The reproduction of the racial order in the United States today is made possible by the invisibility of operations that seem to be about natural dispositions and character rather than about racial fictions.

Children as astute observers are highly conscious of the adult signals that designate rank and status. For one thing, school adults are not subtle or covert about these assessments, but openly assert their judgments. African American youth know that what they bring to school from family and community is seen as deficient, is denigrated, devalued. They know that their family background, their experience, their modes of expression—both verbal and nonverbal—are detrimental to their achievement, must be compensated for, even eradicated. As discerning observers and participants, the boys know they must be actively engaged in discarding or making up for these unbecoming elements of their biography. They must "make themselves over" to succeed in school and to accumulate the cultural capital that is the prerequisite for achievement. They must get rid of the unwanted baggage brought from the streets, the family, the neighborhood. They must shed the distinguishing features of "Blackness" by approximating whiteness, by acting white.

Ethnographic studies have recorded that this institutional imperative for children to "act white" in order to achieve success is known to black kids who use the phrase as a put-down of their peers who are doing well in school. For example, Fordham and Ogbu's study of an all-black high school in Washington, D.C., reports that students forge a collective oppositional identity in the face of institutional racism.[4] In this oppositional culture, school achievement is equated with "acting white"; being a "good" student is equivalent to losing one's racial cultural identity. Black students who do well in D.C. high schools must develop strategies to deal with the accusations and pressures from others who perceive this academic prowess as "acting white." What makes this racial policing seem so troubling is the not-so-subtle insinuation that for students to do well in school they must cut themselves off from blackness by positioning themselves as white. Indeed, the researchers suggest that fear of being accused of "acting white" by peers is a significant factor in deterring a number of youth from adopting the behavior required for success.

This research adds significantly to our knowledge about the crucial relationship between racial identification and school success, but the conclusions drawn are considerably weakened by a misplaced emphasis. There is overemphasis on the role of peers as the principle force holding back students. This emphasis tends to give credence to the notion that it is primarily African Americans who hold individual

4. Signithia Fordham and John Ogbu, "Black Student School Success: Coping with the 'Burden of Acting White,'" *Urban Review* 18, no. 3 (1986).

members back from success by constantly policing and ostracizing those who seem to be "bettering" themselves. It downplays the hegemonic power of the institution that operates through normalizing practices to push certain students to the margins and produce the condition in many of active "not-learning."

There is overwhelming evidence from case studies and from autobiographical work that African American kids enter school not with an oppositional orientation at all, but full of promise and eager to learn.[5] There is also evidence that somewhere early in the fourth grade this motivation and intense excitement about school learning dwindles, markedly so for African American boys, in what has come to be called "the fourth-grade syndrome."[6] This is the point at which African American males appear to begin to disidentify with school and to look to other sources for self-valuation. It is my contention that this diminished motivation to identify as a "scholar" is a consequence of the inhospitable culture of school that African American children encounter, rather than a consequence of peer pressure.

When the institution and not the peer group is understood to be determinate, the claim that "acting white" is a prerequisite for success becomes an insight *on the part of youth* into the normalizing techniques of the institution. The kids are in fact circulating a radical critique by recognizing and pointing out processes and relationships observed and elaborated by eminent social theorists who argue that schooling is organized to affirm, elevate, and valorize the cultural forms and expressive modes of the dominant group in society and to devalue those of the subordinate group.[7] This theory emphasizes the reproduction of class relations through schooling. It propounds that success and social mobility, from this perspective, is dependent on the mastery of middle-class linguistic codes, lifestyles, disciplinary modes, and relational manners; that schools reflect the familial and neighborhood practices of upper- and middle-class students who fit smoothly into its forms of communication and social organization. These youth do not have to

5. For case studies see Kotlowitz, *There Are No Children Here;* and Kunjufu, *Countering the Conspiracy.* For autobiographical work see Gilyard, *Voices of the Self.*

6. Kunjufu, *Countering the Conspiracy.*

7. See, for example, Basil Bernstein, "Social Class, Language, and Socialization," in *Power and Ideology in Education,* ed. Jerome Karabel and A. H. Halsey (New York: Oxford University Press, 1977); Pierre Bourdieu, "Symbolic Power," in *Identity and Structure: Issues in the Sociology of Education,* ed. Dennis Gleeson (Driffield, England: Studies in Education, 1977), 112–19; and Bowles and Gintis, *Schooling in Capitalist America.*

make the kind of profound adjustments made by children from working-class and poor families. Black youth are pointing out a similar institutional relationship in the context of a racialized culture when they point out that "acting white" is a prerequisite for fitting in at school and is absolutely basic to any kind of success. This requirement ruthlessly excludes African American cultural modes as relevant and meaningful knowledge practices.

Language use is an excellent example of how the power to determine the standard operates to enforce white middle-class cultural forms as a prerequisite for school success and to present African American kids, especially black males, with difficult dilemmas of identification. The school demands the suppression of language brought from home and imposes Received Standard English as the sole legitimate form of expression as well as the sign of culture, intellect, and a commitment to bettering oneself. The use of Black English, on the other hand, signals both cultural and intellectual deficiency.

Because language is critical at several levels of the formation of subjectivity it is particularly fruitful for exemplifying the connections between the production and performance of conforming and alternative identities. Language is fundamental to the work of representing and constituting self. It bears traces of our geographic origins, the social class we come from, the history we share, our place in systems of power. We use it to express ourselves to others and to register what others say about us in a dynamic interplay and exchange of meanings. Through it we learn about ourselves as autonomous individuals as well as members of social collectives. We are not only produced by language, but we continuously reshape and re-create it under novel circumstances.

While children bring a rich variety of language systems into school, the institution imposes a profoundly restricted and jealously guarded monolingual system through the sanction of only one form, Received Standard English, as the legitimate form of expression and exchange in the classroom. Children who come from families who speak other languages such as Chinese, Spanish, Russian, Vietnamese at home are pulled out of the regular classroom for several periods a week for English lessons. Incredibly, their ability to speak and think in more than one language system is not presented to the school population as a marvelous accomplishment to be envied, emulated, applauded, but it is framed as a handicap, a problem to be corrected before their real education can begin.

Many of the African American children come to school speaking Black English. It is a language variant that is not recognized by the school; in fact, it was typically described by teachers at Rosa Parks School as "bad English" or as "ghetto talk." Though Black English remains unrecognized by the school as an acceptable medium of communication, a number of sociolinguists and other scholars conclude that rather than being merely bad grammar, Black English is a full-blown language with a grammar and syntax of its own that emanates from and reflects the historical and lived experience of Americans of African descent.[8] This is not to say, by any means, that all black Americans naturally use or speak Black English. There is great variation in our use of language; social class, for instance, influences whether a child grows up in a household where Received Standard English or Black English is the norm. Many are fluent in both and switch between the two, using Received Standard English in "white" settings, especially where one needs to downplay one's Blackness to be acceptable, and Black English with family, with black friends, or in social situations where one wants to downplay class divisions and emphasize racial ties and unity.

The school actively seeks to suppress and eradicate Black English. "Ghetto talk" is seen as symptomatic of the ignorance, backwardness, and uncouth nature of the speaker. Children who use it are corrected, ostracized, and marginalized as dumb. Ironically, African American teachers in the school were the ones most actively engaged in enforcing the use of proper English; yet many of these teachers would themselves lapse into Black English as they conducted everyday conversations with their peers and talked to students.

The kids know that the use of Received Standard English is the absolute baseline for an active commitment to the school agenda. We can understand why they would choose to adopt this sanctioned language form. But why do some hold on to Black English and invite trouble in school? The choice is not by any means due to lack of exposure to the standard form as a result of social isolation or a culture of

---

8. See Smitherman, *Talkin and Testifyin;* J. L. Dillard, *Black English: Its History and Usage in the United States* (New York: Vintage, 1973); W. Labov, *Language in the Inner City: Studies in the Black English Vernacular* (Philadelphia: University of Pennsylvania Press, 1972); and June Jordan, *On Call: Political Essays* (Boston: South End Press, 1985), chap. 16.

poverty; they are exposed daily to Received Standard English through family, community, television, movies, and the classroom. Why do they choose to use a stigmatized language?

First of all, to exorcise "ghetto talk" and speak Received Standard English, especially in the early school years, does not entail a simple decision to speak "properly" on the part of black children. It involves a violent and painful assault on their very sense of self and on those with whom they most closely identify that can inflict long-term psychic damage to self-esteem:

> Language . . . is also very important as a symbol of identity and group membership. To suggest to a child that his language, and that of those with whom he identifies, is inferior in some way is to imply that *he* is inferior. This, in turn, is likely to lead either to alienation from the school and school values, or to a rejection of the group to which he belongs. It is also *socially* wrong in that it may appear to imply that particular social groups are less valuable than others. . . . The fact must also be faced that, in very many cases, speakers will not *want* to change their language—even if it were possible.[9]

In this atmosphere of denigration of what one brings to school, many black children are forced to choose between identification with school or with family and social group. To accept the superiority of one means rejecting the value of the other, so a decision must be made to adhere to one source of knowledge and become alienated from the alternative.

Most children become bidialectal or bilingual, switching back and forth between the two systems. But there are severe psychological costs involved in the effort to negotiate both. Keith Gilyard, in a moving account of his own childhood acquisition of language and literacy, reflects on the severe psychic strain that black children undergo as they try to fashion selves in both worlds. In a poignant illustration of Du Bois's concept of "double consciousness," Gilyard describes how he decides to use another name, Raymond, as the one he will use in school in an act of psychic survival:

---

9. P. Trudgill, *Sociolinguistics: An Introduction* (Harmondsworth: Penguin, 1974), 80–81.

Nobody had ever called me Raymond before. Uptown it was always Keith or Keithy or Little Gil. Raymond was like a fifth wheel. A spare. And that's what I decided to make these people call me. They cannot meet Keith now. I will put someone else together for them and he will be their classmate until further notice. That will be the first step in this particular survival plan. Of course it wasn't thought out in those specific terms, but the instinct and action were there. And from that day on, through all my years in public school, all White folks had to call me Raymond.[10]

He points out that this work of "splitting" in order to survive under the duress of maintaining two identificatory systems took a toll on his schoolwork. The cause of this change was unrecognized by the school, which looked to family problems for the explanation:

My teachers in Queens could not appreciate just how hard I worked to fit in socially or how effective I actually was at finding a niche that would be acceptable to the class as a whole. By the end of the third grade, in addition to the marks indicated above, my occasional resentment of group control and my occasional evading of responsibility had become constants. Also, that my relationship with my parents seemed disturbed was duly noted. Unfortunately, the only conclusion they drew from them was that I needed "supervision." They were nowhere near the whole truth about me, which was, in short, that I was showing some cracks under the strain of all the various role-playing I was engaged in. Nonetheless, I held myself together enough emotionally to handle the academic requirements of those one-level classes.[11]

A second reason for holding on to Black English is eminently practical. Language is not only a vital aspect of enunciating self; it emanates from a specific historical context as a medium for coping in one's social and material environment. Perkins contends that black children use it because it is more in harmony with the milieu in which they must survive compared with Received Standard English that does not provide them with the pliable speech they need to navigate the locale. The child "makes no effort to emulate so-called standard language because it acts

10. Gilyard, *Voices of the Self,* 43.
11. Ibid., 66.

as a conduit for articulating a way of life which is inconsistent with his own."[12]

The choice to use Black English as one's primary mode of communication, therefore, is grounded in several decisive moments for the African American child. It serves as a means of self-identification and an assertion of one's group identity. It reflects a commonality of social experience enabling one to negotiate and cope in a specific milieu. When spoken it vociferously announces one's rejection of the school's strategies that erect barriers of social distinction between self and family. This choice, however, is not made freely, but under severe duress. The enforcement of a language hierarchy can therefore be considered a crucial "external circumstance" to be taken into consideration as we seek to understand the effect of racial identification on school commitment.

Identification: Double Consciousness

For African Americans, "race" as an identity and as a nexus of identification has never been theorized or experienced as a simple, unitary, decontextualized subject position. At the beginning of the twentieth century—long before the poststructuralist discovery of the socially invented, multiply positioned, nature of "self"—W. E. B. Du Bois was describing the African American experience of self as unstable and dualistic.[13] Blacks identified both as Americans, as "citizens," and as a racially subordinated minority that was excluded politically and socially. This "double consciousness," as he described it, has served as the matrix for identification as "black" culturally and politically, grounding a culture of resistance and struggle against denial of the full rights of "citizens" because of "race."

Identification with and through "Blackness" is itself split through the work of representations. Blackness is doubly constituted: as systematically demeaning, derogatory, and dehumanizing through the representational system of the dominant social order; as well as resourceful, creative, diverse through the cultural production of black communities. This splitting means that on the one hand, black identity is always refracted through the norm—whiteness—and inscribed with distort-

---

12. Useni Eugene Perkins, *Home Is a Dirty Street: The Social Oppression of Black Children* (Chicago: Third World Press, 1975), 30.

13. Du Bois, *Souls of Black Folk.*

ing, disfiguring images the internalization of which results in a self-hatred that often manifests itself in an uneasy, ambivalent embrace of whiteness.[14]

On the other hand, subordination is the site of resistance in Du Bois's original formulation and that of subsequent African American scholars.[15] The position of Outsider becomes the vantage point for the production of a powerful critique of the social order and can foster a self-representation that contests the order as it stands. It is a position that is "a central location for the production of a counter-hegemonic discourse that is not just found in words but habits of being and the way one lives."[16]

Schoolboys and Troublemakers manifest this duality, this peculiar mixture of embrace and rejection. All of those I interviewed were physically identifiable as African American, though the wide differences in skin color and hair type manifested the rich diversity of people who identify as black in the United States today. All were identified in the school records as black. How did they identify themselves? When I asked the boys to identify themselves in terms of their race, the typical self-description was African American and/or black. But, there was a strong tendency for Schoolboys to identify themselves as multiracial or to distance themselves from the concept of race as a meaningful form of social distinction. Ricky, for example, described a preference for a race-blind language that invoked the school as his authenticating source for this definition:

> I just think of myself as a human being. Like our teacher was discussing like there's really no such thing as a black or a white race. White—that's just like a color and black is a color. African American, that's what people call black. So like I really don't like to think of others like that. So I have to say—a human being. On a test or something like that I'd say African American.

---

14. Fanon, *Black Skins, White Masks;* also Kenneth Clark, *Dark Ghetto: Dilemmas of Social Power* (New York: Harper and Row, 1965). Kenneth Clark argues that "Human beings who are forced to live under ghetto conditions and whose daily experience tells them that almost nowhere in society are they respected and granted the ordinary dignity and courtesy accorded to others, will, as a matter of course, begin to doubt their own self worth" (63–64).

15. For example, Collins, *Black Feminist Thought;* and bell hooks, *Yearning: Race, Gender, and Cultural Politics* (Boston: South End Press, 1990).

16. hooks, *Yearning,* 149.

While Ricky sees himself as "officially" black in terms of filling out forms, he rejects the notion that race is a meaningful social category in practice. He is critical of using it as a form of differentiation. Izrael, another Schoolboy, also eschewed black and white as categories for pigeonholing himself. He was proud of his mixed racial heritage when he described himself as Cherokee Indian, white, and black.

Schoolboys were more likely to make the link with being black and black culture in an abstract sense removed from their own daily experience. Tyrone, for instance, said that he preferred to be called African American rather than black, "because that's the mother land—Africa. It means that they was like the first people that was living on the earth. Because Adam and Eve was black."

In contrast, none of the Troublemakers identified themselves in multiracial terms, even though two of them came from households with white mothers, while a third boy who was extremely light-skinned clearly came from a mixed-race household. The Troublemakers were also more likely to talk of race as a tangible factor in their present existence. Jamar described racial identification as a feature of his everyday life when he mentioned church and being black as the two things that he "would never be afraid to stand up for."

Identification as black, even for Troublemakers, was not a total and seamless attachment. The discourse of individualism and choice ran through all of their explanations, especially when it came to describing their own life-chances. Along with the notion that race made a difference, they positioned themselves as agents of their own futures in a society in which "you can be whatever you want to be, as long as you work hard for it." They bring this image to their preparation for future careers.

Identification is a process of marking off symbolic boundaries through embodied performances of self that call up and draw on idealized figures and cultural representations as a reference to one's rightful membership and authenticity. Identification in this sense is a series of public acts of commitment to a subject position; this performance is fraught with anxiety about loss of self through exclusion and banishment as an outsider relative to that position. Both Schoolboys and Troublemakers work at these public acts of commitment, Schoolboys in visibly demonstrating attachment to school; Troublemakers demonstrating their disidentification with school through performance of Blackness that emphasizes their attachment to a raced subject position.

Before examining the differences between the Schoolboys and Troublemakers, I want to emphatically underscore the fluidity and lack of permanence of these two identities even as I invoke them for analytical purposes. Boys who are Troublemakers in school can be highly disciplined, obedient, and mindful of authority in specific contexts in school (jazz band, for example) and out of school (the baseball team). While it is extremely difficult to be recategorized from Troublemaker to Schoolboy, the latter are highly vulnerable to demotion to Troublemaker. The dilemmas of self-fashioning and tensions around group identification and commitment that Schoolboys face are not easily resolved and intensify in junior and senior high school, where many of them join the ranks of the Troublemakers.

Balancing Acts: Schoolboys

The Schoolboys are discussed first because their patterns of behavior and the dilemmas of subjectivity that they face reveal pressures and strains that boys now categorized as Troublemakers may have already faced and resolved. The Schoolboys work at conforming to the school's linguistic and relational codes in order to be seen as committed to the school's agenda. They are concerned with enactment of the details of fitting in, with achieving on the school's terms, with not getting into trouble. This means distancing themselves from "Blackness," which is represented as trouble and the disruption of order. While they do not labor under the burden of negative expectations from the school adults, their performative work is nonetheless difficult and emotionally taxing. Stressing one's identity as a human being or one's multiracial antecedents dilutes that part of yourself—the black part—which is defined as a problem.

Schoolboys must work to strike a balance between the expectations and demands of adults and peers in and out of school. They experience psychic strain as they weave back and forth across symbolic boundary lines. The ability to "act white," to perform the citational acts of that identity, is a tactic of survival, and a passport to admission to the circle of children who can be schooled. This difference may be rewarded in school by the adults but can be a problem in the construction of self among one's peers and with family and community outside the school. To perform this act too realistically, to appear to adopt whiteness not as a guise but an identity, is seen as an expression of self-hatred and race shame. The kids define this distancing oneself from Blackness as a loss of self-respect. Kids who perform "whiteness" too well, without any black undertones, are viewed dubiously by their peers. As Jamar pointed out,

> There's a lot of people—they black, right—they're like ashamed. They act white and stuff like that. If you black, you should be black. It's not any people out there who's white is ashamed of being white. They want to act like they are.

Ricky's mother worried about how his participation in his extended family or in the more abstract community of Blackness had been affected after he spent four years in a small private school in which he was the only African American pupil:

> When he'd go around his cousins—and I'm from a large family— he was always kinda made fun of because he spoke differently from the rest of the kids and he was like [she hesitates for several seconds, then laughs, embarrassed] white! But black! And I'm looking at this big tall kid and I told my husband, you know we really have to do something, make some changes here because that is not the real world that Ricky is in.

The change was to remove him from the private school and enroll him at Rosa Parks. Unlike Ricky, who identifies himself as a human being, his mother believes that because others will see him as black he must be prepared for a reality in which his race will make a difference. Ricky's mother, Shirley, went on to describe how the way he spoke differentiated him from other children in public school:

> There were some things like picking up the bad language. I mean not bad language like profanity, I mean bad language like bad grammar, dialect, and all of that. I didn't like that. One time he came home, that was when he first started public school, and he said, "Mom, you know what this kid said to me?" He was making the point that the kid spoke bad English. And so he was repeating what the kid said. "Isn't that funny?" he said. And I thought, golly, well, this is public school, the real world! Another time, he told me, "A kid said, 'I got a dollah! I got a dollah!' Mom, he didn't say

'dollar,' he said 'dollah.'" I thought, oh Lord and told him, "Well, don't you say anything!"

Because language is a significant marker for distinguishing "whiteness" and "Blackness," Shirley assumes that racialized difference is a feature of the "real world" inhabited by Ricky. She works to prepare him for it. Private school will give him access to the "cultural capital" symbolized through language use and demeanor that will make possible his upward mobility. On the other hand, she is concerned that Ricky has become estranged from an identity that knits him to family. Though diversity of language use has long been a feature of class divisions in black communities, language has become a marker of some racial solidarity, even for the middle class. His isolation from other black kids in a private school has meant that he has not acquired even the bicultural skills and interpretive frame to move back and forth between the worlds of the school and that of the family. By the end of the sixth grade, Ricky's parents have decided to send him back to private school because they feel that he has begun "falling behind" in public school. The strategies of class mobility as survival supersede notions of the importance of family and racial group solidarity.

In this delicate balancing act, a boy's multicultural mode of identification that blurs lines of difference helps to resolve the conflicting expectations from schools, peers, and family. It is both an expression of internalization of the institution's discourse of racelessness as well as a liberatory critique. As a critique it affirms the multiple possibilities of human connection and the many communities in which we learn about self and other. But the liberatory aspect of the insight is weakened by the context in which it is formulated, which enforces a hierarchy in the range of possibilities of becoming and being variously human. Under these circumstances, a multicultural mode of identification is more likely taken up to dilute, to de-emphasize the part of yourself, the black part, that is a problem.

The balancing act also poses dilemmas for gender identification: positioning oneself as indubitably masculine while at the same time sincerely embracing the role of Schoolboy is fraught with the potential for doubts about the authentic performance of both race and gender. As Harper points out, the performance of Blackness is marked by the "very uncertainty, tentativeness and burden of proof seen to characterize conventional masculinity."[17] A too careful observance of school rules, an adherence to Standard English, for example, undermines the representation of black boy–ness. Yet, as soon as African American boys begin to enact masculinity in referential acts of the Good Bad Boy, they risk demotion to the category of Troublemaker.

Fordham and Ogbu's study of older students corroborates this dilemma. They found that to "act white" had very different consequences for boys than for girls. Males who were seen to "act white" were also deemed less masculine. The researchers claimed that for a boy to be labeled a "brainiac" was to simultaneously call into question his manhood; while to be taking college preparatory courses was tantamount to being gay.[18] African American boys who were "doing well" had to deal not only with the possibility of exile from the racial community, but with being "unmanned."

This finding that being a Schoolboy exerts increasing pressure on individuals to "prove" their masculinity was confirmed in a series of interviews I conducted with African American men who were college students. Some of these men described strategies they had devised for managing to be seen as committed students by the school and "real" boys by their peers. The ability to fight or to be exceptionally gifted in some field of sports were the most prominent skills mentioned. Boys who had gained a reputation for being able to physically defend themselves were admired for their prowess; their ability in the classroom then became something admirable, an indicator that they could compete in many arenas. But the reputation for fighting had to be acquired outside of school, since fights in school would jeopardize one's standing with the teachers and undermine one's apparent academic commitment. Another strategy was to be extremely quick verbally so they could play "the dozens" with the best. This game of verbal aggression and competition only signifies male prowess when played in the vernacular. Therefore, the reputation for being a rap artist must be acquired out of earshot of most teachers. Certainly, the kind of classroom performances described earlier would undo positive reputations with the teachers. Many Schoolboys disidentify with school and join the ranks of the Troublemakers by the time they get into high school because of this tug of war. Troublemakers are not born, they are made.

17. Harper, *Are We Not Men?* 40.
18. Ibid., 194.

Race Matters: Acting Black

The Troublemakers have resolved the dilemma of subjectivity differently. They emphasize race rather than exorcise it as the school demands; turning it up, rather than down. They make race difference visible in school as an assertion of the "we," of a group rather than an individual condition. Troublemakers are less likely to hide their use of Black English and are likely to use it in moments of discipline. These are situations where they are being "shamed," and saving face demands a response that speaks of masculinity in a grammar of power. Unity is also affirmed through physical displays such as clothing style, through the formation of a group presence, as well as through open challenges and tests of the race-blindness of the institution.

From a marginalized space in school, Troublemakers constitute alternative notions of self around a group identity, specifically around a notion of Blackness. This unity is galvanized through observation and experience, through current events and their racial frame, through the decoding of race representations, through the active performance of "Blackness" and the consequences of self-fashioning through this identity.

Troublemakers are more likely to wear symbolic badges of their identification; to dress the part. These badges are not just the predictable items of youth "style" such as baseball caps turned back or with sales tags still attached; baggy pants sagging down low on the hips; sports shoes; Chicago Bulls jackets. While this style has its roots in a black popular culture and is seen by school as representing a subversive presence that they work to rule out of school, it is one that has been adopted by youth across a wide spectrum of race and class and is now mass-marketed globally. So to identify one's "Blackness," one's difference as a group from other youth symbolically through clothing and style requires a special touch. Horace wears a T-shirt with a picture of Malcolm X and the quote "By any means necessary" to the jazz band recital when all the other kids are wearing white shirts and black pants. Claude wears a black hooded sweatshirt with the hood up in a gangster style that references black rappers who are folk heroes.

A common experience and common identities in school encourages the crystallization of friendship groups among the Troublemakers, who hang out together on the playground and network during the day. The school has its own perspective on these groups and their power to pose alternative agendas and activities. This perspective draws on cultural images of gender and race in assessing their challenge to school order. A group of African American girls walking around the Rosa Parks schoolyard at recess is not viewed as a threat, a mass that needs to be dispersed into separate parts or channeled into organized sports. In fact, a group of girls talking or just hanging out together is a typical scene in the yard. Boys who are engaged in hanging out, who are not involved in a game, are likely to be watched closely and with some suspicion by adults. Most of these are small groupings of three or four boys, but some become especially visible to the school as they grow in size. The school personnel also pay close attention to which of the children are in the group.

One group of boys at Rosa Parks makes its racial presence highly visible. It is made up of the most marginalized kids in the school. The adults on the schoolyard at recess pay special attention to this crew of between five and seven African American boys who hang out together generally and are not involved in the football or baseball games. They band together at the edges of the games under the watchful eye of the playground aides and vice principal, who actively attempt to keep other children from joining them. They loiter, they linger, they observe, they are deep in a circle of conversation or they are frozen in silent and ominous deliberation. All the adults are aware of their presence as they congregate, disperse on an adult's command, only to reconvene in some other spot not too far away. Unlike some of the other kids who get in trouble for defying the orders of the adults who police the playground, this group of friends seemingly avoids unnecessary contact with the adults. Their surveillance is so vigilant, however, that they are often implicated in trouble.

The name they have chosen to call themselves is a statement of their identification. They have appropriated NFL, the initials of the National Football League, as their group's tag changing it's meaning to "Niggers for Life." They make themselves visible as a crew by tagging their logos onto stop signs, bus benches, even the poster with the code of school rules in the Punishing Room. It is an identity that they are not afraid to flaunt at the school, and the adults know who they are and what NFL signifies. It is their bond, their statement, their pledge to each other and to themselves. It is a statement of collective racial identity as it simultaneously expresses their defiance and distance from school.

You have to notice Claude, the boy who is always at the center of the group. Though he is short for his age, skinny—a real runt—he has a presence that draws my attention. It says look at me. He had been described as a "a little Napoleon" by one of the student specialists. No matter how hot the day, Claude wears his black Raiders jacket and baseball cap. His cap today says "Pooh Man" on it, which I am quite sure is not a reference to Winnie-the-Pooh. Later when I ask him, I find that Pooh Man is an Oakland, California, rapper in the gangster style. He tells me that one of Pooh Man's best-known songs is from the movie *Juice* and is called "Sex, Money, and Murder." Under his jacket, Claude wears a thin, worn-out, dingy T-shirt. All of his friends wear baseball caps. Two of them wear black hooded sweatshirts and big wide-legged pants.

The style tells who they are to the world of the school and the streets. They have power, they are a presence: watch out for us, we're bad, we're cool. They drift from one edge of the playground to another. They do not participate in the organized games at the end of the yard. Because of this, I assumed that they, unlike the other boys I had interviewed, were not practicing to be baseball or football stars. However, I discovered when I attended the tryouts for the citywide football program that Claude and some of his friends were in the competition for the city league.

These boys were not participating in school games partly because school adults hemmed them in, isolated them, and in fact, stigmatized their inclusion in approved social activities. One boy heading over to their group on the playground was warned away by the student specialist: "You'd better not go over there. You know that you'll get in trouble if you do." This caution emphasized that by virtue of being with those kids you became more visible, more likely to be singled out for punishment.

Claude has a bulging file in the cabinet where all the punishment records are kept. I asked the vice principal why he had not been put in the PALS program because he seemed to me to be a prime candidate, given the general profile of the students the program was said to serve. Claude is one of those boys who is deemed "unsalvageable." "It's a waste of time and energy to do anything with him," was the vice principal's diagnosis. "There are a lot of kids who can use some help, but the good kids always get neglected and the kids who will never make the grade get the attention." Here is precisely the way that the concept of the endangered species is brought into the school and used as a resource for determining the allocation of scarce and precious funding.

The baddest kids in school are the most visibly black-identified as they construct subjectivity around cultural representations of an "authentic" Blackness derived from cultural icons of the gangster as a renegade, transgressive masculinity. By encoding the NFL logo with the name Niggers for Life they are attaching themselves to potent symbols of race/gender power as well as identifying with a specific class. The initials NFL as the acronym for the football league conjures up images of male power at its extreme: ruthlessly competitive and physically awesome men of enormous bulk and unbelievable salaries.

This is a masculine power that is animated through the figure of the Nigger, undoubtedly the name that most epitomizes the stigmatization and denigration of Blackness in the racial hierarchy of the United States. At the same time, *Nigga* has been reappropriated by black males as a term for recognizing and hailing each other; as a gesture of camaraderie and a shorthand acknowledgment of a shared knowledge and history. The group at Rosa Parks claims this membership and connection as they distance themselves from a worldview that requires disassociation from the community of origin. There is a class identity as well as a racial community being claimed. The designation *Nigga,* as naming of self, makes the link between race and class. Social historian Robin Kelley suggests the term is rooted in "the hood," the urban, inner-city black community characterized by staggering levels of unemployment and poverty. He contends that the term is employed to differentiate

> urban black working-class males from the black bourgeoisie and African Americans in positions of institutional authority. Their point is simple: the experiences of young black men in the inner city are not universal to all black people, and, in fact, they recognize that some African Americans play in a role in perpetuating their oppression.[19]

The NFL youth distance themselves from the class mobility strategy preferred by the school and identify with the poor, black, rebellious "hood," whose very presence the school deplores.

---

19. Robin Kelley, *Race Rebels: Culture, Politics, and the Black Working Class* (New York: Free Press, 1994), 210. For a discussion of the use and meaning of the term *nigger* in black communities see pages 209–14.

Special Treatment: Reverse Discourse

Another mode of making race visible in school is through direct confrontation; by speaking out and charging racial discrimination. The
Troublemakers have developed theories about the external circumstances they encounter. This formulation is based on the observations
of kids, in general, that overwhelmingly the children who are marginalized within the school are black.

> My teacher this year . . . she be racist. When she tells us to put
> something away—mostly all the black kids—she says I'm taking it.
> When it's like the white kid—she say, one more time play with that
> and I'm taking it away. And then she gives them another chance.
> Everybody, everybody knows that it's so! My friend, Lucas, he's
> white and he says it's not fair. It's definitely not fair. But he's not
> racism [sic] at all. He's okay. He's nice. He's funny. He plays around
> in class sometimes.

This comment reveals one of the features of the Troublemakers'
well-elaborated theory about how race operates in the school to differentiate among children. In their analysis, racism involves a complex set
of social relations that have to do with differential power and its
enforcement rather than being about a simple congruence between skin
color and racial politics. Trey points out that his white friend has
observed that the teacher treats African American students more puni-
tively and takes an antiracist position. Many black youth identified
African American teachers as racist. One boy, describing his classroom
teacher, said, "She don't like the black kids. She be racist. And she be
black." It is important to note that both African American and white
teachers identified by kids as racist were characterized similarly by some
of their African American colleagues in the school, though far more
guardedly and in the safe-coded language of the day, as in, "She has a
hard time dealing with black boys."

The ideology that the educational system is race-blind is also contested by adults in the school. African American staff members and a
few white adults speak bitterly and with frustration—but cautiously
and privately—about the way that race makes a difference in the treatment of children. In public discussions, however, they rarely mention
race because they know that raising the issue is volatile, divisive, and

will result in their own marginalization. They fear becoming labeled "troublemakers" themselves.

Not only did the boys observe and create theories about teachers, but they tested their observations and challenged the assumption of race-blindness in spontaneous demonstrations. It is instructive to recount one of these challenges from the three different standpoints that were told to me. The teacher involved, a white woman, told me about the "couch incident" in this way:

> Y'know, I don't let the children sit on the couch during silent read-ing because they just congregate and start talking. Mark [a white boy] finished all his work and he went to sit on the couch. Then I caught Trey sitting there reading and told him he had to get back to his seat. Of course he had to talk back, saying I pick on certain kids and let others get away with murder. He kept up the arguing, so I sent him to the office. Then Trey's father calls up after school and yells at me on the phone that I'm a racist! That I'm always picking on the black kids. Of course when he comes in with the mother, he was pretty quiet. She just reeked of alcohol—made me sick to my stomach. So today Horace goes and sits on the couch during silent reading. Testing me! When I called him on it, he said, then how come you let Mark do it. I just told him, Horace, you know better than this. Better go back to your seat or you're not going on the field trip.

The teacher referred to this incident more than once in conversa-tions with me. She was genuinely upset that her action was considered racist since she prided herself on being highly conscious of race as dis-crimination and worked at being color-blind in her relationships. I also heard more about the incident from one of the African American stu-dent specialists:

> Horace and Trey, that's a bad combination! That kid [Trey] has a jail-cell with his name on it. He says Mrs. Deane picks on black kids. He was mouthing off the other day and wants to make it a race thing. That is so passé. He brought his parents in. His father is a pathetic, weedy guy. Hardly bigger than Trey. The father yells at Mrs. D. on the phone and then comes into the office and was really meek. [The specialist snorts contemptuously. He is very

worked up about this.] Right there, in front of everybody, Trey asks why the "Friday News" [weekly newsletter sent home to all the parents] is just full of *good* things and doesn't report on any of the *bad* things in the school. I told him that wasn't the purpose of the "Friday News."

Both school adults, one African American, one white, refuse the racial interpretation of the incident and invalidate the perspective of the boy and his family. They affirm the official position that it is not the boy's race that determines the punishment that is meted out, but the boy's character, his inherent criminality. This rejection of the plausibility of the accusation is bolstered by representation of the mother as "drunk" and therefore not to be taken seriously. The delegitimation of the father is specifically gendered; he is "unmanned" as small and weak. The power of the parents to advocate on behalf of their kid is dismissed.

Trey tells me the story at a much later date. He recalls it in a rather offhand, no-big-deal way. For him, these skirmishes are part of the everyday experience of school. He witnesses the lack of legitimacy and power that his parents bring to his defense against school adults. Trey knows that just as his own tests and charges against the school are discounted and marginalized, so are those of his mother and father. He cannot factor in adult power to bolster his claims within the school against adult authority.

The official discourse of school insists that the "difference" among schoolchildren emerges out of standardized tests and psychological examinations; that in a hierarchy of worthiness "difference" is about individuals, not about a social collective; that being identified as African American within the racialized accounting system of the school district is of no further account. The couch story brings into the open "race" as a feature of social relations in the school; as a basis for differentiation. Trey positions himself as black and, as such, racially marked for special (mis)treatment. The teacher is adamant about discrediting this interpretation of the event because to allow it to be credible is to call into question the neutral, universalistic, impartiality of the rule/authority structure. It is also to call into question her own sincere presentation of self as unbiased.

I have situated getting in trouble in the context of the workday. The Troublemakers constitute alternative modalities of identification for themselves in the face of the school's classification of them as academic failures, troublemakers, bound for jail. They use the performance of masculinity through dramatic performances and disruptions in class, through making a name through fighting as a strategy for recouping a sense of self as creative, powerful, competent in the face of the tedium of the school's workday. They refuse the school's assessment of them as failing because of their own individual problems and incapacities by affirming a group identity. They assert that they are receiving special treatment because they are black. They invoke racism as a discourse to counter the discourse of individual choice of the school.

For African American males at Rosa Parks, to be normalized within the school's individualizing discourse is to agree to the school's explanatory frame that not only failure in school but one's very life chances, prison or profession, are a matter of personal choice rather than the consequences of structures of inequality and relations of power. Success or failure, it's up to you. You, rather than external forces, are the problem. To embrace the school agenda is to distance oneself from a group identification in the process of fashioning one's individuality. The Troublemakers refuse the school's characterization of the problem as solely about individuals. They reframe the school's criteria for evaluation and assessment of worthiness and competence of students by asserting that race is used as a criteria for teacher judgments and interactions with children. This reverse discourse draws on a popular knowledge sedimented in family and public space to interpret their experience. As the Troublemakers disidentify with school and take up alternative identities they engage in social mobility strategies and paths to adult careers that diverge drastically from the school's and make the formal curriculum seem irrelevant.

The Schoolboys negotiate both race and gender identities among peers, school adults, and family. They are more likely to have internalized the school's position that academic prowess is a matter of individual capacity and choice. They are more likely to constitute themselves through multicultural language and representations. While Schoolboys may employ similar strategies for enlivening the tedium of the workday such as fights and class disruptions, they are more likely to be spectators or to engage in these practices in less public circumstances.

Moments of public punishment are powerful learning experiences about social location and worthiness for everyone involved. These cultural spectacles signal profound meanings of "racial" difference through a performance that engages audience as well as actors in a reenactment of social roles within relations of power. In these spectacles, the singling out, the naming, the displaying of that which is "bad" affirms the institutional power to stigmatize. D'Andre, like Gary, like Horace becomes a lesson to other children in the room about what it means to be caught in the spotlight of disciplinary power. They learn that to get in trouble with authority is to risk becoming the example, the spectacle for the consumption of others. It is to risk, not mere momentary humiliation, but the separation from one's peers as different. The racial message that structures the interaction is that Blackness in general is a problem, makes trouble, gets in the way of learning, doesn't know how to behave properly, must be expelled.

PROMOTION EXERCISES

The sixth-grade promotion exercises were to be held on the playground, and all of the sixth-grade classes rehearsed for the big event each day for four days. Not all of the children are present at the rehearsal, however. Some, like Claude, have been eliminated from the procedure, and he sits watching the lines of kids file out on the playground through the window of the Punishing Room.

Each teacher, all women, stands watching her class issue out of the building in straggly lines and continually bark out orders about space, pace, and proper bodily demeanor. "Hands out of pockets," "Straighten up that line," "So-and-so, you're too close to the person in front of you. Slow down," or "So-and-so, walk a little faster." One of the teachers says smugly, "This is your graduation, you know."

Once the kids are assembled alphabetically and by class, they practice reciting together the Kahlil Gibran poem that they have learned by heart.

The morning of the promotional activity ("We don't call it graduation because it's not strictly speaking a graduation from anything," one of the teachers tells me) is sunny and beautiful. Extended families stream onto the playground, which is covered with neat rows of folding chairs, and take their seats. The kids come filing out of the building, the seriousness of the ritual written all over their solemn faces. There is no problem with pace or space now. They know how to conduct themselves when it's time to do so; they just have little patience for regimentation and too much control.

Lamar, who had been suspended and forbidden to participate in the exercises, appears in the line, looking the clichés of angelic all rolled into one: he is as good as gold, as neat as a pin, as if butter wouldn't melt in his mouth. His head is completely shaven, the teachers have decided to turn a blind eye to his presence. I hear one of the student specialists saying that he and his mom think he got away with something but "she goin'ta be real sorry later."

I see Horace's mother and sister, Terrence's family, D'Andre's grandmother. Everyone has dressed up for the occasion. I am struck by the generational mix—grandmothers, mothers, fathers, many babies. Babies are passed around with oohs and aahs of approval.

Principal, teachers, and students all perform the ceremony with impressive displays of approval and respect. The valedictorian is an African American girl. Tears come to my eyes as she speaks so seriously and wisely. Everyone is listening attentively.

At this moment, we are all at our very best.

chapter eight
dreams

The purpose of education, finally, is to create in a person the ability to look at the world for himself, to make his own decisions, to say to himself this is black or this is white, to decide for himself whether there is a God in heaven or not. To ask questions of the universe, and then learn to live with those questions, is the way he achieves his own identity. But no society is really anxious to have that kind of person around. What societies really, ideally, want is a citizenry which will simply obey the rules of society. If a society succeeds in this, that society is about to perish.

—JAMES BALDWIN, "A TALK TO TEACHERS"

This book began with an anecdote about the school's vice principal identifying a small boy as someone who had a jail-cell with his name on it. I started with this story to illustrate how school personnel made predictive decisions about a child's future based on a whole ensemble of negative assumptions about African American males and their life-chances. The kids, however, imagined their future in a more positive light. They neither saw themselves as being "on the fast track to prison," as predicted by school personnel, nor did they see themselves as working at low-level service jobs as adults. The boys, in fact, had a decidedly optimistic view about their future.

This scenario, at such variance with that of the administrator's, became clear to me in my final semester at Rosa Parks, when the sixth-graders wrote an essay on the jobs they would like to have as adults. As I scanned these written accounts of students' dreams, I became conscious of a striking pattern. The overwhelming majority of the boys aspired to be professional athletes—playing basketball, baseball, or football—when they grew up. The reasons they gave for this choice were remarkably similar: the sport was something they were good at; it was work they would enjoy doing; and they would make a lot of money.[1] They acknowledged it would be extremely difficult to have such a career, but, they argued, if you worked hard and had the talent, you could make it.

These youthful essays confirmed what the boys had told me in interviews about the adult occupations they imagined for themselves. While a few had mentioned other options such as becoming a stand-up comedian, a Supreme Court justice, or a rap musician, almost all expressed the desire to play on an NBA or NFL team. This was not just an empty fantasy. Most of the boys with whom I had contact in my research were actively and diligently involved in after-school sports, not just as play, but in the serious business of preparing themselves for adult careers. This dream was supported in tangible ways by parents who boasted about their sons' prowess, found time to take them to practice, and cheered their teams on at games. I had assumed initially that these after-school sports activities were primarily a way of parents keeping kids busy to guard against their getting into drugs and sex. However, after talking to parents and kids I realized that what I observed was not just about keeping boys out of trouble but was preparation for future careers.

The occupational dreams of these boys are not at all unique. A survey by Northeastern University's Center for the Study of Sport in Society found that two-thirds of African American males between the ages of thirteen and eighteen believe they can earn a living playing professional sports.[2] Nor is this national pattern for black youth really surprising. For African American males, disengagement from the school's agenda for approval and success is a psychic survival mechanism; so imagining a future occupation for which schooling seems irrelevant is eminently rational. A career as a professional athlete represents the possibility of attaining success in terms of the dominant society via a path that makes schooling seem immaterial, while at the same time affirming central aspects of identification.

I have argued that the boys distance themselves from the school's agenda to avoid capitulating to its strategies for fashioning a self for

---

1. It is interesting to note that the girls in the class all responded in a stereotypical way. The vast majority wanted to have "helping" careers in traditional female occupations: teachers, nurses, psychologists. None of the girls gave money as a reason for their choice.

2. Survey reported in *U.S. News and World Report*, March 24, 1997, 46.

upward mobility—strategies requiring black youth to distance themselves from family and neighborhood, to reject the language, the style
of social interaction, the connections in which identities are grounded.
From the highly idealized viewpoint of youth, a career in sports does
not appear to require these strategic detachments. Their heroes—players like Michael Jordan, Scottie Pippen, Dennis Rodman, Rickey Hen-
derson, to name just a few—have achieved the highest reaches of success without disguising or eradicating their Blackness.

But these are only dreams, for the chances of getting drafted by
professional teams are slim to nonexistent. The probability has been
calculated as somewhere in the region of one in ten thousand that a
youth will end up in pro football or basketball.[3] Based on these facts, a
plethora of popular and scholarly literature, as well as fiction and documentary films, have underscored how unrealistic such ambitions are,
making the point that few youths who pour their hearts, energy, and
schooling into sports will actually make it to the professional teams
where the glory lies and the money is made.[4] They point out this discouraging scenario in order to persuade young black males to rechannel
their energies and ambitions into conventional school learning that
allows for more "realistic" career options.

Yet, in reality, for these youth efforts to attain high-status occupations through academic channels are just as likely to fail, given the conditions of their schooling and the unequal distribution of resources
across school systems.[5] Children attending inner-city public schools are
more likely to end up in dead-end, minimum-wage, service sector jobs
because they do not have the quality of education available in the sub-
urban public or elite private schools. Today's dreams will be transformed into tomorrow's nightmares.

----

3. Raymie E. McKerrow and Norinne H. Daly, "The Student Athlete," *National
Forum* 71, no. 4 (1990): 44.

4. For examples see Gary A. Sailes, "The Exploitation of the Black Athlete: Some
Alternative Solutions," *Journal of Negro Education* 55, no. 4 (1986); Robert M. Sellers and
Gabriel P. Kuperminc, "Goal Discrepancy in African-American Male Student-Athletes'
Unrealistic Expectations for Careers in Professional Sports," *Journal of Black Psychology* 23,
no. 1 (1997); Alexander Wolf, "Impossible Dream," *Sports Illustrated,* June 2, 1997; and
John Hoberman, *Darwin's Athletes: How Sport Has Damaged Black America and Preserved
the Myth of Race* (Boston: Houghton Mifflin, 1997).

5. For a shocking demonstration of the difference between schools see Kozol, *Savage
Inequalities.*

While I rejected the labeling practices of the school vice principal, in my opening chapter, I also reluctantly admitted that by the end of the school year I, too, had come to suspect that a prison cell might have a place in the future of many Rosa Parks students. In contrast to the vice principal, this foreboding was not by any means rooted in a conclusion I had come to about individual children's proclivity for a life of crime, nor was it grounded in any evidence that, as some labeling theories hold, individuals stigmatized as deviant come to internalize this identity and adopt delinquent behaviors at rates higher than other youth. Rather it emanated from my increased awareness of the way that racial bias in institutions external to school, such as the media and criminal justice system, mirrored and converged with that of the educational system. This convergence intensifies and weights the odds heavily in favor of a young black male ending up in jail. School seems to feed into the prison system, but what exactly is the connection between the two? What are the practical links between the punishing rooms, jailhouses, and dungeons of educational institutions and the cells of local, state, and federal prison systems? There are both long-term causal links as well as visible, immediate connections.

There are serious, long-term effects of being labeled a Troublemaker that substantially increase one's chances of ending up in jail. In the daily experience of being so named, regulated, and surveilled, access to the full resources of the school are increasingly denied as the boys are isolated in nonacademic spaces in school or banished to lounging at home or loitering on the streets. Time in the school dungeon means time lost from classroom learning; suspension, at school or at home, has a direct and lasting negative effect on the continuing growth of a child. When removal from classroom life begins at an early age, it is even more devastating, as human possibilities are stunted at a crucial formative period of life. Each year the gap in skills grows wider and more handicapping, while the overall process of disidentification that I have described encourages those who have problems to leave school rather than resolve them in an educational setting.

There is a direct relationship between dropping out of school and doing time in jail: the majority of black inmates in local, state, and federal penal systems are high school dropouts.[6] Therefore, if we want to begin to break the ties between school and jail, we must first create educational systems that foster kids' identification with school and encourage them not to abandon it.

One significant but relatively small step that could be taken to foster this attachment would be to reduce the painful, inhospitable climate of school for African American children through the validation and affirmation of Black English, the language form that many of the children bring from home/neighborhood. As I pointed out earlier, the denigration of this form and the assumptions made about the academic potential of speakers of Ebonics pose severe dilemmas of identification for black students—especially for males. The legitimation of Black English in the world of the school would not only enrich the curriculum but would undoubtedly provide valuable lessons to all students about sociolinguistics and the contexts in which standard and nonstandard forms are appropriate. The necessary prerequisite for this inclusion would be a mandatory program for teachers and school administrators to educate them about the nature and history of Ebonics. This was of course the very change called for by the Oakland School Board in 1996. However, it is clear from the controversy that ensued and the highly racialized and obfuscatory nature of the national media's coverage of the Oakland Resolution that there is serious opposition to any innovations that appear to challenge the supremacy of English.[7]

There is also an immediate, ongoing connection between school and jail. Schools mirror and reinforce the practices and ideological systems of other institutions in the society. The racial bias in the punishing systems of the school reflects the practices of the criminal justice system. Black youth are caught up in the net of the juvenile justice system at a rate of two to four times that of white youth.[8] Does this mean that African American boys are more prone to criminal activity than

---

6. United States Department of Justice, *Profile of Jail Inmates* (Washington, D.C.: U.S. Government Printing Office, 1980). Two-thirds of the black inmates have less than a twelfth-grade education, while the rate of incarceration drops significantly for those who have twelve or more years of schooling.

7. For an excellent overview of the debate that ensued over the Oakland School Board's resolution and a discussion of Ebonics, see Theresa Perry and Lisa Delpit, eds. *The Real Ebonics Debate: Power, Language, and the Education of African American Children* (Boston: Beacon Press, 1998).

8. Miller, *Search and Destroy,* 73.

white boys? There is evidence that this is not the case. A study by Huizinga and Elliot demonstrates that the contrast in incarceration statistics is the result of a different *institutional response* to the race of the youth rather than the difference in actual behavior. Drawing on a representative sample of youth between the ages of eleven and seventeen, they compare the delinquent acts individual youth admit to committing in annual self-report interviews with actual police records of delinquency in the areas in which the boys live. Based on the self-reports, they conclude that there were few, if any, differences in the number or type of delinquent acts perpetrated by the two racial groups. What they did find, however, was that there was a substantially and significantly higher risk that the minority youth would be apprehended and charged for these acts by police than the whites who reported committing the same kind of offenses. They conclude that "minorities appear to be at greater risk for being charged with more serious offenses than whites involved in comparable levels of delinquent behavior, a factor which may eventually result in higher incarceration rates among minorities."[9]

Images of black male criminality and the demonization of black children play a significant role in framing actions and events in the justice system in a way that is similar to how these images are used in school to interpret the behavior of individual miscreants. In both settings, the images result in differential treatment based on race. Jerome G. Miller, who has directed juvenile justice detention systems in Massachusetts and Illinois, describes how this works:

> I learned very early on that when we got a black youth, virtually everything—from arrest summaries, to family history, to rap sheets, to psychiatric exams, to "waiver" hearings as to whether or not he would be tried as an adult, to final sentencing—was skewed. If a middle-class white youth was sent to us as "dangerous," he was more likely actually to be so than the black teenager given the same label. The white teenager was more likely to have been afforded competent legal counsel and appropriate psychiatric and psychological testing, tried in a variety of privately funded options, and dealt with more sensitively and individually at every stage of the juvenile justice processing. For him to be labeled "dan-

9. David Huizinga and Delbert Elliot, "Juvenile Offenders: Prevalence, Offender Incidence, and Arrest Rates by Race," paper presented at "Race and the Incarceration of Juveniles," Racine, Wisconsin, December 1986, quoted in ibid., 72.

gerous," he had to have done something very serious indeed. By contrast, the black teenager was more likely to be dealt with as a stereotype from the moment the handcuffs were first put on—easily and quickly relegated to the "more dangerous" end of the "violent-nonviolent" spectrum, albeit accompanied by an official record meant to validate each of a biased series of decisions.[10]

Miller indicates that racial disparities are most obvious at the very earliest and the latest stages of processing of youth through the juvenile justice system, and African American male youth are more likely to be apprehended and caught up in the system in the very beginning. They are also more likely "to be waived to adult court, and to be adjudicated delinquent. If removed from their homes by the court, they were less likely to be placed in the better-staffed and better-run private-group home facilities and more likely to be sent into state reform schools."[11]

Given the poisonous mix of stereotyping and profiling of black males, their chances of ending up in the penal system as a juvenile is extremely high. Even if a boy manages to avoid getting caught within the juvenile justice system through luck or the constant vigilance of parents, his chances of being arrested and jailed are staggeringly high as an adult. A 1995 report by the Sentencing Project finds that nearly one in three African Americans in his twenties is in prison or jail, on probation or parole, on any given day.[12]

The school experience of African American boys is simultaneously replicated in the penal system through processes of surveillance, policing, charges, and penalties. The kids recognize this; the names they give to disciplinary spaces are not just coincidence. They are referencing the chilling parallels between the two.

A systematic racial bias is exercised in the regulation, control, and discipline of children in the United States today. African American males are apprehended and punished for misbehavior and delinquent acts that are overlooked in other children. The punishment that is meted out is usually more severe than that for other children. This racism that systematically extinguishes the potential and constrains the

10. Ibid., 78.
11. Ibid., 73.
12. Sentencing Project, *Young Black Americans and the Criminal Justice System: Five Years Later* (Washington, D.C.: Sentencing Project, 1995). This unprecedented figure reflects an increase from the 1990 Sentencing Project findings that one in four black males in their twenties was under the supervision of the criminal justice system.

world of possibilities for black males would be brutal enough if it were restricted to school, but it is replicated in other disciplinary systems of the society, the most obvious parallel being the juvenile justice system.

Open Endings

Whenever I give a talk about my research, I am inevitably asked what ideas or recommendations I have for addressing the conditions that I describe. What do I think should be done, listeners want to know? The first few times this happened I felt resentful partly because I knew my colleagues who did research on subjects other than schooling were rarely asked to come up with policy recommendations to address the problems they had uncovered. This request for solutions is made on the assumption that schools, unlike the family and workplace, are basically sound albeit with flaws that need adjusting.

My hesitation to propose solutions comes from a conviction that minor inputs, temporary interventions, individual prescriptions into schools are vastly inadequate to remedy an institution that is fundamentally flawed and whose goal for urban black children seems to be the creation of "a citizenry which will simply obey the rules of society." I stand convinced that a restructuring of the entire educational system is what is urgently required if we are to produce the thoughtful, actively questioning citizens that Baldwin describes in the epigraph to this chapter. To make the point, however, that small programs at Rosa Parks school such as PALS—always underfunded, always dependent on grants of "soft" money that required big promises of quick fixes—served always too few and would inevitably disappear entirely or be co-opted by the institution, was so disheartening, so paralyzing that I am forced to rethink my reply. Is it all or nothing? Can we eradicate forms of institutional racism in school without eliminating racism in the society at large? Are the alternatives either quick hopeless fixes or paralysis because small changes cannot make a difference in the long run? How can the proliferation of local initiatives that spring up, in hope and with enthusiasm, be sustained without taking on institutional goals and attitudes? How can emergent forms appear alongside and out of the old? Most important of all, will attention be paid to the counterdiscourse of the Troublemakers themselves?

When I asked the kids, Schoolboys and Troublemakers, how they thought schooling might be improved, they looked at me blankly. I think they shared my sense of despair. The responses that I wrung out of them seemed trivial, even frivolous. It was all about play, about recreation: a longer recess, bigger play areas, playgrounds with grass not asphalt—and so on. The list that I had dreamed up was the opposite of frivolous. It was all about curriculum: smaller classes, Saturday tutoring, year-round school, antiracist training for student teachers, mutual respect between adults and youth. One thing I am convinced of is that more punitive measures, tighter discipline, greater surveillance, more prisons —the very path that our society seems to be determined to pursue—is not the approach to take. Perhaps, allowing ourselves to imagine the possibilities—what could, should, and must be—is an indispensable first step.

works cited

American Psychiatric Association. *Diagnostic and Statistical Manual of Mental Disorders.* 4th ed. Washington, D.C.: American Psychiatric Association, 1994.

Anderson, Elijah. *Streetwise.* Chicago: University of Chicago Press, 1990.

Ariès, Phillipe. *Centuries of Childhood: A Social History of Family Life.* New York: Vintage, 1962.

Aronowitz, Stanley, and Henry A. Giroux. *Education under Siege: The Conservative, Liberal, and Radical Debate over Schooling.* South Hadley, Mass.: Bergen and Garvey, 1985.

Barrett, Michele. *Women's Oppression Today: Problems in Marxist Feminist Analysis.* London: New Left Books, 1980.

Bernstein, Basil. "Social Class, Language, and Socialization." In *Power and Ideology in Education,* ed. Jerome Karabel and A. H. Halsey, 473–86. New York: Oxford University Press, 1977.

———. *Towards a Theory of Educational Transmission.* Vol. 3 of *Class, Codes, and Control.* London: Routledge and Kegan Paul, 1974.

Billingsley, Andrew. *Climbing Jacob's Ladder: The Enduring Legacy of African-American Families.* New York: Simon and Schuster, 1992.

Bourdieu, Pierre. "The Economics of Linguistic Exchanges." *Social Science Information* 26, no. 6 (1977): 645–68.

———. "Symbolic Power." In *Identity and Structure: Issues in the Sociology of Education,* ed. Dennis Gleeson, 112–19. Driffield, England: Studies in Education, 1977.

Bourdieu, Pierre, and Jean-Claude Passeron. *Reproduction in Education, Society, and Culture.* Trans. Richard Nice. Beverly Hills: Sage, 1977.

Bowles, Samuel, and Herbert Gintis. *Schooling in Capitalist America: Educational Reform and the Contradictions of Economic Life.* New York: Basic Books, 1976.

Brewer, Rose M. "Theorizing Race, Class, and Gender: The New Scholarship of Black Feminist Intellectuals and Black Women's Labor." In *Theorizing Black Feminisms: The Visionary Pragmatism of Black Women,* ed. Stanlie M. James and Abena P. A. Busia, 13–30. New York: Routledge, 1993.

Butler, Judith. *Bodies That Matter: On the Discursive Limits of "Sex."* New York: Routledge, 1993.

———. "Performative Acts and Gender Constitution: An Essay in Phenomenology and Feminist Theory." *Theatre Journal* 40, no. 4 (1988): 519–31.

Carmichael, Stokely, and Charles V. Hamilton. *Black Power: The Politics of Liberation in America.* New York: Vintage, 1967.

Casanova, Ursula. "Rashomon in the Classroom: Multiple Perspectives of Teachers, Parents, and Students." In *Children at Risk: Poverty, Minority Status, and Other Issues in*

Educational Equity, ed. Andres Barona and Eugene E. Garcia, 135–49. Washington, D.C.: National Association of School Psychologists, 1990.

Cassidy, Frederic G., ed. *Dictionary of American Regional English.* Vol. 2. Cambridge: Harvard University Press, 1991.

Clark, Kenneth, *Dark Ghetto: Dilemmas of Social Power.* New York: Harper and Row, 1965.

Collins, Patricia Hill. *Black Feminist Thought: Knowledge, Consciousness, and the Politics of Empowerment.* Boston: Unwin Hyman, 1990.

Commission for Positive Change in the Oakland Public Schools. *Keeping Children in School: Sounding the Alarm on Suspensions.* Oakland, Calif.: The Commission, 1992.

Connell, R. W. "Teaching the Boys: New Research on Masculinity and Gender Strategies for Schools." *Teachers College Record* 98, no. 2 (1996): 206–35.

Connell, R. W., et al. *Making the Difference: Schools, Families, and Social Division.* London: George Allen and Unwin, 1982.

Crenshaw, Kimberle. "Beyond Racism and Misogyny: Black Feminism and 2 Live Crew." In *Words That Wound: Critical Race Theory, Assaultive Speech, and the First Amendment,* ed. Mari J. Matsuda et al., 111–32. Boulder, Colo.: Westview Press, 1993.

Dalla Costa, Mariarosa. "Women and the Subversion of the Community." In *The Power of Women and the Subversion of Community,* ed. Mariarosa Dalla Costa and Selma James, 19–54. Bristol, England: Falling Wall Press, 1973.

De Lauretis, Teresa. *Technologies of Gender: Essays on Theory, Film, and Fiction.* Bloomington: Indiana University Press, 1987.

Dillard, J. L. *Black English: Its History and Usage in the United States.* New York: Vintage, 1973.

Du Bois, W. E. B. *Souls of Black Folk.* 1903. Reprint, New York: Bantam, 1989.

Eder, Donna. "Ability Grouping and Students' Academic Self-Concepts: A Case Study." *Elementary School Journal* 84, no. 2 (1983): 149–61.

Eder, Donna, Catherine Colleen Evans, and Stephen Parker. *School Talk: Gender and Adolescent Culture.* New Brunswick, N.J.: Rutgers University Press, 1995.

Fanon, Frantz. *Black Skins, White Masks.* Trans. Charles Lam Markmann. New York: Grove Press, 1967.

Feagin, Joe, and Melvin Sikes. *Living with Racism: The Black Middle-Class Experience.* Boston: Beacon Press, 1994.

Fiedler, Leslie A. *Love and Death in the American Novel.* New York: Criterion, 1960.

Filby, N. N., and B. G. Barnett. "Student Perceptions of 'Better Readers' in Elementary Classrooms." *Elementary School Journal* 82, no. 5 (1982): 435–49.

Foley, Douglas E. *Learning Capitalist Culture: Deep in the Heart of Tejas.* Philadelphia: University of Pennsylvania Press, 1990.

Fordham, Signithia, and John U. Ogbu. "Black Student's School Success: Coping with the 'Burden of Acting White.'" *Urban Review* 18, no. 3 (1986): 176–206.

Foucault, Michel. *Discipline and Punish.* Trans. Alan Sheridan. New York: Vintage, 1979.

———. *Power/Knowledge: Selected Interviews and Other Writings, 1972–1977.* Ed. and trans. Colin Gordon. New York: Pantheon, 1980.

Gibbs, Jewelle Taylor. "Young Black Males in America: Endangered, Embittered, and

Embattled." In *Young, Black, and Male in America: An Endangered Species,* ed. Jewelle Taylor Gibbs et al., 1–36. New York: Auburn House, 1988.

Gilmore, Perry. " 'Gimme Room': School Resistance, Attitude, and Access to Literacy." *Journal of Education* 167, no. 1 (1985): 111–28.

Gilroy, Paul. *Small Acts: Thoughts on the Politics of Black Culture.* New York: Serpent's Tail, 1993.

Gilyard, Keith. *Voices of the Self: A Study of Language Competence.* Detroit: Wayne State University Press, 1991.

Goodwin, Marjorie Harness. *He-Said–She-Said: Talk as a Social Organization among Black Children.* Bloomington: Indiana University Press, 1990.

Gouldner, Helen. *Teachers' Pets, Troublemakers, and Nobodies: Black Children in Elementary School.* Westport, Conn.: Greenwood Press, 1978.

Grant, Linda. "Helpers, Enforcers, and Go-Betweens: Black Females in Elementary School Classrooms." In *Women of Color in U.S. Society,* ed. Maxine Baca Zinn and Bonnie Thornton Dill, 43–63. Philadelphia: Temple University Press, 1994.

Hall, Stuart. "The Rediscovery of 'Ideology': Return of the Repressed in Media Studies." In *Culture, Society, and the Media,* ed. Michael Gurevitch et al., 56–90. New York: Methuen, 1982.

Hargreaves, David H., Stephen K. Hester, and Frank J. Mellor, eds. *Deviance in Classrooms.* London: Routledge and Kegan Paul, 1975.

Harper, Philip Brian. *Are We Not Men? Masculine Anxiety and the Problem of African-American Identity.* New York: Oxford University Press, 1996.

Hoberman, John M. *Darwin's Athletes: How Sport Has Damaged Black America and Preserved the Myth of Race.* Boston: Houghton Mifflin, 1997.

Hochschild, Arlie Russell. *The Managed Heart: Commercialization of Human Feeling.* Berkeley and Los Angeles: University of California Press, 1983.

———. *The Second Shift: Working Parents and the Revolution at Home.* New York: Viking, 1989.

Hochschild, Jennifer L. *The New American Dilemma: Liberal Democracy and School Desegregation.* New Haven: Yale University Press, 1984.

hooks, bell. *Yearning: Race, Gender, and Cultural Politics.* Boston: South End Press, 1990.

Hull, John D. "Do Teachers Punish according to Race?" *Time,* April 4, 1994, 30–31.

Jaynes, G., and R. Williams Jr., eds. *A Common Destiny: Blacks and American Society.* Washington, D.C.: National Academy Press, 1989.

Jordan, June. *On Call: Political Essays.* Boston: South End Press, 1985.

Kelley, Robin. *Race Rebels: Culture, Politics, and the Black Working Class.* New York: Free Press, 1994.

Kohl, Herbert. *I Won't Learn from You: The Role of Assent in Learning.* Minneapolis: Milkweed Editions, 1991.

Kotlowitz, Alex. *There Are No Children Here.* New York: Doubleday, 1991.

Kozol, Jonathan. *Savage Inequalities: Children in America's Schools.* New York: HarperCollins, 1991.

Kunjufu, Jawanza. *Countering the Conspiracy to Destroy Black Boys.* 2 vols. Chicago: African American Images, 1985.

Labov, W. *Language in the Inner City: Studies in the Black English Vernacular.* Philadelphia: University of Pennsylvania Press, 1972.

Levine, Lawrence. *Black Culture and Black Consciousness: Afro-American Folk Thought from Slavery to Freedom.* New York: Oxford University Press, 1977.

Mac an Ghaill, Mairtin. *The Making of Men: Masculinities, Sexualities, and Schooling.* Buckingham, England: Open University Press, 1994.

MacKinnon, Catharine A. *Feminism Unmodified: Discourses on Life and Law.* Cambridge: Harvard University Press, 1987.

MacLeod, Jay. *Ain't No Making It: Leveled Aspirations in a Low-Income Neighborhood.* Boulder, Colo.: Westview Press, 1987.

Majors, Richard, and Janet Mancini Billson. *Cool Pose: The Dilemmas of Black Manhood in America.* New York: Lexington, 1992.

Marsh, P., E. Rosser, and R. Harre. *The Rules of Disorder.* London: Routledge and Kegan Paul, 1978.

Massey, Douglas S., and Nancy A. Denton. *American Apartheid: Segregation and the Making of the Underclass.* Cambridge: Harvard University Press, 1993.

McKerrow, Raymie E., and Norinne H. Daly. "The Student Athlete." *National Forum* 71, no. 4 (1990): 42–44.

McNeil, Linda M. *Contradictions of Control: School Structure and School Knowledge.* New York: Routledge and Kegan Paul, 1986.

Mehan, Hugh, Alma Hertweck, and J. Lee Miehls. *Handicapping the Handicapped: Decision-Making in Student's Educational Careers.* Stanford: Stanford University Press, 1986.

Messerschmidt, James W. *Masculinities and Crime: Critique and Reconceptualization of Theory.* Lanham, Md.: Rowman and Littlefield, 1993.

Miller, Jerome G. *Search and Destroy: African American Males in the Criminal Justice System.* New York: Cambridge University Press, 1996.

Mills, C. Wright. *The Sociological Imagination.* New York: Oxford University Press, 1959.

Minnesota Department of Children, Families and Learning. *Student Suspension and Expulsion: Report to the Legislature.* St. Paul: Minnesota Department of Children, Families and Learning, 1996.

Mullings, Leith. "Images, Ideology, and Women of Color." In *Women of Color in U.S. Society,* ed. Maxine Baca Zinn and Bonnie Thornton Dill, 265–89. Philadelphia: Temple University Press, 1994.

Oakes, Jeannie. *Keeping Track: How Schools Structure Inequality.* New Haven: Yale University Press, 1985.

Ogbu, John U. "Class Stratification, Racial Stratification, and Schooling." In *Class, Race, and Gender in American Educational Research: Toward a Nonsynchronous Parallelist Position,* ed. Lois Weis, 163–82. Albany: State University of New York Press, 1988.

Omi, Michael, and Howard Winant. *Racial Formation in the United States: From the 1960s to the 1980s.* New York: Routledge and Kegan Paul, 1986.

Perkins, Useni Eugene. *Home Is a Dirty Street: The Social Oppression of Black Children.* Chicago: Third World Press, 1975.

Perry, Theresa, and Lisa Delpit, eds. *The Real Ebonics Debate: Power, Language, and the Education of African-American Children.* Boston: Beacon Press, 1998.

Pettigrew, Thomas, ed. *Racial Discrimination in the United States.* New York: Harper and Row, 1975.

Polakow, Valerie. *Lives on the Edge: Single Mothers and Their Children in the Other America.* Chicago: University of Chicago Press, 1993.

Rist, Ray C. "Student Social Class and Teacher Expectations: The Self-Fulfilling Prophecy in Ghetto Education." *Harvard Educational Review* 40, no. 3 (1970): 411–51.

———. *The Urban School: A Factory for Failure, a Study of Education in American Society.* Cambridge: MIT Press, 1973.

Sadker, Myra, and David Sadker. *Failing at Fairness: How America's Schools Cheat Girls.* New York: C. Scribner's Sons, 1994.

Said, Edward. *Orientalism.* New York: Vintage, 1978.

Sailes, Gary A. "The Exploitation of the Black Athlete: Some Alternative Solutions." *Journal of Negro Education* 55, no. 4 (1986): 439–42.

Sellers, Robert M., and Gabriel P. Kuperminc. "Goal Discrepancy in African-American Male Student-Athletes' Unrealistic Expectations for Careers in Professional Sports." *Journal of Black Psychology* 23, no. 1 (1997): 6–23.

Sentencing Project. *Young Black Americans and the Criminal Justice System: Five Years Later.* Washington, D.C.: Sentencing Project, 1995.

Smitherman, Geneva. *Talkin and Testifyin: Language of Black America.* Detroit: Wayne State University Press, 1977.

Stack, Carol B. *All Our Kin: Strategies for Survival in a Black Community.* New York: Harper and Row, 1974.

Sudarkasa, Niara. "African-American Families and Family Values." In *Black Families,* ed. Harriette Pipes McAdoo, 9–40. Thousand Oaks, Calif.: Sage, 1997.

Tattum, Delwyn P., ed. *Management of Disruptive Pupil Behavior in Schools.* New York: John Wiley and Sons, 1986.

Thorne, Barrie. *Gender Play: Girls and Boys in School.* New Brunswick, N.J.: Rutgers University Press, 1993.

Trudgill, P. *Sociolinguistics: An Introduction.* Harmondsworth: Penguin, 1974.

Turner, Patricia. *Ceramic Uncles and Celluloid Mammies: Black Images and Their Influence on Culture.* New York: Anchor, 1994.

United States Commission on Civil Rights. *Teachers and Students: Differences in Teacher Interaction with Mexican American and Anglo Students.* Washington, D.C.: U.S. Government Printing Office, 1973.

United States Department of Justice Statistics. *Profile of Jail Inmates.* Washington, D.C.: U.S. Government Printing Office, 1980.

Wolf, Alexander. "Impossible Dream." *Sports Illustrated,* June 2, 1997, 80–82.

Weinstein, Rhonda Strasberg, and Susan E. Middlestadt. "Student Perceptions of Teacher Interactions with Male High and Low Achievers." *Journal of Educational Psychology* 71, no. 1 (1979): 421–31.

West, Candace, and Don H. Zimmerman. "Doing Gender." *Gender and Society* 1, no. 2 (1987): 125–51.

Willis, Paul. *Learning to Labor: How Working Class Kids Get Working Class Jobs.* New York: Columbia University Press, 1977.

———. "Cultural Production Is Different from Cultural Reproduction Is Different from Social Reproduction Is Different from Reproduction." *Interchange* 12, nos. 2–3 (1981): 48–67.

index

acting white, 203–5; gender significance of, 215; schoolboys and, 212–15; youth critique of, 204

adultification, 80–85; black boys as hypersexualized, 174–75; of black children, 89–90; of black children fighting, 194; and masculinity, 96; and oral performance, 179; and punishment, 90; and rule-breaking, 179

adult power. *See* power, adult

Airès, Phillipe, 81n

alternative sites of knowledge. *See* knowledge, alternative sites of

American Psychiatric Association (APA), 195n, 195–96, 196n, 200n

Anderson, Elijah, 124n

Arcadia, 4; crime in 6–7; police, 135–61

Arcadia School District: busing, 4–5, 5n; and CTBS scores by race, 55; desegregation, 4–6, 18–19; high school segregation, 5; high school tracking, 5; location, 4; race and schools, 5; racial segregation of teachers, 18; Rosa Parks School neighborhoods, 4–5, 5n; white flight from, 5

Aronowitz, Stanley, 21n

"at-risk": black boys as, 91–96; intervention program for, 3; labeling for, 9; and normalizing judgment, 90–96; and race, 17–18; and race and sex, 4; and ranking practices, 54–55; and reputations, 95–96; tests determine, 54

Barnett, B. G., 98n

Barrett, Michele, 170n

behavior: adultified, 90; and counseling, 43; defiance as mental disorder, 195–96; disruptive as (un)reasonable, 199–202; explaining, 21–22; and images, 77–88; and reputations, 95–96

Bernstein, Basil, 50n, 204n

Billson, Janet Mancini, 78n, 124n

Black English. *See* language

black masculinity. *See* masculinity, black

bodies: of adult black males, 66–67; adult-child contact, 43; adult power over, 61–73; docile as norm, 72; drawings in discipline files, 33, 46; and eye contact, 65–66; fighting as practice of, 185–93; gender and physicality, 43; gender power through, 99; movement as trouble, 62–73; and nonverbal communication, 67; at play, 62–63; presentation of, 41; at rest, 62–64; school rules regulate, 49; styles in public, 125; stylized sulking, 68; teacher control of, 62–73

Bourdieu, Pierre, 21n, 50n, 51n, 204n; concept of cultural capital, 50; concept of symbolic violence, 51

Bowles, Samuel, 21n, 50n, 204n

Brewer, Rose M., 22n

Butler, Judith, gender as performance, 170–71, 171n

Mehan, Hugh, 59n
Mellor, Frank J., 54n; on labeling
  principles, 88n, 88–89, 89n
Messerschmidt, James W., 165n
methodology, 7–23; children's perspective, 11–17, 97–99; fieldwork
  site, 2; institution as focus, 73; personal agency and social structure,
  21, 21n, 22, 22n; popular knowledge in, 105; race, class, and gender
  in, 22, 22n, 23; rap music as
  epigraphs, 16–17; research assistance, 14–17; rethinking strategies,
  11–12. See also children's perspective; interviews; participant observation
Michigan public schools, corporal
  punishment, 3, 3n
Middlestadt, Susan E., 98n
Midland neighborhood, 5. See also
  social class
Miehls, J. Lee, 59n
Miller, Jerome, 82n, 113n, 231n,
  232–33, 233n
Mills, C. Wright, on social terror,
  116, 116n
Minnesota Department of Children,
  Families and Learning, 3n
mothers: as incompetent, 41; Mariana's lament, 134–61; and masculinity, 41; practices as problem,
  78; in son's outcome, 37
Mullings, Leith, 79n, 170n
My Girl (film), 25–26

neighborhoods: "bad," described,
  105–6; and children's fears,
  117–20; crime in, 6–7, 46; drugs
  in, 46, 106; friends as homies,
  120–21; Heartland, 5n, 5–7, 10n;
  Highlands, 5, 5n, 10n; in identity
  formation, 105; and legitimizing
  discourse, 45–47; Midland, 5, 5n,
  10n; and oppositional discourse,
  98; popular knowledge in, 105;

racial composition, 6, 6n; Rosa
  Parks School, 4–5, 5n; Schoolboys
  in, 105; Troublemakers in, 105. See
  also knowledge, popular; Rosa Parks
  School; social class
normalizing judgment: being "at-risk,"
  90–96; Foucault's concept defined,
  51; instrument of discipline, 52;
  range of, 90–96; and reputation,
  95–96; and teacher practices,
  88–96; and unsalvageable students,
  96

Oakes, Jeannie, on remedial classes,
  59, 59n
Oakland, Calif.: punishment in public
  schools, 3, 3n; School Board Resolution on Ebonics, 231
Ogbu, John, 21n, 203n, 215, 215n
Omi, Michael, 20n
Oppositional Defiant Disorder
  (ODD), 195–96, 200; challenged,
  197–202
oppositional discourse. See discourse,
  oppositional
Oprah Winfrey Show, 11
Other, 21; blacks as, 79–80; racist category, 79–80

Parker, Stephen, 170n
participant observation: by children,
  97–98; cinema, 24–27; field trips,
  7–8; hallway, 64–65; Jailhouse,
  34–44; methodology, 7–23; Miss
  Lyew's class, 92–95; Mrs. Daly's
  class, 7–8; Mrs. Smythe's class,
  56–59; Myelisha and candy,
  101–4; in neighborhood, 105–6;
  promotion exercises, 225–26; Punishing Room, 84–85; reason for, 4;
  rent board hearing, 114–16;
  rethinking strategies, 11–12; school
  day routine, 166–69; Special Day
  Class (SDC), 60; transforming
  experience, 26–27. See also chil-